NEW TOWNS
THE RISE, FALL AND REBIRTH

KATY LOCK & HUGH ELLIS

RIBA Publishing

IMAGE CREDITS

Introduction
1.1 Katy Lock/TCPA; 0.2 ncjMedia Ltd

Chapter 1
1.2, 1.4, 1.5, 1.6 TCPA; 1.3 Reproduced by permission of the Garden City Collection; 1.7 Stevenage Museum, 1.8 Estate of Abram Games; 1.9a, 1.10 Homes England; 1.9b, 1.9c, 1.9d, 1.14a; TCPA Collection; 1.11 Foundation Le Corbusier; 1.12a David F. Bostock, The Radburn Association; 1.12b Yoostar; 1.13, 1.20 RIBA Collections; 1.14b Destination Milton Keynes; 1.15, 1.16; Harlow Council; 1.17 Katy Lock/TCPA; 1.18 Carlton Reid/Roadswerenotbuiltforcars.com; Harlow Council; 1.21 John Donat/RIBA Collections; 1.22 Boyd & Evans; 1.23 JR James Archive/Flickr

Chapter 2
2.1 TCPA; 2.2 Evening News/Associated Newspapers Ltd; 2.3 John McCann/RIBA Collections; 2.4, 2.6, 2.9a, 2.9b, 2.11, 2.13 Homes England; 2.5 TCPA Archive/Stevenage BC; 2.7 Garden City Collection; 2.10 Mary Evans Picture Library; 2.12 MK Parks Trust

Chapter 3
3.1 Tony Ray-Jones/RIBA Collections; 3.2 Mark Rae; 3.3, 3.4, 3.5, 3.6, 3.7, 3.9 TCPA; 3.8 a2dominion

Chapter 4
4.1a Milton Keynes Council; 4.1b Destination Milton Keynes; 4.2, 4.3, 4.4, 4.6, 4.7, 4.10, 4.11, 4.12, 4.14, 4.15, Katy Lock/TCPA; 4.5 Mace; 4.8 Caroline Brown/DLA; 4.9 Destination Milton Keynes; 4.13a, 4.13b, 4.13c, 14.13d Bigg Design; 4.16 Basildon Borough Council; 4.17 Stevenage Bioscience Catalyst; 4.18 Catapult Transport Systems; 4.19 Incredible Edible

Chapter 5
5.1 TCPA; 5.2 Homes England; 5.3, 5.5a, 5.5b, 5.5c, 5.6, 5.8 Katy Lock/TCPA; 5.4 Paul Riddle; 5.7 Harlow Art Trust

Chapter 6
6.1 TCPA; 6.2, 6.4 RIBA Collections; 6.3 Homes England; 6.5, 6.7 Durham County Archives; 6.6, 6.8 TCPA/Katy Lock; 6.9 Durham County Record Office

Chapter 7
7.1 TCPA; 7.2, 7.3, 7.8 Torfaen County Borough Council; 7.4 Architectural Press Archive/RIBA Collections; 7.5a, 7.5b, 7.6a, 7.6b Katy Lock/TCPA; 7.7 Bron Afon Community Housing

Chapter 8
8.1, 8.2, 8.3 TCPA; 8.4 RIBA Collections; 8.5 John Donat/RIBA Collections; 8.6 RCAHMS courtesy of The Royal Incorporation of Architects in Scotland; 8.7, 8.8a, 8.9 Katy Lock/TCPA; 8.8b Housing Today

Chapter 9
9.1 TCPA; 9.2, 9.4 Homes England; 9.3 West Lancashire Borough Council; 9.5 West Lancashire Borough Council, 2016, The Skelmersdale Story; 9.6 Well North; 9.7, 9.8 Katy Lock/TCPA; 9.9 St Modwen

Chapter 10
10.1 TCPA; 10.2 Wikimedia Commons; 10.3, 10.4, 10.7a, 10.7b, 10.8, 10.9 Armagh City, Banbridge and Craigavon Borough Council; 10.5a, 10.5b, 10.5c, PLACE Built Environment Centre; 10.6 Katy Lock/TCPA

Chapter 11
11.1 TCPA; 11.2 Amazing MK; 11.3, 11.4 Homes England; 11.5, 11.7a 11.7b, 11.7c, 11.8 Katy Lock/TCPA; 11.6 MK Gallery Milton Keynes, photo: Johan Dehlin; 11.9 Amazing MK; 11.10 Caroline Brown/DLA

Chapter 12
12.1 Bill.walford/Wikimedia Commons; 12.2 Katy Lock/TCPA; 12.3 Stevenage Borough Council/Museum; 12.4 Homes England; 12.5 Letchworth Garden City Heritage Foundation reproduced by permission of the Garden City Collection; 12.6 Wikimedia Commons; 12.7 Paul Coleman, 2015, London Intelligence reproduced by permission of London Intelligence Limited

Chapter 13
13.1, 13.3, 13.7 TCPA; 13.2 NIC/5th Studio; 13.4 NIC (Crown Copyright); 13.5 Ebbsfleet Development Corporation; 13.6 © O Street Ltd. 2014

Chapter 14
14.1 Map created by House of Commons Library, Source; 14.2 Photo by Joël de Vriend on Unsplash

---

© RIBA Publishing, 2020

Published by RIBA Publishing, 66 Portland Place, London, W1B 1AD

ISBN 978-1-85946-928-6

The rights of Katy Lock and Hugh Ellis to be identified as the Authors of this Work has been asserted in accordance with the Copyright, Designs and Patents Act 1988 sections 77 and 78.

All rights reserved. No part of this publication may be reproduced, stored in a retrieval system, or transmitted, in any form or by any means, electronic, mechanical, photocopying, recording or otherwise, without prior permission of the copyright owner.

British Library Cataloguing-in-Publication Data
A catalogue record for this book is available from the British Library.

Commissioning Editor: Alex White
Assistant Editor: Clare Holloway
Production: Jane Rogers
Designed and typeset by Studio Kalinka
Printed and bound by Short Run Press, Exeter
Cover illustration: Paul Catherall

While every effort has been made to check the accuracy and quality of the information given in this publication, neither the Author nor the Publisher accept any responsibility for the subsequent use of this information, for any errors or omissions that it may contain, or for any misunderstandings arising from it.

www.ribapublishing.com

Contents

IMAGE CREDITS	II
ABOUT THE AUTHORS	IV
ACKNOWLEDGEMENTS	V
SPONSORS	VI
FOREWORD	VII
INTRODUCTION	IX

PART I: 1
THE BIRTH, RISE AND FALL OF THE UK'S NEW TOWNS

01	THE BIRTH OF THE NEW TOWNS	3
02	THE RISE AND FALL OF THE NEW TOWNS	27
03	NEW TOWN HINTERLAND	45

PART II: 57
THE NEW TOWNS AT MIDDLE AGE

04	THE NEW TOWNS TODAY	59
05	CASE STUDY: HARLOW, ESSEX	79
06	CASE STUDY: PETERLEE, COUNTY DURHAM	87
07	CASE STUDY: CWMBRAN, TORFAEN COUNTY (MONMOUTHSHIRE)	95
08	CASE STUDY: CUMBERNAULD, NORTH LANARKSHIRE	103
09	CASE STUDY: SKELMERSDALE, WEST LANCASHIRE	113
10	CASE STUDY: CRAIGAVON, COUNTY ARMAGH	121
11	CASE STUDY: MILTON KEYNES, BUCKINGHAMSHIRE	129

PART III: 141
REBIRTH OF THE NEW TOWNS

12	TOP LESSONS FROM THE NEW TOWNS	143
13	THE FUTURE OF THE NEW TOWNS IDEAL	157
14	CONCLUSION	169
	NOTES AND REFERENCES	173
	INDEX	179

About the TCPA

Founded by Sir Ebenezer Howard in 1899 to promote the idea of the garden city, the Town and Country Planning Association (TCPA) has been at the forefront of delivering new communities for over a century. The TCPA is an independent charity campaigning for transformation of the planning system to realise social and environmental justice. The association occupies a unique position, overlapping with those involved in the development industry, the environmental movement and those concerned with social justice, and prides itself on leading-edge, radical thinking and problem-solving.

ABOUT THE AUTHORS

Katy Lock

Katy is an urbanist and campaigner for social justice and the environment. She has over 18 years experience in planning and environmental practice with particular expertise in policy development, analysis and thought leadership in relation to new communities, housing, green infrastructure, urban design and sustainability.

Katy is Director of Communities and Frederic Osborn Fellow at TCPA and leads on the Association's campaigns and promotion of garden city principles in policy, legislation, education and the arts. Katy also leads the TCPA's ongoing research on transferable lessons from the new towns, currently looking at new town renewal and modernising the New Towns Act- and a series of practical guides to delivering new communities today. In 2017 Katy co-authored *The Art of Building a Garden City: Designing New Communities for the 21st Century* with Hugh Ellis and Kate Henderson.

Katy is a Chartered Town Planner (MRTPI) and has a background in planning, urban design and sustainability. Before joining the TCPA in 2011, she worked for several years in the private sector as an environmental planning consultant. Katy is currently a trustee for Planning Aid for London, and a Design Review panellist for Design South East. Katy was born in Milton Keynes and has been defending the new town ever since.

Dr Hugh Ellis

Dr Hugh Ellis is a planner and screenwriter. He is Director of Policy at the TCPA, and has worked on policy development, briefings and engagement with central government and politicians. In 2018 he led the secretariat for the Raynsford Review, setting out a blueprint for a new planning system in England. Since 2015 Hugh has co-authored three books, including *Rebuilding Britain* and *Town Planning in Crisis* with Kate Henderson, and *The Art of Building a Garden City: Designing New Communities for the 21st Century* with Katy Lock and Kate Henderson. He has led on TCPA campaign work on 'planning out poverty' and planning for people, and he is a strong critic of the deregulation of planning and policies such as Permitted Development. He is currently leading work on planning for the climate crisis.

Prior to joining TCPA in March 2009, Hugh was the National Planning Advisor to Friends of the Earth England, Wales and Northern Ireland, before which he spent a number of years working for the Coalfield Planning Cooperative on community planning projects. He has a Doctorate in Land Use Planning from the University of Sheffield where he was a lecturer in the utopian art of town planning.

ACKNOWLEDGMENTS

This is a book that reveals what we can do as nation when we turn the hope of a better life into practical action. We are indebted to the generations of garden city and new town pioneers who, in the face of apparently impossible odds, proved that a good condition of life for ordinary people was not just a desirable pipe dream but a practical necessity. This utopian legacy continues to provide us with a mixture of inspiration and a sense of responsibility!

We would like to thank all of our colleagues and the Trustees, Policy Council and Vice Presidents of the TCPA for their enthusiasm for planning and belief in the utopian tradition. We are particularly grateful to Kate Henderson who help us conceive of this project. We are also indebted for the wisdom of many of those involved in the new towns programme and particularly to David Lock for his detailed comments. We would like to thank those who helped us bring this book alive with images, including our colleagues Lizzie Simpson and Nick Matthews, and contributors Caroline Brown at David Lock Associates, Letchworth Garden City Heritage Foundation, The Milton Keynes City Discovery Centre, Mark Rae, Hertfordshire Archives, the various New Town Local Authorities and Homes England.

The book would also not have been possible without the generous support of our sponsors.

Many thanks to the team at RIBA Publishing, in particular to Alex White for having the faith to let us do this again and for supporting us throughout the process along with Jane Rogers, Clare Holloway and Kathryn Glendenning.

Finally, we would like to thank our families and friends for their continued patience, love and support.

This book is dedicated to the memory of Wyndham Thomas 1924 – 2019, Former director of TCPA and driving force behind Peterborough Development Corporation. A brave and a compassionate advocate of planning for people.

SPONSORS

We are grateful to the following organisations for sponsoring this book.

Gascoyne Cecil Estates

Gascoyne Estates manages the historic Hatfield Park estate on behalf of the Cecil family who have owned land and property in Hertfordshire for over 400 years. Gascoyne sold land to Ebenezer Howard to assist the construction of Welwyn Garden City. Later, following the Second World War much of Hatfield New Town and post war elements of Welwyn Garden City was also built on estate land. Gascoyne's principle of responsible business has been practiced for many generations and its sense of responsibility and commitment to community is fundamental to the way the estate has been managed, both in the past and to the present today..

Lady Margaret Patterson Osborn Trust

The Lady Margaret Patterson Osborn Trust was set up by the children of Sir Frederic Osborn and his wife in memory of their mother. The Trust's remit is to promote interest in garden cities, new towns and other new settlements, and in Welwyn Garden City.

Welwyn Hatfield Borough Council

FOREWORD

This book gives a flavour of the most extraordinary and misunderstood programme of urban development in our national history. Our post war new towns transformed the lives of millions of working people giving them affordable and well-designed homes with all the social facilities they needed. I was born in Washington new town and my mum and sisters still live there. My childhood was shaped by the freedom to play in safe streets and with the kind of generous green space that marked the humanity and generosity of its designers. That experience has defined my passion for the value of well-planned and affordable places. But it's also the source of real anger that we have forgotten the value of providing decent homes in beautiful surroundings at an affordable cost.

The great value of this book is that it challenges head on the myths about the new towns programme and reveals the lessons we should have learned about their success. They weren't part of some centrally imposed conspiracy and they were highly profitable for the Government. It is simply ridiculous to regard them as a failure. But neither does this account seek to hide the real problems in some of our new towns. Instead it explains why so many struggled with their regeneration after central government asset striped them in the 1980s.

The contrast between many of the homes and the communities we deliver now could not be starker. Do we really want our children to be brought up in tiny flats with no windows? Is that really the best we can do? Above all this is book about the hope we could create if we started to care about the basic quality of life of all members of our society. I hope it will be uncomfortable reading for modern politicians because it sets out what can be achieved when we have brave and compassionate leadership. It is a powerful call for a new start in UK housing policy and I hope will be the beginning of new debate not just about our existing new towns but how we could seize the exciting opportunity of building the very best for future generations.

George Clarke: architect, TV presenter, campaigner and a founder of TV production company *Amazing Productions*

0.1
HENRY MOORE'S FAMILY GROUP, UNVEILED IN HARLOW IN 1956. THE SCULPTURE ENCAPSULATES THE NEW-TOWN DREAM OF A SOCIALLY JUST FUTURE.

INTRODUCTION

In an era marked by political inertia and division, it is hard to conceive that we were once capable of taking bold action to solve the problems confronting our society. Even though we now face the challenges of growing inequality and poverty and the existential threat of climate change, which are comparable in scale to the postwar reconstruction of Britain, the idea of beginning a programme to transform the living conditions of ordinary people (Figure 0.1) seems almost dream-like. And yet that is what the British New Towns programme did, and that, despite the mistakes, is why it's worth understanding and celebrating.

In *The Art of Building a Garden City*,[1] we told the overall story of garden cities and new towns in the context of 500 years of thinking and agitation for the creation of ideal places. This book drills down further into one of the most remarkable and globally significant aspects of that story, the British New Towns programme. Often dismissed with lazy references to roundabouts and concrete cows, the new towns story is one defined by hope, bravery and betrayal. Shaped by anarchists, artists and visionaries, new towns promised a new beginning for millions of people (Figure 0.2). If their ambition was monumental, their fall from grace was equally spectacular. Forgotten by the public and politicians, ridiculed in the media and regarded as a curious past experiment by many in the built environment sector, new towns have been thoroughly misunderstood and disregarded, despite their obvious relevance in dealing with our housing crisis.

The aim of this book is not to repeat the many excellent, detailed histories of the new towns, but instead to explore the big-picture lessons the programme offers us for 21st-century place-making. The book seeks to address the myths and realities of the New Towns programme and to capture a flavour of the rich legacy of the places it delivered. In the context of our current housing crisis and with government repeatedly talking about 'new towns' in the Cambridge–Milton Keynes–Oxford Arc, these lessons are particularly relevant.

Three rounds of New Town designations, beginning in 1946 and lasting barely 25 years, created 32 new or expanded communities which are now home to 2.8 million people. If we had continued with the programme, even in a modest way, we would have avoided the blight on people's lives created by decades of not building the right-quality homes at affordable prices in beautiful communities. In turning our back on the new towns, we also disregarded the immensely valuable learning of all aspects of design and governance that could have transformed the quality of what we build now.

Far from being a public-sector financial burden, the model of capturing the uplift in land values resulting from development enabled by the

NEW TOWNS: THE RISE, FALL AND REBIRTH

0.2
ROY AND EVELYN GILBERT RECEIVE THE KEY TO THEIR NEW HOME IN WASHINGTON, IN 1976. THEIRS WAS THE 10,000TH HOME TO BE BUILT IN THE NEW TOWN.

powers of Development Corporations made the first generation of new towns highly profitable. Even with all the unfavourable terms applied when the programme was prematurely wound up in 1980, the new towns have paid back all their loans and go on yielding profits to the government and Homes England.

The break-up of a national approach to housing delivery by the forced winding up of the Development Corporations and the discounted sale of their assets could be seen as a betrayal of new towns and their citizens. It undermined the long-term version of the programme due to a short-sightedness that is unfortunately common in planning.

The asset-stripping of the towns had major and damaging long-term impacts on their development. In some cases, this meant the last generation of new towns were 'half baked' and remain unfinished. The obvious lesson is that the towns needed to build legacy funds for renewal to deal with the unique challenge of building new places and the simultaneous aging of key infrastructure. Even with these problems, the economic success of towns such as Milton Keynes, Warrington or Stevenage is real and impressive.

These big-picture themes have key lessons but so does the micro history of the new town communities. The commitment to community development, to balanced employment provision, to art and culture and to generous civic facilities and green space is in sharp contrast to the majority of housing developments we build now. While the upheaval of people moving from communities in existing towns and cities was real, this needs to be balanced with the testimony of those whose lives were immeasurably improved by finding a high-quality home in a new town.

The rich experience set out in the case studies is complex, but there is much more real achievement than most of us assume. It would be short-sighted, though, to ignore the mistakes. Innovation in housing design in Peterlee may have been cutting-edge architecture but it was a practical failure. Cost constraints and shortages of materials led to some poor-quality homes, and monolithic concrete town centres in some of the new towns have proved particularly inflexible. The later new towns took accommodating the car to new heights, which is challenging to our notions of sustainable transport. Neither can a new town, simply because is it 'new', avoid the wider problems of regional economic decline or changing retail habits.

But all the new towns, with their diverse challenges, have space to adapt and innovate. They were and are places of opportunity for new design solutions. Ironically enough, their future success depends on the very qualities possessed by their founding Development Corporations. They need comprehensive master-planning for the future, backed by a powerful local authority or even the redesignation of a Development Corporation which can coordinate change. One of the biggest barriers to success was the privatisation of whole town centres in a way that makes control and regeneration difficult for the community to achieve. So, while the iconic Aneurin Bevan swimming pool may be about to be demolished and renewed in Skelmersdale, there is much to learn from the legacy of how these places were delivered. Some lessons are self-evident, like the vital role of active and creative public authorities in driving delivery and renewal. Others remain uncomfortable. Will a future government ever fully recognise the vital need to house its population in places that secure their happiness and wellbeing?

One final piece of context is vital to a fair description of the new towns. We can't expect new towns (or any place) to escape the wider economic and social context in which they sit. Neither can we assess the record without reflecting on the wider quality of housing units we now build for people. Much of this new housing is of poor design quality, badly located in relation to sustainable transport, unaffordable and lacking the full range of walkable services, from GP surgeries to corner shops. Set against this modern reality, the new towns approach demonstrates a genius for coordination and breathtaking design ambition.

We hope this book gives a flavour of the most extraordinary and misunderstood programme of urban development in our national history; one which was an attempt to solve strategically and comprehensively the challenges of postwar reconstruction and population change and deal with the legacy of poor-quality industrial housing. Part 1 sets out the background to the programme and charts the complex history of the first 50 years of the new towns. Part 2 is focused on the rich and diverse state of the new towns today, supported by seven case studies which bring the current achievements and challenges alive. Part 3 offers a reflection on the key lessons for the future and what these mean for the potential of a new generation of new towns.

PART I

THE BIRTH, RISE AND FALL OF THE UK'S NEW TOWNS

01 THE BIRTH OF THE NEW TOWNS **02** THE RISE AND FALL OF THE NEW TOWNS
03 NEW TOWN HINTERLAND

01

THE BIRTH OF THE NEW TOWNS

It is a long cry from [Thomas] More's Utopia, to the New Towns Bill, but it is not unreasonable to expect that Utopia of 1515 should be translated into practical reality in 1946 ... Our aim must be to combine in the new town the friendly spirit of the former slum with the vastly improved health conditions of the new estate, but it must be a broadened spirit, embracing all classes of society ... We may well produce in the new towns a new type of citizen, a healthy, self-respecting, dignified person with a sense of beauty, culture and civic pride.

Lewis Silkin, Minister of Town and Country Planning, introducing the second reading of the New Towns Bill, 1946.[1]

Introduction

The New Towns programme, with its three phases, was the most ambitious town-building programme ever undertaken in the UK and has been described as 'perhaps the greatest single creation of planned urbanism ever undertaken anywhere'.[2]

It is difficult to imagine a contemporary politician giving a speech with the same passion as that of Lewis Silkin as he introduced the New Towns Bill in 1946. But a government with the ambition to transform the nation and enable no less than 'a new kind of citizen' does not appear overnight. Understood as a response to the need for postwar reconstruction, the New Towns programme emerged in the wake of half a century of thinking about how we might live. This rich history, which we set out in detail in *The Art of Building a Garden City*,[3] underpinned the postwar government's response to the immediate drivers of population growth, deindustrialisation, modernism and the political transformation which total war had produced. In this chapter we touch on these key influences and drivers before setting out the mechanics of the New Towns Act, and the delivery of 32 new towns that followed.

NEW TOWNS: THE RISE, FALL AND REBIRTH

Growing new towns from garden cities

The words 'new town' and 'garden city' are frequently used interchangeably when talking about new communities today but these terms are in fact two related but distinct concepts. The garden city story starts half a millennium ago with Thomas More's *Utopia*,[4] and there is no doubt that the New Towns programme would never have happened without the transformational Garden City Principles distilled by Ebenezer Howard.

Howard's genius lay in combining a vision of a socially just community with a key financial measure that would make that vision a reality. The garden city was not simply a design concept but an attempt to create a fair and cooperative society. These new, self-contained towns would replace slums (Figure 1.1) with high-quality housing for working people; each house would have a decent garden and generous play space for children. The garden cities would provide for the best blend of town and country, allowing not just access to the natural environment but also bringing that environment into the heart of the city. This union of town and country would encourage healthy communities, not just through physical activity and fresh air but a healthy social life. The garden cities would also have integrated transport systems and a strong emphasis on democratic community governance. Each garden city would have its own employment to limit commuting. They would be towns 'designed for industry and healthy living; of a size that makes possible a full measure of social life, but not larger; surrounded by a permanent belt of rural land; the whole of the land being in public ownership or held in trust for the community'.[5]

1.1
TENEMENT HOUSING IN GLASGOW IN 1868. THE GARDEN CITY IDEA AIMED TO PROVIDE AN ALTERNATIVE TO THE 19TH-CENTURY SLUM HOUSING THAT BLIGHTED THE LIVES OF SO MANY WORKING PEOPLE.

01 THE BIRTH OF THE NEW TOWNS

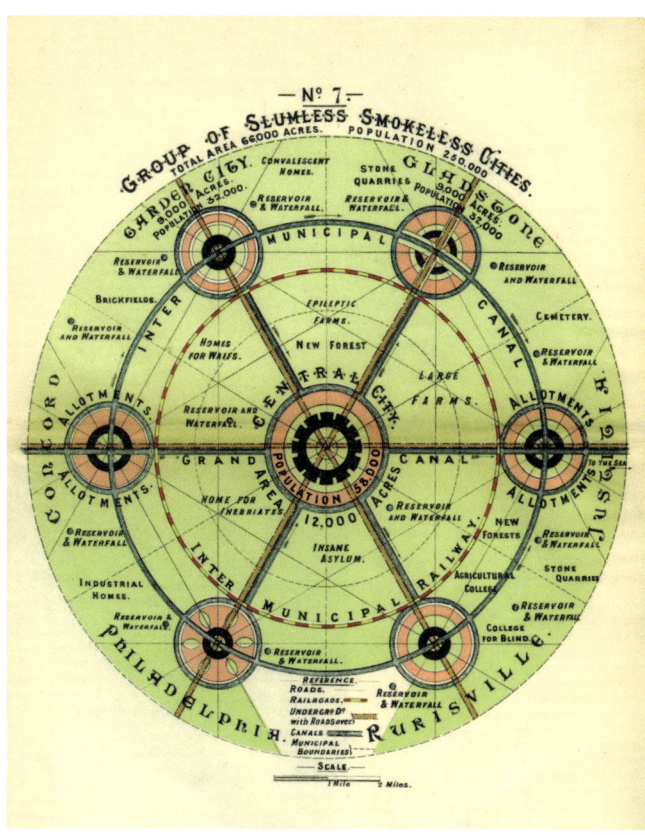

1.2
SOCIAL CITY DIAGRAM. EBENEZER HOWARD'S VISION FOR A NETWORK OF GARDEN CITIES HAD A PROFOUND INFLUENCE ON THE POSTWAR NEW TOWNS PROGRAMME.

Howard did not envisage isolated communities. He set out a vision for a garden city that would reach an ideal population of around 32,000 people. Once this planned limit had been reached, a new city would be started a short distance away, followed by another, and another, until a network of such places was created, with each city providing a range of jobs and services, but each connected to the others through excellent public transport, providing all the benefits of a much larger city but with each resident having easy access to the countryside. Howard called this network of connected settlements the 'Social City' (Figure 1.2).

By the 1920s, the garden city movement had already transformed the way Britain – and indeed the world – thought about dealing with urban growth and renewal.

Ebenezer Howard's seminal work *To-morrow: A Peaceful Path to Real Reform* (1898) led to the creation of the Garden Cities Association (now the Town and Country Planning Association) in 1899 and to the first garden city experiment at Letchworth by 1903.[6]

Howard's blueprint for beautiful, healthy and cooperative new communities was revolutionary not just in the importance it attached to good planning, but in the inclusion within his model of practical ways of both paying for development and giving the community a permanent financial share in the place where they live (possibly sufficient, he thought, to provide pensions, healthcare and education, none of which were freely available at that time).

NEW TOWNS: THE RISE, FALL AND REBIRTH

1.3
RUSHBY MEAD, LETCHWORTH GARDEN CITY. EARLY HOUSING IN LETCHWORTH WAS THE EMBODIMENT OF THE ARTS AND CRAFTS DESIGN IDEALS, PROVIDING BEAUTY IN HUMAN SCALE, HOMES SENSITIVE TO THE PAST AND PRESENT, USING LOCAL MATERIALS.

Howard's holistic and principled vision has proved to be an elegant and durable ideal of social transformation. The concepts of land value capture, 'marrying town and country', community development and a spirit of innovation and experimentation were the key principles that evolved between the garden cities and new towns.

The garden city financial model

Under Ebenezer Howard's garden city model, the land ownership (in today's terms, the freehold) of the entire development would be retained by a limited-profit, semi-philanthropic body similar to a community interest company or trust: income earned from capitalising on the increasing land values which result from development – known as 'betterment' – and from residential and commercial leaseholders (with uplift on reversion at the end of lease periods) would be used to repay the original development finance debts. As these debts were gradually paid off, and as land values rose, the money could be increasingly invested in community assets and services, building up what we might think of as the garden city 'mini-welfare state'.

The garden city idea progressed at an astonishing speed; a year after publishing To-morrow, Howard and his supporters formed the Garden Cities Association (which became the Garden Cities and Town Planning Association in 1909 and the Town and Country Planning Association in 1941). By 1903, the Association's Garden City Pioneer Company was set up to find a site, and First Garden City Limited was formed to build the first garden city at Letchworth, Hertfordshire, designed by Barry Parker and Raymond Unwin (Figure 1.3).

But it was not a straight trajectory. Letchworth Garden City struggled to assemble enough low-interest loans for the start-up phase of capital works, and although the outbreak of war in 1914 gave a boost to the local economy (the dust-cart building company, for example, switched over to making armoured vehicles), building materials and labour were in short supply. Even so, Letchworth inspired countless developments around the world, and its cooperative spirit and socialist ideals attracted 'every sandal-wearing, vegetarian, teetotaller',[7] an association which later the new towns tried their best to shrug.

Another key prewar moment came in 1912, when Raymond Unwin, who had left Letchworth to work on Hampstead Garden Suburb, published *Nothing Gained by Overcrowding!*, an influential pamphlet which set out how an alternative to bylaw terraces – the housing standard at the time – could improve the way people live.[8]

Nothing Gained by Overcrowding! was influential in the design and layout of new homes but its publication was also to mark Unwin's second transformation, from campaigning outsider to the UK's most influential chief planner. The year 1912 was also notable as the time when Frederic James Osborn, a former clerk, aged just 27, joined the Howard Cottage Society at Letchworth as secretary and manager. Osborn went on to be the driving force behind the postwar New Towns programme that followed (Figure 1.4).

1.4
FREDERIC JAMES OSBORN, AN ENDURING AGITATOR FOR THE GARDEN CITY IDEALS.

1918 to the early 1940s:
The New Townsmen and the rise of the new garden cities

In 1918, just six years after joining Letchworth, Frederic Osborn's experience at the first garden city led him to publish a book calling for a programme of new towns to deal with the reconstruction efforts after World War I. *New Towns after the War* combined Osborn's learning from the early days of Letchworth with his reaction to the detrimental effects of the chaotic prewar policy of allowing the urban sprawl of existing cities and 'the grave results of that policy on the lives of town-dwellers and the efficiency of industry'.[9] Osborn and colleagues C.B. Purdom and Letchworth publisher W.G. Taylor – calling themselves 'The New Townsmen' – argued that 100 garden cities should be built under state direction and with the state providing 90% of the £500-million capital required.[10] Alongside its emphasis of the state's role in delivery and finance, the book was also significant in that it specifically distanced itself from the argument that garden cities were a utopian socialist programme. This was an attempt to allow the idea to embed in mainstream politics and distance its association with 'sandal-wearing vegetarians'.

Ebenezer Howard remained sceptical of the ability of government to organise itself to deliver new communities as needed and in 1919 he secretly bought land (using money from private investors) for a second demonstration project – Welwyn Garden City – which happened to be not far away from Letchworth. Howard employed Osborn to be estates manager for the new garden city. Osborn would become one of its first residents and the garden city would in turn fuel his learning and campaigning for a New Towns programme.

The end of World War I meant housing was again top of the national agenda and as servicemen returned from the horrors of the trenches the nation called for 'homes fit for heroes'. Given the urgent need for substantial amounts of new housing, in 1918 the Tudor Walters Committee, heavily influenced by Raymond Unwin, recommended a massive programme of subsidised cottage homes to be built by local authorities.

The government subsequently committed to expanded public housing programmes in the Addison Act of 1919. The standard of these new homes was a spectacular improvement on what had gone before and was inspired by the garden city design ideals of Letchworth. However, the expediency of delivering at speed meant that many of these new homes were built in large-scale estates on the edge of existing settlements. The resulting development of new housing was considered by some to be 'the antithesis of the garden city idea'.[11] To the dismay of the garden city movement, it seemed that Howard's garden city vision 'would be lost for a generation'.[12]

Laying the political foundations

The interwar years saw the impact of the public housebuilding programmes and a series of reports and interventions that would lay the foundations for the postwar New Towns Act.

A 1921 committee report looking at how to deal with unhealthy areas had recommended in favour of garden cities and the New Townsmen, led by C.B. Purdom, published *The Building of Satellite Towns* (1925), which included in its pages potential locations for a ring of satellite towns round London to deal with London's expanding population (Figure 1.5).[13]

By now Raymond Unwin was an influential establishment figure and in 1933 he published a special report of the Greater London Regional Planning Committee. This led to the creation of the Departmental Committee on Garden Cities and Satellite Towns, which reported in 1935 and

01 THE BIRTH OF THE NEW TOWNS

in turn led to the Green Belt Act 1938, which enabled local authorities to buy and protect land around cities. In the same year, the Barlow Commission was appointed to consider the causes of the existing distribution of the industrial population, future trends and the social, economic and strategic disadvantages of concentration, and to propose remedies.[14] The Commission's report recommended the decentralisation of industry from congested areas and indicated that the problems were of national urgency, proposing a central national authority – a board for industrial location responsible to the Board of Trade – to deal with them.

The decentralisation plan for London's population was set out in Patrick Abercrombie's *1943 County of London Plan*.[15] Osborn criticised the plan for its 'half-hearted' approach to decentralisation compared to that proposed by the New Townsmen 20 years earlier. The Greater London Plan followed a year later and included proposals for a ring of eight satellite towns around London (Figure 1.6).

Building the new towns would take place alongside the demolition of inner-city slum housing, which would be replaced by modern housing estates. There was discussion of radical initiatives to be taken when peace arrived. Meanwhile, the Garden Cities Association – by now called the Garden Cities and Town Planning Association – continued to campaign for regional planning beyond the London region.

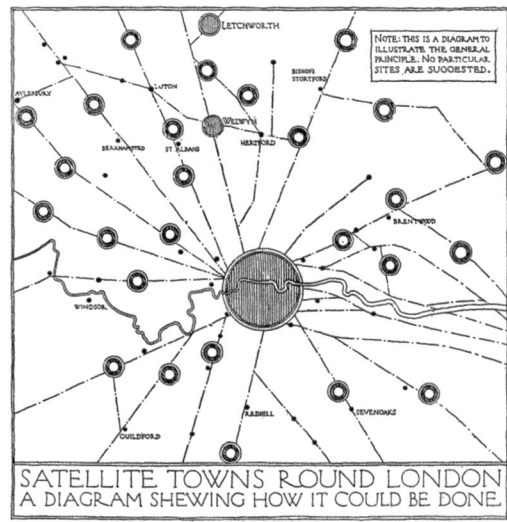

1.5
C.B. PURDOM'S VISION FOR SATELLITE TOWNS IN 1925. AS A THEATRICAL PRODUCER, PURDOM EMBODIED THE COLLISION OF THE CREATIVE ARTS AND PRACTICAL PLANNING THAT MADE THE GARDEN CITY MOVEMENT SO POWERFUL.

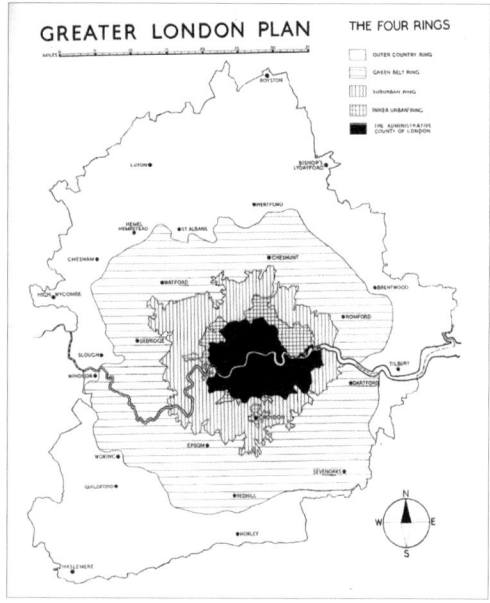

1.6
THE GREATER LONDON PLAN, 1944. THE PLAN PROPOSED A RING OF SATELLITE TOWNS AROUND LONDON, 20 YEARS AFTER PURDOM HAD SHOWN THE SAME FOR THE GARDEN CITIES AND TOWN PLANNING ASSOCIATION. (THE TOWNS MARKED WITHIN THE RING ON THIS MAP WERE EXISTING TOWNS, NOT THE PROPOSED NEW TOWNS.)

After World War II

World War II left the country with a severe housing shortage, not only as a result of enemy action, but also because of six years of lost housebuilding and a longer legacy of slum housing. But it was not only physical and demographic changes that furthered a need for radical change: there was a recognition that postwar Britain deserved a new future. The Labour Party's landslide victory of 1945 reflected that mood, and a programme of new towns would be visible proof of the government's pledge to build a new society on the ruins of the old.

In 1945 Lewis Silkin (Figure 1.7), the newly appointed Minister of Town and Country Planning, appointed a New Towns Committee under the chairmanship of Sir John Reith, who had established the BBC (the British Broadcasting Corporation) before the war. Within a year the committee had published three succinct but detailed and profoundly influential reports on how to deliver a programme of new towns. The committee recommended that the new towns should be built by public development corporations rather than local authorities and directly funded by grants from HM Treasury. Its reports set out how this large upfront investment would later result in a huge financial return for the government. The committee began by assuming that there should be no private-sector role in the overall management of the new towns. This view was modified partly because of private-sector enthusiasm for the new town model and the interim report included provision for some involvement from authorised private-sector organisations. Lewis Silkin set aside this recommendation partly because of the real difficulties involved in giving the private sector such extensive legal powers and the issue of how such power could made accountable. As a result, the final New Towns Bill allowed only for public development corporations.

The New Towns Act

The committee had realised that it would not be possible for local authorities to deliver such ambitious schemes, in terms of resources, expertise or, crucially, the political will to ensure delivery could take place where it was needed most. The New Towns Act was passed in 1946 even as the committee's last report was being published. Never before had Britain seen a government with such an ambitious programme of housebuilding designed to provide high-quality housing in well-designed communities as part of a wider public programme addressing public health and social justice (Figure 1.8).

1.7
LEWIS SILKIN FAMOUSLY DEFENDING THE STEVENAGE DESIGNATION AT A PUBLIC MEETING HELD IN MAY 1946.

01 THE BIRTH OF THE NEW TOWNS

1.8
POSTERS LIKE THIS ONE BY ABRAM GAMES, 1942, PROMISED A BETTER FUTURE THAT EVERYONE COULD HELP TO BUILD.

The New Towns Act 1946 was an element of a comprehensive postwar planning settlement. The Act sat alongside the Town and Country Planning Act 1947, which instituted the nationalisation of the right to develop land, the capture of land values (betterment[16]) and a reformed system of statutory development plan-making by local authorities. Although the taxation of land value was abolished by the Conservative government in 1954, the power to create whole new towns was retained.

How the New Towns Act worked

The success of the New Towns legislation was founded on a simple but powerful combination of site designation followed by the establishment of a New Town Development Corporation to acquire land at existing-use value and do all that was necessary to bring the town into being. While elements of this law, such as the compulsory purchase of land, were not new, the concept of the Development Corporation was a key and brilliant innovation allowing for a powerful and focused master developer.

11

The need for a state-sponsored new town, together with its location, was typically identified by regional or subregional studies undertaken by various agencies of central and local government. Such studies usually identified the role, purpose and scale of the proposed development. Where the minister felt that the New Towns legislation should be used, consultation took place with relevant local authorities and legislation (called a Designation Order) was drafted, explaining the purpose of the project, addressing concerns raised through the consultation process, and setting out details of suggested boundaries. The draft legislation was open to objection and inquiry under a planning inspector, who reported back to the minister. It was not uncommon for small boundary changes to be made in response to objections. In Warrington, for example, the boundaries and Designation Order were amended after concerns about impacts on infrastructure, air pollution and existing services, and the loss of green belt and agricultural land.[17] Eventually, a final Designation Order would be adopted and development could begin.

New Town Development Corporations

New towns were built by public Development Corporations directly financed by a combination of HM Treasury loans, budgets from other agencies (such as highways and health authorities) and the per-capita budgets for local government services (for example schools). The powers and remit of New Town Development Corporations were set out in the New Towns Act 1946. Once a site had been designated, the Development Corporation acted as the 'engine' of the new towns approach.

New Town Development Corporation core powers

The success of the New Town Development Corporations was directly related to their ability to deploy the following core powers:

- to compulsory purchase land if it could not be bought by voluntary agreement

- to buy land at current-use value (later, after the Myers legal ruling, some 'hope value' also had to be paid[18]) and capture the betterment for HM Treasury (and thus, ultimately, the public)

- to borrow money (initially primarily from HM Treasury but later in the programme from other sources as necessary), repayable with interest

- to control development within the new town designated area

- to grant or refuse planning permission for development within the new town designated area (with certain small exceptions, such as advertisements, although local 'partnership' agreements sometimes extended that range so long as they helped in the mission to deliver the new town)

- to procure housing subsidised by central government grant and by other means, and to act as a housing association in the management of housing

- to do anything necessary for the development of the town, such as providing cash flow for the delivery of utilities or entering into partnership working with other agencies, investing in social and community development, promoting economic development, marketing the new town in the UK and overseas (Figure 1.9), etc.

01 THE BIRTH OF THE NEW TOWNS

1.9
PROMOTIONAL MATERIAL FOR WARRINGTON AND RUNCORN, 1970S. THE DEVELOPMENT CORPORATIONS WERE HIGHLY EFFECTIVE IN MARKETING AND PROMOTING THE NEW TOWNS.

Importantly, the interlocking nature of the plan-making, development-management and land-ownership powers of the New Town Development Corporations made them very effective instruments of delivery. The role of central government was clear, and responsibility for the design, ownership and consent for new development was held by a single public body, ultimately accountable to the minister. In Northern Ireland, the corporations were called New Town Commissions, and importantly also had municipal functions that New Town Development Corporations elsewhere did not have.

In the Development Corporations, the New Towns Act created a new opportunity for those who delivered them to be part of the most exciting task in urbanism. The well-resourced corporations were able to cherry-pick the best – or simply luckiest – talent from a worldwide pool of planners, architects, landscape architects, artists, ecologists, community development workers, economists and countless others who came together to design and deliver unprecedentedly ambitious schemes. In short, the corporations had the dedicated staff in the numbers and with the skills to drive delivery (Figure 1.10).

Creating 'balanced' communities

Reflecting the spirit of the garden city movement, the purpose of the new towns was not simply to provide homes and jobs, but to create socially balanced communities. This notion of social balance was partly Howard's original ideal of people of different backgrounds living together, in sharp contrast to the class segregation of much prewar development. In practice, it was reflected in trying to create integrated employment, mixed-tenure homes and a social life that provided opportunities for all. In some cases, such as Peterlee, it meant an explicit commitment to create new employment for women. New development (and its residents) was to be well integrated with pre-existing communities. This was more easily achieved in some places than others, reflecting local geography, the design of the master plan in promoting physical integration, the effort invested in social development and community cohesion, and the complexity and challenges inherent in such an endeavour.

NEW TOWNS: THE RISE, FALL AND REBIRTH

1.10
THE STAFF OF THE MILTON KEYNES DEVELOPMENT CORPORATION, PHOTOGRAPHED IN 1972. YOUTH AND ENTHUSIASM (AND TREE-CLIMBING SKILLS?!) WERE A VITAL PART OF THEIR SUCCESS.

Financing

New Towns were financed by a combination of 60-year, fixed-rate loans from central government, budgets from other agencies (such as highways and health authorities) and the per-capita budgets for local government services (for example for schools). Initially, the New Town Development Corporations were allowed to borrow only from HM Treasury. In the early stages, land was bought by the Development Corporation at near existing-use values (in the main, agricultural price levels fixed at current prices), which provided the new towns with the financial wherewithal for subsequent development. Infrastructure such as roads and parks had to be built in advance of population growth and demand, and thus before any increase in local taxation. New town construction, therefore, required significant investment over a considerable period of time. As the new towns progressed, the Development Corporations sold freeholds, as well as acquiring land. Land for schools and hospitals, for example, was sold to the relevant authorities or given away for free. Open space was typically given with an endowment, either to the local authority or to some other not-for-profit body, such as a land trust, in perpetuity.

The financing of housing built for rent in the new towns operated in a way similar to that applying to local authorities, with central government providing subsidies to the Development Corporations. In terms of revenue, new town housing activities evolved over time alongside central government's changing housing policy. Each of the new towns built up very large housing revenue accounts, which, with inflation on the one hand and controls on rents on the other, led to significant liabilitiesfor later new towns.

The New Town Development Corporations did not finance all aspects of the town's development. HM Treasury loans were supplemented by funds from the relevant existing public-sector programmes in the area, refocused towards the new town (to pay for key facilities, such as schools and hospitals, and some utilities, such as water infrastructure), and by attracting inward investment from the private sector.

The first generation of new towns proved so financially successful that, assisted by relatively low interest on the loans to the Development Corporations (set at a rate of 2% above Libor), they were net lenders to other public bodies. For example, Harlow repaid all its loans within 15 years and started to produce a surplus for HM Treasury. However, the cost of borrowing was a major financial burden for the 'Mark Three' new towns during the 1970s and 1980s, when interest rates rose dramatically, up to 16%. In addition, the forced sale of Development Corporation commercial assets (both mature and immature) from 1981 onwards removed income growth from this source.

This limited the ability of the new towns to reinvest in their renewal and upkeep. The total £4.75-billion loan made to the New Town Development Corporations by HM Treasury was repaid in early 1999 (assisted by the sale of sites). After that, by 2002, land sale receipts had generated around a further £600 million, of which only £120 million was reinvested in the new towns.[19] More recently, between 2010 and 2014 alone, land sale receipts generated a further £70.3 million for HM Treasury.[20]

The New Towns Act in Scotland and Northern Ireland

The New Towns programme in Scotland

Like the rest of the UK, housing conditions in Scotland after World War II were a major issue. Overcrowded slum dwellings were still present in Scottish cities. Between the two world wars there had been some slum clearance and new building programmes, but in many cases what had been built was not much better than what it had replaced. By the time the New Towns Act was passed in 1946, the population of Glasgow and the Clyde Valley region had reached such high levels that Patrick Abercrombie and Robert Matthew's Clyde Valley Regional Plan (1946) made provisions to depopulate Glasgow by half (36% of Scotland's population was concentrated in the region, with 22% living in Glasgow alone[21]). Decentralisation would be achieved by expanding existing towns in the region, encouraging industrial growth in other parts of Scotland, and building new towns.

The New Towns programme in Northern Ireland

As a result of a mix of complex historical, economic and political factors, a statutory system of town and country planning in Northern Ireland did not develop at the same speed as it did in Britain. Consequently, the new towns concept did not materialise in Northern Ireland until the mid-1960s, when a plan for the Greater Belfast region (the Belfast Regional Survey and Plan, published in 1963 – the 'Matthew Report') recommended a new regional city of approximately 100,000 people to help address Belfast's acute housing issues. This need was driven by a legacy of poor and overcrowded housing conditions in Belfast and the perceived failure of the Belfast Corporation to grapple with the problem. This, combined with a concern for industrial modernisation, led the government to intervene.

NEW TOWNS: THE RISE, FALL AND REBIRTH

The approach in Northern Ireland was unique in that the designated area was usually much bigger than the area to be developed. It included surrounding villages and towns so that there could be a strategic approach to renewal and delivery of an entire subregion.

The New Towns Act (Northern Ireland) was passed in 1965, empowering the Minister of Development to designate an area as a new town and constitute a New Town Commission to carry out both development and municipal functions.

Designing the new towns

The design ethos of the new towns was not simply to provide homes and jobs, but to create socially balanced communities that integrated employment, homes and social life to provide opportunities for all. Lewis Silkin, the Minister of Town and Country Planning, encouraged the corporations to be no less than 'daring and courageous in their efforts to discover the best way of living'.[22] With central government funding, the corporations were able to attract the best young design talent from across the UK and Europe.

While the design of the garden cities had been heavily influenced by the Arts and Crafts movement, the design characteristics of the new towns were heavily influenced by Modernism, interpreted in a way which aimed to retain the garden city vision of marrying town and country. It was in the new towns that the goals of the garden city and Modernist movements collided – for the former in terms of town planning and the latter in terms of architecture (Figure 1.11).[23] While the vision of this approach is to be applauded, the success of this marriage remains one of the great areas of debate of the new towns' legacy, and the almost complete abandonment of the ideas of Raymond Unwin and Barry Parker in space standards and housing design quality seems,

1.11
LE CORBUSIER, LA VILLE RADIEUSE. THE GARDEN CITY AND MODERNIST MOVEMENTS, EXEMPLIFIED BY LE CORBUSIER'S LA VILLE RADIEUSE, COLLIDED IN THE DESIGN OF THE NEW TOWNS.

01 THE BIRTH OF THE NEW TOWNS

(a)  (b)

1.12
A COMPARISON OF RADBURN, IN NEW JERSEY (A), AND GLENROTHES, IN FIFE (B). RADBURN (BUILT IN 1928) WAS DESIGNED TO ACCOMMODATE SEPARATE VEHICLE AND PEDESTRIAN MOVEMENT, USING GREEN SPACE TO CONNECT NETWORKS OF WALKWAYS, PROVIDING SPACE FOR CHILDREN TO PLAY IN COMMUNAL AREAS IN FRONT OF HOUSES. THIS GAVE A PERCEPTION OF HEALTHIER AND SAFER SPACES, AND CLEARLY INFLUENCED THE LAYOUT OF GLENROTHES NEW TOWN (DESIGNATED IN 1948).

in retrospect, short-sighted. Just as Letchworth was shaped by the design orthodoxy of its time, so the new towns could be viewed as a product of our brief love affair with Modernism.

The detailed designs of the new towns were influenced by the evolution of architecture and design thinking across the world, but most notably and directly were the result of an important UK-US dialogue on planning and design. American urbanist Clarence Perry had developed the concept of 'neighbourhood units', taking inspiration directly from Parker and Unwin's prewar designs, where key amenities were within a short walking distance of homes and at a scale which encouraged social interaction and a sense of place. His concept included self-contained neighbourhood units consisting of cul-de-sacs, surrounded by major roads with shops at the edge and a school at the centre, exemplified by the development at Radburn in New Jersey (Figure 1.12).

The development at Radburn, by architect-planner Clarence Stein, introduced a new design principle – the separation of vehicles and pedestrian movement networks. This approach was recommended by Patrick Abercrombie in the Greater London Plan, in 1944, and in the Dudley Report on the design of dwellings, also in 1944. The separation of people and traffic and the creation of extensive walk and cycle ways became one of the signature design approaches of the new towns and part of a new consensus in Britain's urban design in this postwar period.

There were two important changes to Stein's approach which had an impact on how the new towns developed. Firstly, early new town homes were often terraces rather than detached villas (Figure 1.13). Secondly, garages were grouped into courts, often a short distance away from homes, with poor surveillance. A consequence was that homes often had poorly identifiable fronts and backs. People would often use the back door – closer to their car – removing activity from the street in front of homes.[24] These characteristics continue to be visible in many contemporary developments.

17

1.13
HOUSING WITH MONO-PITCHED ROOFS, MARK HALL NORTH, HARLOW, BY FRY, DREW & PARTNERS, 1952.
HOUSING IN EARLY NEW TOWNS WAS OFTEN FORMED OF TERRACES RATHER THAN DETACHED HOMES.

In addition to design theory, a number of other practical and political realities influenced new town design. For the early new towns, the cost and availability of materials were major factors. For later new towns, the dominance of the motorcar affected whole approaches to movement and layout. Changing economic and social policy also proved to be a major influence. The new town pioneer residents moving from London's East End were pleased enough to have an indoor toilet and garden – cars were the reserve of the wealthy few. By the 1970s and 1980s, disposable income and social mobility for an increasing number of new town residents brought with them expectations of a wider range of amenities and consumer choice.

New town master plans

The new towns followed the garden city tradition of development by master plan. This holistic approach allowed the corporations to think strategically about how design and layout would help or hinder their goal of creating 'balanced communities'. A layout plan would be accompanied by a series of supporting documents on specific issues such as water or green space, much like today.

The designers of the first wave of new towns, often fresh from the army and therefore used to building bridges and big infrastructure, created rigid blueprints for development, which provided little flexibility for change over the long lifetime of a new community. Later, new towns learnt from this experience and recognised that the most effective approach was to create a framework for development which was strong enough to guide future development patterns but flexible enough to allow for innovation over time, 'a trellis on which the roses can grow where they will'.[25]

01 THE BIRTH OF THE NEW TOWNS

(a)
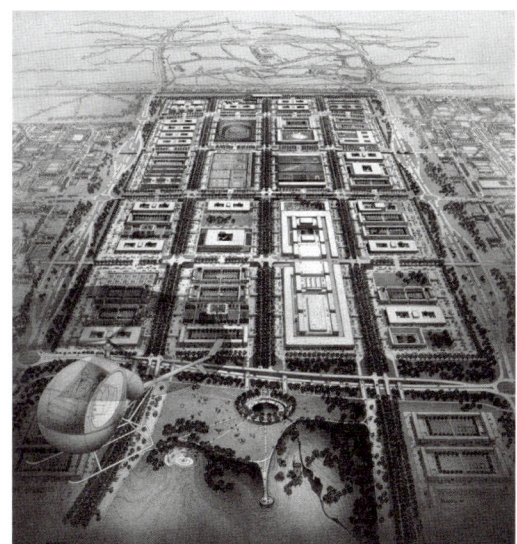

(b)

1.14
HELMUT JACOBY'S 1976 VISION OF CENTRAL MILTON KEYNES (A) AND AN AERIAL VIEW OF CENTRAL MILTON KEYNES TODAY (B). SEEN SIDE BY SIDE, THEY ILLUSTRATE THE POWER OF A STRONG MASTER PLAN.

The new town master plans (Figure 1.14) continue to guide future development in many of the new towns, and in many cases provided a valuable framework for councils to continue the job of the Development Corporations when they were prematurely wound up. The concept of walkable neighbourhoods with a range of local community facilities, set within a comprehensive framework of green infrastructure, was promoted by the garden city pioneers and developed further through the new towns. These principles have now been embedded as good practice in urban design.

Common design characteristics

Design varied, of course, from place to place and between different periods of development. However, in many cases designers moved from one Development Corporation to another, taking their design approaches with them, and it is possible to identify a number of characteristics which are recognisable across many of the new towns. These include the following.

Neighbourhood units

Influenced by the garden cities and later Radburn (*see* page 17), housing was developed in 'neighbourhood units', built around a primary school and other local facilities (Figure 1.15), creating a sense of community and allowing people to be within a short walk of key amenities. This was intended to reinforce local identity and serve day-to-day needs, with the town centre providing larger facilities.

NEW TOWNS: THE RISE, FALL AND REBIRTH

1.15
PRENTICE PLACE, HARLOW, 1956. THE PHOTOGRAPH SHOWS A TYPICAL NEIGHBOURHOOD SHOPPING AREA.

1.16
THE JOURNEY HOME FROM WORK AT TEMPLEFIELDS, HARLOW, IN 1953. INDUSTRIAL AREAS WERE SEPARATED FROM RESIDENTIAL AREAS IN THE NEW TOWNS AND LINKED BY FOOTPATHS AND CYCLEWAYS TO ENABLE ACCESS TO CLEAN AIR AND ENCOURAGE HEALTHY LIFESTYLES.

Low-density living

A combination of relatively cheap land, emphasis on green space and recognition that high-rise development did not necessarily equate to healthy living conditions meant that, in general, first-phase new towns were built at low densities. In Harlow this was as low as four dwellings per hectare in some places. However, there was no fixed approach and in reality densities varied within and between the new towns (Harlow was later home to the first high-rise residential block in Europe – The Lawn). The designers of some new towns, such as Cumbernauld, specifically sought to explore higher-density living for new town residents.

Zoning of industrial and residential areas

First envisaged by the garden city pioneers, the housing and industrial areas were separated in the new towns to distance residents from the polluting noise, smells and traffic of industry. Excellent pedestrian and transport links encouraged people to walk to work (Figure 1.16) or take public transport.

01 THE BIRTH OF THE NEW TOWNS

Pedestrian-friendly town centres

Pedestrianised town centres (in the first generation) and covered shopping malls in town centres (in the later new towns) would not only allow for a safe and pleasant environment for commercial activity but would also emphasise the public space between buildings and the social life and positive environment that can be created (Figure 1.17). This was consciously a radical departure from the traditional high street, where traffic went through town centres rather than around them. It was a feature envisaged earlier by Ebenezer Howard and later influenced by design in Sweden, for example Vällingby, and the United States, which featured early examples in Ohio, Seattle and Illinois.[26]

1.17
BASILDON TOWN CENTRE, PHOTOGRAPHED IN 2018. THE PEDESTRIANISED TOWN CENTRE CONTINUES TO PROVIDE SPACE FOR A RANGE OF SOCIAL AND COMMERCIAL ACTIVITIES, BUT GETTING THE RIGHT MIX CAN BE A CHALLENGE.

Ease of movement

Pedestrians and vehicles were often separated into different networks – allowing people to move freely and safely from place to place, with underpasses and overpasses making it unnecessary to cross busy roads (Figure 1.18). This also allowed for rapid movement by public transport and private car. The natural layout to achieve this was a grid, as explored at Washington and Milton Keynes. The rise of the motorcar proved to be a fundamental influence on the design of the new towns and represented a core challenge for their ongoing sustainability, particularly those delivered in the 1960s. The result is convenience for the car user but a street scene in which the car is king.

Integrated green infrastructure network

The new towns continued the garden city tradition of combining town and country, using networks of green space throughout the master plan. These green networks were deployed along transport corridors, to ease movement for pedestrians and cyclists and to separate transport from the neighbourhood units. This was achieved through parks and 'green wedges' (Figure 1.19) providing access to green space throughout the town, including formal and informal parks, and with neighbourhoods that were often at densities that allowed for green verges and front gardens. Following the introduction of the concept in Patrick Abercrombie's Greater London Plan of 1944, and the Clyde Valley Regional Plan of 1946, the Reith New Towns Committee recommended a green belt around each of the new towns – to prevent them from sprawling and to help realise Howard's vision of towns surrounded by a belt of open country for agriculture and access to countryside, as at Letchworth and Welwyn garden cities. But at designation, the requirement for an agricultural green belt was lost, and no new town master plan has a fixed perimeter of agricultural land – a big departure from Howard's idea, and a weakness.

Innovative architecture and design

Architects were positively encouraged to be innovative and use the latest materials (Figures 1.20 and 1.21). The Development Corporations often employed artists to create public art (Figure 1.22) and sometimes to design whole housing estates (such as Archigram in Milton Keynes or Victor Pasmore at Peterlee). Young architects were keen to prove their worth but were often under unrealistic pressures to build at speed, and some later attracted criticism for putting design aesthetics before the needs of residents. The new towns also pioneered sustainable design innovations through initiatives such as Energy World in Milton Keynes.[27]

1.18
SIX HILLS ROUNDABOUT, STEVENAGE, PHOTOGRAPHED IN 2013. SEPARATING CARS AND PEDESTRIANS WAS A DRAMATIC DEPARTURE FROM THE MOVEMENT PATTERNS IN TRADITIONAL TOWNS.

01 THE BIRTH OF THE NEW TOWNS

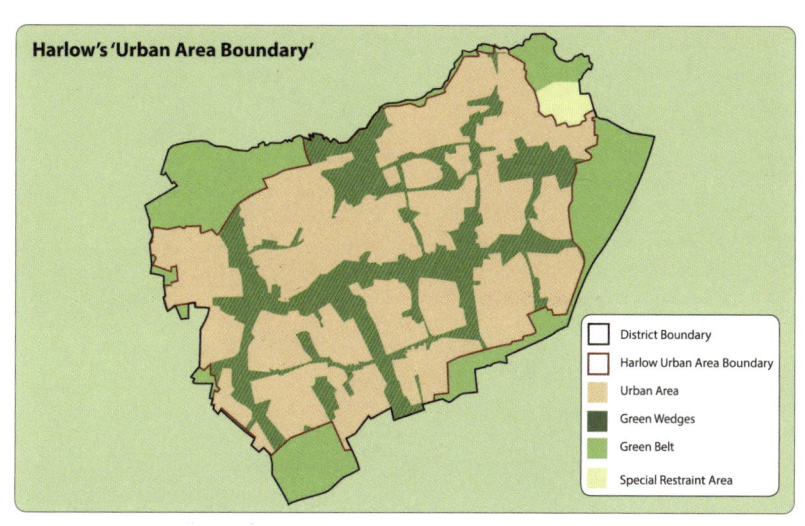

1.19
A MAP SHOWING HARLOW'S 'GREEN WEDGES'. WHEN DESIGNING HARLOW IN 1947, SIR FREDERICK GIBBERD AIMED TO ENSURE THAT THE EXISTING LANDSCAPE OF THE AREA WAS RESPECTED, HENCE THE TOWN'S ICONIC 'GREEN WEDGES'.

1.20
THE SOUTHGATE ESTATE, IN RUNCORN. JAMES STIRLING DEVISED A RADICAL NEW HOUSING TYPE FOR THIS ICONIC ESTATE, WHICH HAS SINCE BEEN DEMOLISHED. MANY SUCH ESTATES WERE LATER WHOLLY OR PARTIALLY DEMOLISHED FOLLOWING PROBLEMS WITH ANTISOCIAL BEHAVIOUR OR THE USE OF POOR-QUALITY MATERIALS.

1.21
MILTON KEYNES DEVELOPMENT
CORPORATION'S ARCHITECTS' OFFICE.
THE CORPORATION DEVELOPED
NEW CONSTRUCTION APPROACHES –
THIS BUILDING WAS CONSTRUCTED
USING THE SYSTEM BUILDING FOR
INDUSTRY DEVELOPED BY THE
CORPORATION'S INDUSTRY GROUP. THE
CONSTRUCTION TOOK ONLY 24 WEEKS
BUT THE BUILDING HAS NOW BEEN
DEMOLISHED.

1.22
FICTION, NON-FICTION AND REFERENCE (1984), A MURAL INSIDE MILTON KEYNES CENTRAL LIBRARY, BY BOYD & EVANS, ARTISTS IN RESIDENCE AT MILTON KEYNES. ARTISTS PLAYED A PROMINENT ROLE IN THE NEW TOWNS.

Emphasis on social housing

The early new towns were dominated by housing that the Development Corporation built and then rented out as landlords – between 69% (at Basildon) and 97% (at Peterlee) of housing in the 'Mark One' new towns was for social rent.[28] Such housing was later transferred to local authorities or housing associations. The later new towns had a more diverse housing mix, but still included a significant proportion of housing for social rent.

Self-containment

The new towns aimed to be as 'self-contained' as possible (to avoid the creation of commuter towns), in that sufficient homes and facilities were to be provided to enable new residents to work and live within the new town. The approach taken included industrial strategies which, for several of the early new towns, dictated that people could only move to the new town if they were employed there. In practice, self-containment was a nearly impossible objective, as everywhere has a daily flow of people in and out for various purposes. However, the emphasis on generating sufficient jobs to balance the incoming populations ensured that none of the new towns suffered the fate of becoming 'commuter suburbs'.

1.23
THE FURNACE GREEN COMMUNITY CENTRE, IN CRAWLEY, PHOTOGRAPHED C. 1971. COMMUNITY FACILITIES WERE PROVIDED AT THE EARLY STAGES OF DEVELOPMENT AND WERE AN ESSENTIAL RESOURCE FOR NEW RESIDENTS. THIS BUILDING IS STILL USED AS A COMMUNITY CENTRE TODAY.

Space for social and community development

Provision of space for social and community development included locating community facilities within a short walking distance of homes (Figure 1.23) and using multifunctional spaces (a school doubling up as a community centre, for example). The Development Corporations also made a conscious effort to encourage participation in the arts as part of community development. This was a strength that can be seen in all three waves of the new towns.

The New Towns Act laid the foundation for a new approach to housing delivery, based on high ambition and innovation.

02

THE RISE AND FALL OF THE NEW TOWNS

Introduction

The New Towns Act 1946 set out the mechanics of the New Towns programme, but the reality of its delivery was subject to the rapid political, social and economic change which characterised the 50 years of the programme. This chapter looks at the delivery of the new towns themselves, and how the meteoric rise of the programme was matched by its sharp decline.

Delivering the new towns

Thirty-two new towns were designated in the United Kingdom between 1946 and 1970 (plus the subsequently abandoned Stonehouse in Scotland). The programme was delivered in three phases: 'Mark One', designated between 1946 and 1950; 'Mark Two', designated between 1961 and 1966; and 'Mark Three', designated between 1967 and 1970 (Figure 2.1).

Of these 32 new towns, 21 were in England, two in Wales, five in Scotland and four in Northern Ireland. The 'Mark One' new towns were those built in the immediate years after the New Towns Act 1946 was passed. Between 1946 and 1950 the Labour government oversaw the designation of 14 of the 32 new towns. Following the vision set out in Patrick Abercrombie's Greater London Plan (1944), the first eight were in a ring around London and the others were in: the English Midlands, at Corby; the Northeast of England, at Aycliffe and Peterlee; South Wales, at Cwmbran; and Central Scotland, at East Kilbride and Glenrothes.

The first new towns experienced significant opposition, in no small part due to the fact that many of the locations around London and in the shire counties were in Conservative constituencies, reluctant to import thousands of working-class (Labour) voters. In the 1950s the Conservative government decided to halt the designation of new towns (with the exception of Cumbernauld in Scotland in 1955) and instead focus on continued development using the Town Development Act 1952. This saw the planned expansion of existing smaller towns, with HM Treasury funding the basic infrastructure through agreement between 'importing' and 'exporting' local authorities.

NEW TOWNS: THE RISE, FALL AND REBIRTH

2.1
MAP SHOWING THE LOCATIONS AND DESIGNATION DATES OF THE UK'S 32 NEW TOWNS, PLUS LETCHWORTH AND WELWYN GARDEN CITIES. THE NEW TOWNS PROGRAMME WAS DELIVERED IN THREE PHASES.

Delivery under this programme was slow, and it was difficult to reach the necessary political agreements between big cities like London and the host authorities. The baby boom of the 1960s signalled the need for large-scale action, too, so the New Towns programme had to continue.

Between 1961 and 1970, 17 more new towns were started ('Mark Two' and 'Mark Three'): three more for London, but this time further away from the capital (Milton Keynes, Northampton and Peterborough); two for the Midlands (Redditch and Telford); four in the Northwest (Runcorn, Skelmersdale, Warrington and Central Lancashire); one in the Northeast (Washington); one in Wales (Newtown); two in Scotland (Livingston and Irvine); and four in Northern Ireland (Craigavon, Antrim, Ballymena and Derry-Londonderry). (Derry-Londonderry was one of several places where the New Towns Act was used for the expansion and renewal of existing towns. Other examples included Peterborough and Central Lancashire.)

Patrick Abercrombie's Greater London Plan of 1944 had identified potential locations or areas of search for eight new towns around London. In Scotland, in 1946 the Clyde Valley Regional Plan made provisions to depopulate Glasgow by half and East Kilbride was designated a year later. Regional plans led to the designation of Glenrothes in 1948, Cumbernauld in 1955, Livingston in 1962 and Irvine in 1966. Stonehouse was designated in 1963 but de-designated in 1974 following the publication of the West Central Scotland Plan, which prioritised the rebuilding of inner Glasgow. The new towns were among the largest towns in Scotland and were later seen as important economic growth points for the country.

In Northern Ireland, the Matthew Report (Professor Sir Robert Matthew's Belfast Regional Survey and Plan, published in 1963) led to the designation of Craigavon as a new regional city in 1965. The Matthew Report also called for seven other 'centres for development' to be designated, although only four (including Craigavon) were taken forward. A plan for Antrim was drawn up in 1965, and Antrim was designated under the New Towns Act a year later; a plan for Ballymena was drawn up in 1966, and designation followed in 1967. The fourth and final new town in Northern Ireland was Derry-Londonderry. The Matthew Report classified it as a 'key centre' and the 1965 Wilson Report called it 'Ulster's second city'. It was physically peripheral and in need of investment – in 1967 unemployment was 20.1% (compared with 2.1% and 8.1% in Britain and Northern Ireland, respectively). An outline plan was developed and Derry-Londonderry was designated in 1969 under the New Towns (Amendment) Act 1968.[1]

Throughout the UK, subregional studies formed a basis for approving or discarding proposals for new town locations. Other new towns, such as Peterlee and (later) Milton Keynes, were voluntary proposals put forward by the relevant county councils, keen to relieve development pressures in their areas (Figure 2.2). Compared with today's procedures, where securing planning permission for large sites on average between 5 and 10 years, the site designation process was fast – progressing from a recommendation in a study to a confirmed Designation Order typically in three years, and sometimes less than 12 months.[2]

Delivering at speed

The postwar economy meant it took until 1952 for construction of the first-wave new towns to really get going, but when it did they delivered at speed, soon reaching a rate – across all 14 towns – of around 10,000 homes per year.[3] Following a brief dip in 1955, new town delivery had reached 12,000 homes per year across the programme by 1957. Progress with completions mirrored the economic status of the country, but completions accelerated significantly from 1975 onwards as the third-wave new towns got going. The peak build-out rates in the individual new towns would be the envy of contemporary government. At its peak, Milton Keynes was delivering 3,370 homes per year[4] through the combined action of a powerful Development Corporation and sufficient public-sector funding. Today, a recent study of 70 large sites showed the highest average annual build rate for the schemes assessed was 321 per year (albeit on a site where delivery had only been taking place for three years).[5]

2.2
A CARTOON BY JOSEPH LEE, PUBLISHED IN THE EVENING NEWS IN 1949. ONE OF THE KEY MISCONCEPTIONS ABOUT THE NEW TOWNS PROGRAMME WAS THAT THE LOCATIONS WERE DECIDED CENTRALLY – IN FACT, IT WAS OFTEN A LOCAL AUTHORITY-LED PROCESS.

2.3
HOUSING AT WILLOWFIELD, HARLOW, DESIGNED BY SIR FREDERICK GIBBERD FOR HARLOW DEVELOPMENT CORPORATION, 1965. THE HIGH PROPORTION OF SOCIALLY RENTED HOMES BUILT BY THE CORPORATIONS SHAPED THEIR COMMUNITIES AND PROVIDED AFFORDABLE HOMES FOR THOUSANDS OF PEOPLE.

Providing a mix of tenures

The New Towns programme successfully delivered a high number of homes across different tenures, with the Development Corporation model allowing for diversity in the build-out achieved. In the early years of the New Towns programme, before the private housebuilding market had faith that the new town would actually be built, and when the primary purpose of the new town was to accommodate people in need from nearby overcrowded cities, the Development Corporations built housing for rent, acting as landlord. This gave them control over letting and management policies (typically, a small proportion of stock was kept empty, so that incoming employers could relocate their staff quickly). The dominant social rented profile of the early years shaped new town communities markedly (Figure 2.3).

2.4
COMMUNITY HOUSE IN MILTON KEYNES, PHOTOGRAPHED IN THE EARLY 1970S. THE CORPORATIONS WORKED HARD TO CREATE A SENSE OF COMMUNITY FOR THE 'PIONEER' RESIDENTS.

With a degree of maturity, new towns were able to attract developers of housing for sale, and when the first Thatcher government ended the programme of building houses for rent, shared-ownership tenure was devised by the new town movement to try to keep the social mix as wide as possible. Milton Keynes, for example, aimed for a 50-50 split between private homes for ownership and rental housing, and made a clear commitment to mixing housing types, tenure and occupational groups within its grid squares.[6] A lack of housing mix in some of the new towns (for example, a lack of provision for elderly people, or a lack of 'middle class' housing where socially rented housing dominated) prevented the development of truly integrated communities.[7] The early new towns were also criticised for not attracting the elderly or ethnic minorities, and specific programmes were developed in later new towns to answer these points.[8]

Living in the new towns

The New Towns programme was pioneering not only in terms of the scale of its ambition but also in the spirit of the earliest new town settlers. People moved from the inner cities to the new towns attracted by the prospect of affordable modern housing, work and a better quality of life. The pleasure of newcomers who had never had an inside toilet or separate bedrooms for their children is well documented, as is, conversely, the feeling of isolation that can result from being the first residents of a community.[9] The 'new town blues' was particularly felt by those (mainly women) who had followed their partners to a new life and work in the early new towns but had been removed from their social networks and without the facilities to meet other people. To counteract this, Development Corporations invested in people and activities to welcome new residents. Community centres were set up in homes and residents were offered a welcome pack, with someone employed specifically to make people feel at home and facilitate social gatherings (Figure 2.4). The Development Corporations' investments in social and community development is perhaps one of the most impressive legacies of the New Towns programme. Everything – from high proportions of social housing to ensuring play facilities were put in ahead of families moving in – was designed to foster social development from the outset. Culture and the arts were also key features of new town development (Figure 2.5). Several of the Development Corporations employed 'artists in residence' to design parts of the town as it developed, and public art was a key feature, providing a sense of place and a varied public realm.

2.5
HARLOW CARNIVAL IN THE 1950S OR 1960S. EVENTS SUCH AS THIS WERE USED TO ENGAGE PEOPLE IN THE SOCIAL LIFE OF THE TOWN.

Public engagement

There were some commonly raised objections to new town designations; such objections included concerns of the relevant local authorities over the competitive impact on retail and local economic activity in nearby towns, disquiet over the impact on local services, and concerns about the impact on local agricultural economies. Later new towns put specific efforts into considering the views of residents: as part of the process of developing the master plan for Milton Keynes, consultant planners Llewelyn-Davies, Weeks, Forestier-Walker and Bor undertook a survey of residents living in the villages within the potential designated area of Milton Keynes. Annual surveys of the views of new residents were also conducted by the Development Corporation. These included views on everything from the design of homes to whether 'housewives' felt they had enough employment opportunities. While there is now much cynicism about consultation, there was a real desire on the part of the corporation to understand how people felt about their new environment. Stevenage Development Corporation updated residents on the progress of the new town through a quarterly publication, *Purpose*.

2.6
EARLY MARKETING MATERIALS FOR EAST KILBRIDE, PETERBOROUGH AND MILTON KEYNES. THE DEVELOPMENT CORPORATIONS PUT SIGNIFICANT EFFORT INTO PROMOTING INWARD INVESTMENT FOR THE NEW TOWNS THROUGH BRANDING AND PLACE-MARKETING.

Employment and industry

Central to the new town concept, and part of the near-impossible task of 'self-containment', was the creation of industry and employment to support new town residents. For the early corporations this was restricted by the Board of Trade who, following the Location of Industry Act 1946, had to issue a certificate for new factories over 50,000sq ft.[10] Decentralising industry had been an important part of the Barlow Commission's report (1940; see page 9) which had led to the Act. However, memories of the depression in the 1930s meant that it was challenging for the early new town authorities to invest in new industry as they felt they would be taking a huge risk. Firms were also concerned about having to pay rents to the corporation rather than buying land outright. Yet the postwar period saw an interest in new technology, and emerging firms harnessing this technology were attracted to new towns by the prospect of generous spaces at low rents. Light engineering, food processing, aerospace and synthetic materials all featured in the economies of new towns. In some cases, such as Cwmbran and Skelmersdale, new towns took the high risk of being based on a small number of key manufacturers. By the 1960s, a more liberal approach was taken by the corporations and resources were put into attracting investment from abroad (Figure 2.6).

A short-sighted policy

The New Towns programme had been launched with great ambition and fanfare about the opportunities for a new start, a new future and new approaches to delivery. By the 1950s it emerged that far less political thought had been given to how the programme would end.

Subsequent debate on the end of the Development Corporations would focus on three core issues. The first issue was the Development Corporations themselves – their life span and remit. The second was the assets of the Development Corporation, financial and otherwise, which would be generated through the development process – who would look after them? If not the Development Corporation, then who else, and when and how would they be transferred? A third pivotal issue was one of governance, namely how the corporation would relate to local authorities and, once its job was over, what would be the political boundaries of the new towns? The lack of political commitment to how the corporations would be wound up was inexcusable given the recommendations made by the Reith Committee (1945–47) that the corporations should remain independent from the government.

2.7
EBENEZER HOWARD (CENTRE, IN THE BOWLER HAT) AT THE ANNUAL TREE-PLANTING EVENT IN LETCHWORTH GARDEN CITY, C. 1913. THE EVENT WAS PART OF A COMPREHENSIVE APPROACH TO LONG-TERM STEWARDSHIP IN THE TOWN.

These issues had, of course, been considered decades earlier by Ebenezer Howard and supporters of the garden city movement (Figure 2.7). In Howard's model, the organisation developing the garden city, which invested development profits and income from leaseholders back into the community, would effectively establish a stewardship model in which the 'assets' would be owned by or on behalf of the community, and income from them would be reinvested in perpetuity and linked directly with governance as part of the garden city 'welfare state'. It was independent from the government in order to maintain its values and ensure local ownership and control of assets.

Autonomy and life span of the Development Corporations

Lord Reith's experience at the BBC, and his belief that its independence from the government was crucial to its success, influenced the Reith Commission's views on the Development Corporations. The committee was clear that the corporations should remain independent from the government. As discussed in Chapter 1, that autonomy enabled the corporations to act at speed and 'do the deals'.

The committee's view was that the Development Corporations should continue indefinitely, living side by side with the local authority. However, the view of Lewis Silkin reflected the politics of local government – he expected that '*when its job is substantially done, the corporation must go, and the assets and liabilities handed over to a local authority*'.[11] The Town and Country Planning Association (TCPA) had its own debates about recommended life spans but by 1959 it had formed the view that Development Corporations should be continued until the stage of accommodating 'natural increase' was over (i.e. when children of the first new town migrants had themselves set up households).[12] Because the life span of a corporation was never definitively resolved in law, the minister could decide at any time that their job was over. This vagueness as to their life expectancy left the corporations fatally vulnerable to a government determined to end the New Towns programme.

Handling and transferring the new town assets

A second major flaw in the New Towns law was how it dealt with the transfer of the Development Corporation assets when their job was complete. The New Towns legislation had made clear that when the corporations were wound up the assets would be transferred to the local authority or statutory undertakers. There was no provision or requirement to vest these assets in a community stewardship body like the one at Letchworth. The vagueness about when the job of the corporation was done, combined with the failure to promote community-led stewardship bodies, would later prove to be a major mistake, preventing new towns from looking after their assets in perpetuity.

Although the New Towns Act 1946 was a key part of the 1945 Labour government's agenda, the early delivery of the first wave of new towns took place under the Conservative government of the 1950s. For Winston Churchill's incoming Conservative government, the ambiguity about the wind-up of the corporations and resulting uncertainty over the impact on HM Treasury, which had provided the loans, combined with the economic uncertainty of the time, raised concerns about the programme. Pressure was mounting on the government to provide some certainty, and by 1954 the then Housing Minister Harold Macmillan (Figure 2.8) was recommending that assets were passed to and managed by a single national corporation.

There is some debate about the reasons behind this. Officially the government stated that it did not think the local authorities had the resources or expertise to manage the unique and valuable assets of the New Town Development Corporations. A counter view is that the government was also recognising the potential value of the new town experiments. The first-wave new towns were proving to be profitable and the Conservative government was keen to avoid these assets passing to the (largely Labour-run) authorities.

The forthcoming Act to make this a reality sparked a fierce debate about the activities, remit and objectives of such a body. The need for new legislation to make this change meant that it was not until 1959 that a New Towns Act was passed which established the Commission for the New Towns (CNT) (Figure 2.9).

2.8
HAROLD MACMILLAN WAS THE MASTER OF A CONSERVATIVE ONE-NATION HOUSING POLICY.

2.9
THE LOGO OF THE COMMISSION FOR THE NEW TOWNS (A), AND ON MARKETING MATERIAL FOR LAND IN BRACKNELL TOWNS CENTRE (B). THE CNT PLAYED A SIGNIFICANT ROLE IN THE NEW TOWNS STORY.

The Commission for the New Towns

The Commission for the New Towns (CNT) was established to manage the property of the New Town Development Corporations (and later also the Urban Development Corporations and Housing Action Trusts) transferred to it. The remit of the CNT was explained in the Act as:

> *taking over, managing and turning into account the property previously vested in the development corporation … It shall be the general duty of the Commission to maintain and enhance the value of the land held by them and the return obtained by them from it, but in discharging their functions in relation to any new town the Commission shall have regard to the purpose for which the town was developed under the New Towns Act 1946 and to the convenience and welfare of persons residing, working or carrying on business there.*[13]

The CNT began to absorb the assets of the first-wave new towns once they had reached their target populations and by 1966 had absorbed the corporations at Crawley, Hemel Hempstead (both on 1 April 1962) and the joint Welwyn and Hatfield corporations (1966). It was receiving significant income, with the annual report for 1966 stating, '[These new towns] are a clear indication that the exchequer investment in new towns, far from imposing a burden on the taxpayer, has already proved a far-sighted and rewarding venture.'[14]

For the first 15 years, the CNT was seen to 'symbolise all the contradictions of the new towns policy ... claimed by many to be the most dramatic evidence of the switch from a social to a financial rationale for the new town development ... [but] staffed by people with a long history of involvement in new towns and an intense belief in the concept.'[15]

The 1964 Labour government under Harold Wilson was suspicious of the CNT, seeing it as a form of 'temporary governance'. But Wilson's administration brought with it a renewed interest in the New Towns project. This reached its peak in 1967–68 with the designation of the third and final phase of new towns, such as Milton Keynes, Northampton and Peterborough.

The beginning of the end: urban issues

Despite this ambition and optimism for the New Towns project, and the fact that delivery of those new towns designated in the 1960s was now in full swing, the 1970s brought with it a slow realisation that there was a real and urgent problem emerging in the UK's inner cities, and the new towns were considered part of the problem.

Joining others, such as the Conservative leader of the Greater London Council, Sir Horace Cutler, Labour minister Peter Shore launched a major attack on the programme for draining the inner cities of their most vigorous young people (in fact, only some 17% of those leaving London had actually gone to new towns) and for drawing off money that should be spent on regeneration (in fact, money directed to the new towns was on loan, repayable with interest). Whatever the part played by new towns might have been, the government turned its attention to the problems of the inner cities.

The cities were haemorrhaging population and jobs, primarily driven by deindustrialisation and lack of investment. Meanwhile, the Troubles were well under way in Northern Ireland. In 1978 the Inner Urban Areas Act was passed, following consultants' reports to the Home Office on the problems of inner London, Birmingham and Glasgow. The Act enabled the transfer of resources from the new and expanded towns programmes to urban regeneration. This had already been trialled in Scotland, where in 1974 Stonehouse New Town was abandoned and funds were effectively switched into a major regeneration programme, Glasgow Eastern Area Renewal (GEAR). The focus had turned to partnership and programmes to assist the inner cities.

The 1970s also saw sharp increases in interest rates, which had a direct impact on the loans made to the corporations, forcing them to constantly recalculate budgets based on the changing interest payments, and delaying the dates they thought they could pay back their loans to HM Treasury, making the relationship between the corporations, the CNT and the government increasingly complex.[16]

By the early 1980s, a wave of rioting in areas such as Brixton, in south London (Figure 2.10), and Toxteth, in Liverpool, forced the Conservative government to take action. Margaret Thatcher's government introduced Enterprise Zones and Urban Development Corporations, which retained an emphasis on regenerating inner urban areas. But it was not just the 'pull back' from urban politicians that led to the end of the New Towns programme. There was also a push from Conservative voters in the countryside, who felt that the new towns were bound to lead to more Labour constituencies. Both ideas were indicative of the end of the brief postwar political consensus that national housing problems were a real cross-party social priority.

2.10
BRIXTON, SOUTH LONDON, 1981.
THE INFAMOUS BRIXTON RIOTS
WERE PART OF A PERIOD OF CIVIL
UNREST WHICH FORCED THE
GOVERNMENT TO TAKE ACTION IN
THE INNER CITIES.

The end of the New Towns programme

In this context, Margaret Thatcher's government brought with it a dramatic new approach to the new towns. New Town Development Corporations were not only quangos but were seen to be directly in conflict with ambitions for privatisation and, of course, also represented many of the left-wing metropolitan councils. The timetable for their wind-up was accelerated and targets were set for disposal of their assets to the private sector (Figure 2.11). In the 1980/81 financial year, the Development Corporations were pressured to sell off £120 million worth of the new towns' disposable assets, which were primarily concentrated in commercial and industrial freeholds.

The significance of this change in approach did not go unnoticed. Unsurprisingly, the TCPA was strongly against the government's policy of selling off the new town assets and was strongly critical of the government's 'foolish' policy towards new towns. Its case was based on the premise that a) the policy was contrary to the basic purposes of the new towns; b) the policy was very short-sighted, and short-term economic benefits to public borrowing would be replaced by private borrowing and the assets would not have realised their full value; and c) the policy would prejudice any future consideration of how the new town assets would be managed. The association recognised that some recoiling of assets from the early new towns could work to create funds for public investment, but only where this was done on a prudent and limited basis which recognised the future interests of local citizens.

The Stevenage Development Authority Bill

In 1979 Stevenage Borough Council attempted to save the town's assets through a Private Member's Bill. The Bill, debated in 1980, was based on the legislation that had been used in 1962 to save Letchworth Garden City's assets from the same fate, and proposed the establishment of the Stevenage Development Authority. The authority would take out loans to acquire the assets from the corporation, which it expected might be repayable within 20 years. The Hansard account of the Bill makes fascinating reading, with MPs challenging the government on the legality of selling off the new towns' assets.[17] The government rejected the Bill as a challenge to its authority from local government and with a strong determination to signal a new and free-market approach to housing delivery. Stevenage went on to suffer the fate of other new towns, with many of its assets, including the town centre, ending up in private hands.

The Nene Park Trust, Peterborough

By 1988 some authorities had the benefit of learning from past attempts. Peterborough's development as a new town from 1967 included the creation of the Nene Park to address the stark lack of public green space in the city at the time and '*to provide for the public benefit a park and recreation ground for the inhabitants of Peterborough and visitors with the object of improving the conditions of life for such persons*'.[18] By the time the corporation was wound up in 1988, it had acquired 660 hectares of land in the river valley, secured access agreements with the owners of another 300 hectares, and the park was attracting three quarters of a million visitors a year, and was one of the top ten in Britain.[19] An independent charitable trust was set up to manage the park, with stewardship of the park passing to the newly formed Nene Park Trust. Today the trust is a company limited by guarantee and a registered charity, applying its income to the operation and development of the park.

2.11
THE DOME OF THE CHURCH OF CHRIST THE CORNERSTONE BEING BUILT IN MILTON KEYNES, C. 1991. NEW TOWNS LIKE MILTON KEYNES WERE STILL UNDER CONSTRUCTION WHEN THE DEVELOPMENT CORPORATIONS WERE PREMATURELY WOUND UP.

2.12
AN AERIAL PHOTOGRAPH OF CAMPBELL PARK, CENTRAL MILTON KEYNES. THE PARKS TRUST MANAGES OVER 6,000 ACRES OF PARKLAND IN MILTON KEYNES.

Milton Keynes – Community Foundation and MK Parks Trust

Milton Keynes' network of parks, green spaces and landscaping is undoubtedly one of its crowning glories, and prior to its wind-up the Development Corporation proposed to the Department of the Environment that a Parks Trust should be created to manage the space for public benefit. The Parks Trust, formerly known as Milton Keynes Parks Trust, was established in 1992 to own and manage, in perpetuity, the strategic open space in Milton Keynes. It took a 999-year lease on 4,500 acres of open space and was given an endowment of around £20 million, mainly in the form of commercial property in Milton Keynes, with the rental income providing funding. This figure has now grown to nearly £90 million through investment.[20]

Today, the trust manages over 6,000 acres of parkland in Milton Keynes (Figure 2.12), which includes more than 200 pieces of public art and provides space for income-generating activities such as the World Picnic.

The Milton Keynes Community Foundation was also established in the 1980s, on the initiative of Milton Keynes Development Corporation's Community Development Team. Pioneering the Community Foundation movement in the UK, it was one of many organisations for which the Development Corporation provided premises (for no or peppercorn rent). The foundation has used property and land endowments from Milton Keynes Council, along with commercial and private philanthropic investments, to grow into a profitable enterprise providing a range of support and funding for the voluntary and community sector in Milton Keynes.[21]

Transfer of assets in the rest of the UK

The dissolution of the New Towns programme in Scotland was somewhat different from the procedure in England in that no statutory residuary bodies were created. In the main, the new unitary authorities inherited all the functions of the former Development Corporations. One exception to this is that industrial land was transferred to Scottish Enterprise to market and develop. A memorandum by North Lanarkshire Council stated, 'We would not appear to have suffered the same problems as the English New Towns have experienced when dealing with English Partnerships in this regard.'[22] The new towns were among the largest towns in Scotland and were later seen as important economic growth points for the country. The wider economic role of new towns in Scotland is considered to be the reason that the Scottish New Town Development Corporations had a longer life than those in other parts of the UK.

From 1992 the new towns in England, Wales and Northern Ireland were formally de-listed as a special area of government policy. They were 'reclassified' as equivalent to all other places in the UK within their relevant local authority.[23]

The CNT was instructed to sell its existing portfolio of land and property and any further land or property it received from the remaining Development Corporations as they were wound up. Some of the industrial properties were sold to their occupiers, but many assets were auctioned to the highest private-sector bidder. There was local frustration in the later new towns, which were still in their development phase, as the CNT now had little long-term interest in any new town, and the money raised was taken by HM Treasury to be spent elsewhere.

Assets were also sold before they had a chance to mature to their full value – the surrounding area was not yet developed, for example – to the disadvantage of the taxpayer. A significant proportion of these assets was in the form of socially rented homes. The government wanted these homes to be sold to their tenants, or transferred to housing associations (Registered Social Landlords) where sales were not possible. However, when consulted, many of the tenants chose transfer to the local authority – whom they felt they could trust and would be more accountable – rather than to housing associations.

Between 1977 and 1996, all the remaining Development Corporations were wound up (by 1992 in England and by 1996 in Scotland), with local authorities receiving most of the liabilities but with an endowment (i.e. land/buildings that were expensive to run or maintain – classified as 'community-related assets') and the social housing as chosen by tenants.

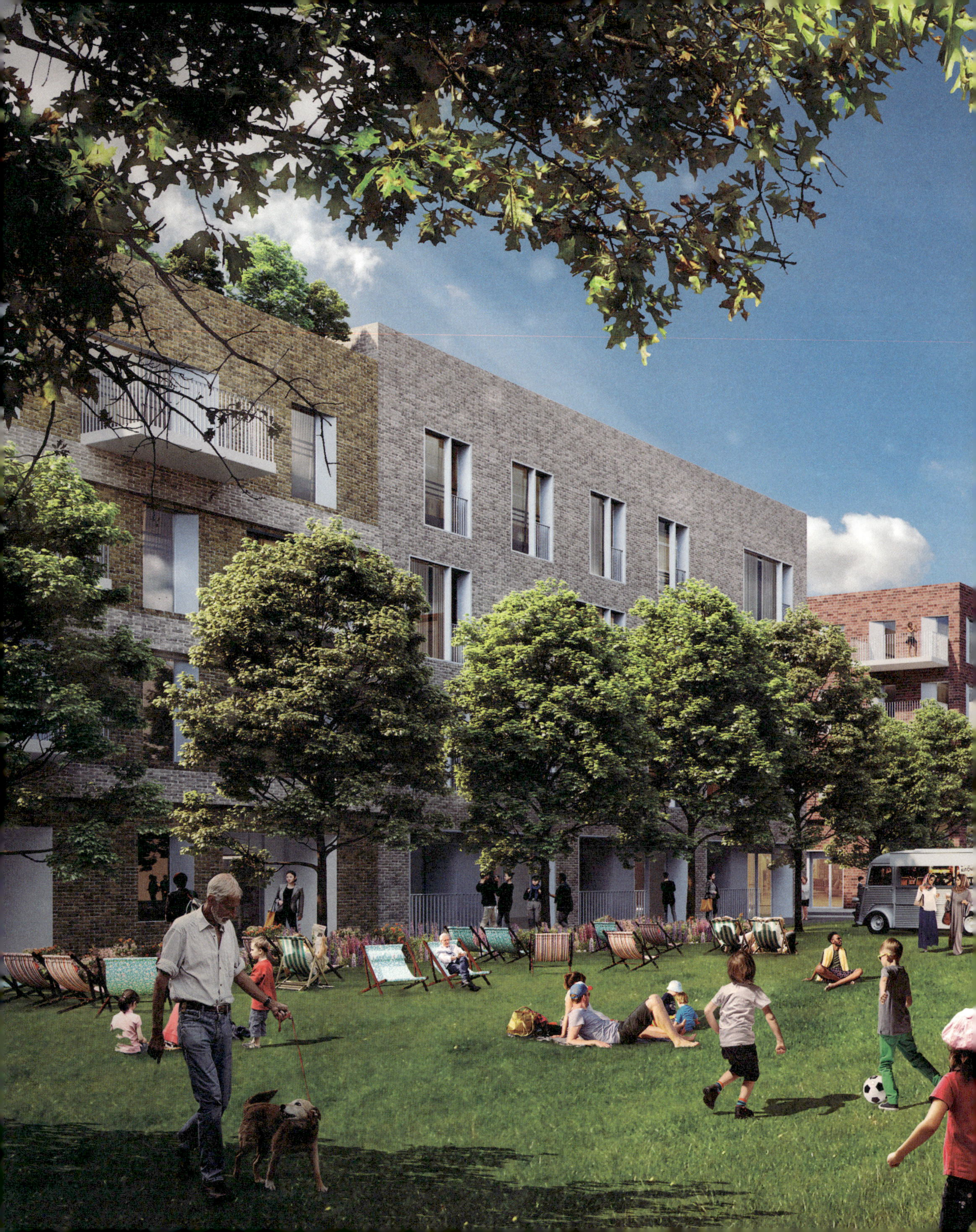

2.13
HOMES ENGLAND'S PROPOSED TOWN CENTRE AT NORTHSTOWE, CAMBRIDGESHIRE. HOMES ENGLAND IS THE SUCCESSOR TO THE COMMISSION FOR THE NEW TOWNS AND IS WORKING WITH COUNCILS TO DELIVER NEW COMMUNITIES TODAY, SUCH AS NORTHSTOWE.

The social housing became an issue as, nationally, the funds to maintain the housing stock were inadequate and maintenance was too onerous to be covered under standard local authority funding streams.

Although many of the assets, including the social housing, were income-generating, many soon became liabilities as authorities struggled to finance their maintenance. There was also some irresponsible behaviour – where endowment money was spent to depress council tax levels, for example. In some cases, the institutional memory that this money had been endowed for a key stewardship purpose was simply lost. Any subsequent sales by local authorities of the assets they had received were subject to 'claw-back', under which the increase in the value from the sale of any of the liabilities for commercial purposes had to be given back to the CNT, of a reducing proportion as years passed. (From 1999 it had to be given to the CNT's successor body, English Partnerships, which combined the CNT and the Urban Regeneration Agency; in 2008 English Partnerships was subsumed into what is now called Homes England, which still operates today as England's national housing and regeneration agency, Figure 2.13.)

It would take a decade for government to begin to consider the impact of its wind-up of the New Towns programme on the new towns themselves. The following chapter considers what happened to the new towns, and wider interest in the new town idea.

3.1
(OPPOSITE)
FOLLOWING THE END OF THE NEW TOWNS PROGRAMME, GOVERNMENT RELIED LARGELY ON THE PRIVATE SECTOR TO DELIVER. THERE HAVE BEEN SOME NOTABLE ATTEMPTS BY THE PRIVATE SECTOR TO DELIVER NEW TOWNS AT SMALLER SCALES, INCLUDING NEW ASH GREEN IN KENT, BUILT BY SPAN – A PROPERTY-DEVELOPMENT COMPANY FORMED IN THE LATE 1950S, LED BY THE ARCHITECT AND DEVELOPER GEOFFREY TOWNSEND IN 1966. THE 2,000 HOME SCHEME, DESIGNED BY ERIC LYONS WAS TO INCLUDE 450 GREATER LONDON COUNCIL HOUSING TENANTS. THE GLC HAD TO PULL OUT AND EVENTUALLY SPAN SOLD THE DEVELOPMENT TO BOVIS HOMES IN 1971. THE DEVELOPMENT WAS CRITICISED FOR ATTRACTING A NARROW DEMOGRAPHIC BUT WAS AN INTERESTING ATTEMPT, WHICH INCLUDED A TWO-TIERED MANAGEMENT MODEL THAT WENT SOME WAY TOWARDS HOWARD'S VISION OF LONG-TERM STEWARDSHIP

03

NEW TOWN HINTERLAND

Introduction

The three decades from the final winding up of the New Towns programme to where we find ourselves in 2020 are marked by two policy decisions that had long-term implications for the new towns and for the legacy of new towns as a solution to our national housing crisis. It is a period that contained some real attempts to deal with growth and reinvent a notion of national urban policy, but in retrospect it was dominated by short-termism and an underlying faith that the private sector could lift the full burden of delivering the homes we need (Figures 3.1 to 3.5). It was an era when the government seemed to move from an ambivalent attitude to the new towns' legacy to offering them limited thought. This position was fuelled by the mythology about the existing programme and a failure to value and understand the special circumstances of the new town communities, some of which were still less than 30 years old. As a result, the housing crisis became more extreme and the existing new towns received no dedicated policy attention from successive national governments.

NEW TOWNS: THE RISE, FALL AND REBIRTH

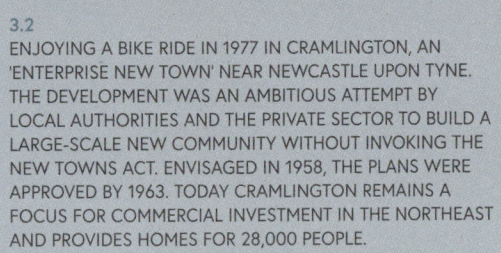

3.2
ENJOYING A BIKE RIDE IN 1977 IN CRAMLINGTON, AN 'ENTERPRISE NEW TOWN' NEAR NEWCASTLE UPON TYNE. THE DEVELOPMENT WAS AN AMBITIOUS ATTEMPT BY LOCAL AUTHORITIES AND THE PRIVATE SECTOR TO BUILD A LARGE-SCALE NEW COMMUNITY WITHOUT INVOKING THE NEW TOWNS ACT. ENVISAGED IN 1958, THE PLANS WERE APPROVED BY 1963. TODAY CRAMLINGTON REMAINS A FOCUS FOR COMMERCIAL INVESTMENT IN THE NORTHEAST AND PROVIDES HOMES FOR 28,000 PEOPLE.

3.3
SOUTH WOODHAM FERRERS, ESSEX. IN THE 1970S, ESSEX COUNTY COUNCIL ACQUIRED LAND TO DEVELOP A NEW COMMUNITY OF 17,500 PEOPLE IN 4,600 HOMES AT SOUTH WOODHAM FERRERS. THE PROJECT WAS DELIVERED (IN THE 1980S) MAINLY BY THE PRIVATE SECTOR BUT WITHIN A TIGHT PLANNING AND DESIGN FRAMEWORK SET BY THE LOCAL AUTHORITY. THE COUNCIL HAD ADOPTED THE RECENT ESSEX DESIGN GUIDE FOR RESIDENTIAL AREAS IN RESPONSE TO CONCERNS ABOUT THE POOR STANDARDS OF SPECULATIVE DEVELOPMENT IN THE COUNTY. WHILE THE DETAILS OF SOME OF ITS DESIGN FEATURES HAVE COME UNDER SCRUTINY, COUNCILS AND DELIVERY PARTNERS TODAY CAN STILL LEARN FROM SOUTH WOODHAM FERRERS' APPROACH TO DELIVERY, AND THE PIONEERING SPIRIT OF ITS DESIGN SOLUTIONS.

In stark contrast to the intense public debate that went with the postwar New Towns programme, recent governments have avoided any serious attempt to have a national conversation about our housing delivery model. In the absence of a long-term national narrative, housing policy has become a sterile debate in which numbers are now more important than people's basic wellbeing. Since 2010 the problems have intensified, partly due to extreme levels of deregulation and partly due to collapse of investment of key tenures such as social rent. This chapter briefly summarises the key policy milestones in this period but the headline is clear: the continuation of the development of new towns, even in a much more limited way, would have made a transformative difference to the amount and quality of places for people.

03 NEW TOWN HINTERLAND

3.4
GREENTOWN WAS A COLLECTIVE-ACTION PROJECT ESTABLISHED IN THE 1980S TO BUILD A 'COOPERATIVELY RUN AND ECOLOGICALLY SOUND VILLAGE COMMUNITY' IN MILTON KEYNES. THERE WERE ALSO SEVERAL ATTEMPTS AT 'DO IT-YOURSELF NEW TOWNS' BY FORWARD-THINKING ORGANISATIONS – NOTABLY, THE GREENTOWN GROUP AT MILTON KEYNES, THE TCPA AT LIGHTMOOR, TELFORD AND FINDHORN ECO VILLAGE IN MORAY, SCOTLAND. IN THESE CASES, GROUPS OF INDIVIDUALS DRIVEN BY THE COLLECTIVE AIM OF A FAIRER AND MORE COOPERATIVE WAY OF LIVING ATTEMPTED TO GAIN CONTROL OF LAND AND START THEIR OWN COMMUNITIES. A COMBINATION OF MARKET FORCES (RISING LAND VALUES) AND FEARFUL LOCAL AUTHORITIES PREVENTED MANY OF THESE SCHEMES FROM BECOMING A REALITY. GREENTOWN WAS A COLLECTIVE ACTION PROJECT ESTABLISHED IN THE 1980S TO BUILD A 'COOPERATIVELY RUN AND ECOLOGICALLY SOUND VILLAGE COMMUNITY' IN MILTON KEYNES.

3.5
CONSTRUCTION IN PROGRESS AT LIGHTMOOR, TELFORD. IN 1980, THE TOWN AND COUNTRY PLANNING ASSOCIATION (TCPA) WORKED WITH TELFORD DEVELOPMENT CORPORATION IN AN ATTEMPT TO BUILD BRITAIN'S THIRD GARDEN CITY AT LIGHTMOOR. IN 2017 THE PROJECT CELEBRATED ITS 30TH BIRTHDAY. THE PROJECT IS NEXT TO THE JOSEPH ROWNTREE HOUSING TRUST LIGHTMOOR VILLAGE DEVELOPMENT OF 1,000 HOMES, WHICH IS ALSO LOCATED ON FORMER DEVELOPMENT CORPORATION LAND.

The existing new towns and national urban policy

Despite the growing literature on new towns and two parliamentary inquiries in the 1990s, successive governments failed to grasp the need for a national policy in relation to the existing new towns. No attempt was made to redress the removal of new town assets nor to confront the implications this disaster was bound to have for their renewal. New towns ceased to be an explicit departmental responsibility of national government and faded from the public policy debate. This meant that their fate rested on national approaches to urban policy and economic development and the ability of local government to finish the job started by the Development Corporations. As Chapter 2 pointed out, this wasn't helped by the frankly chaotic local government boundaries in England, which led some places to have single local councils and others to be governed remotely as part of larger districts. The governance of new towns also changed radically with the drive, after 1997, for devolution. While the management of new towns had always been distinctive in Northern Ireland, the devolution of planning in Scotland to the Scottish government and in Wales to the Welsh Assembly has led to different national planning approaches. Both now and in the future, the nations and regions of the UK will undoubtedly seek diverging approaches to the new towns' legacy.

From 1997, existing new towns benefited from wider programmes of regeneration and investment, but the overall focus was on inner-city renewal and dealing with the housing market failure inside regions, rather than a fundamental attempt to challenge the growing inequalities between the regions. The practical impact of this policy was that new towns reflected the success or failures of the regional economies. This was not simply a crude north–south divide – places like Warrington in the Northwest have proved to be highly successful growth points. But in general, places like Milton Keynes and Stevenage performed extremely well, while Peterlee, Skelmersdale and Cwmbran suffered when key employers, often the ones the towns had been created to serve, closed or relocated. Connectivity was partly a factor in this uneven performance and while all the new towns had strong road links, it now appears very odd that Peterlee had no direct rail connection to Newcastle, nor Skelmersdale to Liverpool.

In retrospect, urban policy up to 2010 was deeply conflicted, seeking the renewal of, for example, the Northern core cities but without ever fundamentally challenging the wider economic geography of the UK. Crudely, the Southeast was dominated by the challenge of rapid growth while much of the ex-industrial North was framed by an impact notion of managed decline exemplified by the much-maligned Housing Market Renewal Initiative (launched in 2002, with funding ending in 2011). This policy resulted in the demolition of low-value and often poor-quality housing in inner-city areas and the regeneration of neighbourhoods with new private and housing association stock.

'New' new towns

Under Tony Blair's premiership, the government saw house prices rise and affordability start to pinch in London and the Southeast and set ambitious housebuilding targets of 2 million new homes by 2016 and 3 million new homes by 2020, based upon a projected need of 240,000 new homes per year. Regional Spatial Strategies provided the evidence base for several smaller new communities that are now being delivered in places like the Cambridge subregion, leading to the development of Cambourne, Longstanton-Oakington and Northstowe, and more recently Alconbury Weald and Waterbeach.[1]

The Sustainable Communities Plan

The high-water mark of this strategic approach to meeting housing need was three related initiatives, beginning in 2003 with the Sustainable Communities Plan.[2] The plan identified four Southeast growth areas – Thames Gateway, Milton Keynes and South Midlands, Ashford and the London-Stansted-Cambridge-Peterborough corridor – to be carried forward through the regional strategy process, to accommodate large amounts of housing and related development. The Growth Areas programme proposed through the Sustainable Communities Plan was perhaps the first time since the new towns that the concept of a planned new community had been considered in a holistic way, highlighting the importance of infrastructure, social and community development and good design. The programme forced all government departments to the table and helped to convince the Treasury that large-scale development could work, even alongside the regeneration of other towns and cities.[3]

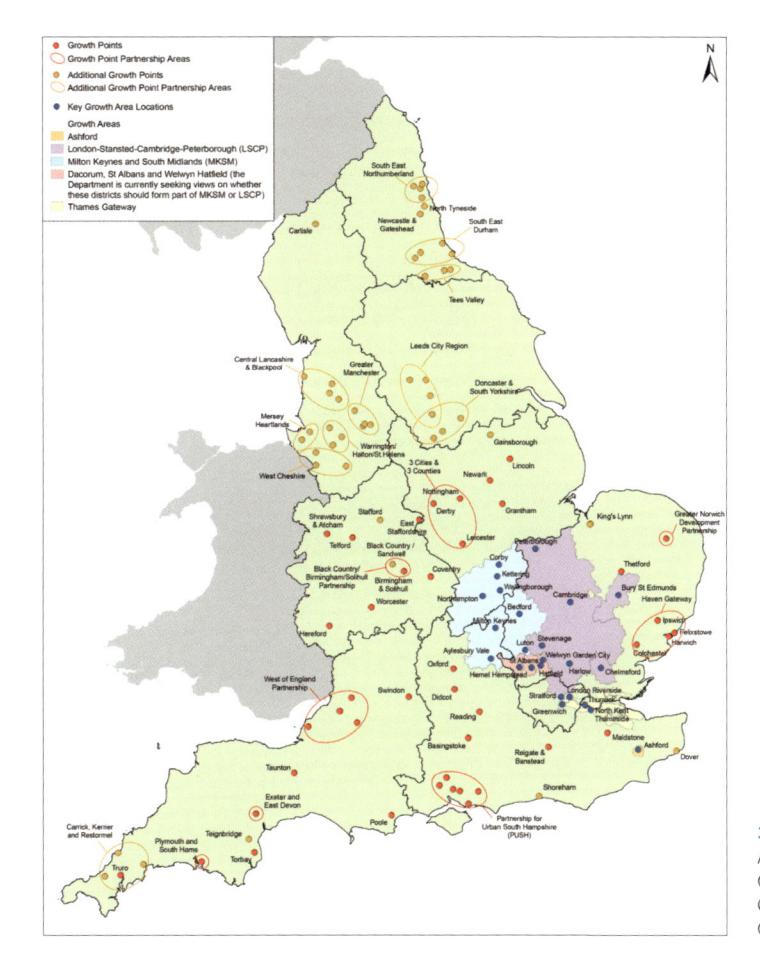

3.6
A MAP SHOWING THE LOCATIONS OF THE 2006 GROWTH AREAS AND GROWTH POINTS IN THE SOUTHEAST OF ENGLAND.

The Growth Points programme

By 2005, within the context of a growing housing affordability crisis, and following Kate Barker's review of housing supply,[4] there was a desire to take further action to stimulate local growth. In 2006 the government established the Growth Points programme (Figure 3.6), in which local planning authorities took the lead.[5] Councils were invited to propose additional housing (a minimum of 20%) beyond existing plans as part of a wider growth strategy, in exchange for government help on infrastructure (particularly transport) and a modest grant to prepare infrastructure and community facilities.

By 2007, 1.6 million homes had been identified in existing Regional Spatial Strategies (RSS) and the 2003 Sustainable Communities Plan laid the foundation for around 650,000 homes in the four Growth Areas, according to a government White Paper.[6] But this was not enough, and in a bid to reach a higher target of 240,000 new homes per year by 2016 and reduce carbon dioxide emissions by 80% below 1990 levels by 2050, the government launched the eco-towns programme.

The eco-towns

In 2007, as the international recession caused by the banking collapse began to hit, the government invited bids for 10 new communities of around 25,000 population each (Figure 3.7). The programme was accompanied by a Planning Policy Statement (PPS) which set out the high objectives to be met.

The eco-towns were intended to be exemplars of good practice in new development, meeting the highest environmental standards while promoting social justice, and inclusive communities (Figure 3.8). The PPS provided a range of minimum standards which were more challenging and stretching than would normally be required for a new development.[7] The eco-towns were to meet zero-carbon and lifetime homes standards, 40% of the total area was to be multifunctional and well-managed green space (at least half of which was to be public open space) and there was to be a net gain in local biodiversity. The eco-town standards set out in the PPS remain the most ambitious set of government-defined development standards ever seen in English policy.

3.7
A MAP SHOWING THE LOCATIONS OF THE SHORTLISTED BIDS FOR ECO-TOWNS. ONLY FOUR BIDS (THE RED DOTS) WERE SUCCESSFUL.

A missed opportunity

The brief strategic renaissance under the Blair administration had many important benefits, not least in recognising the need to work out where growth might take place across the wider South and therefore how to deal with growth in a sustainable and managed way. However, in retrospect it was defined by three key limitations.

3.8
NORTH WEST BICESTER 'ECO-TOWN' IN OXFORDSHIRE. THE NEW COMMUNITY, WHICH INCLUDES 6,000 HOMES, HAS BEEN SUPPORTED BY GOVERNMENT INITIATIVES SINCE THE ECO-TOWNS PROGRAMME AND MADE AN EARLY COMMITMENT TO HIGH ENVIRONMENTAL STANDARDS. TODAY IT IS PART OF THE GOVERNMENT'S 'GARDEN COMMUNITIES' PROGRAMME.

Key limitations of the Blair administration's housing initiatives

1. All these initiatives were strikingly short lived, and none had any opportunity to effectively bed down before they were abolished in 2010. Regional Spatial Strategies had an effective life of around five years; the eco-towns programme less than two years. The English disease of short-termism which had broken out with the disastrous cancellation of the New Towns programme in 1980 had now become paralysing. There was a complete failure to capitalise on the time and effort devoted to regional planning, a process which was well suited to identification of new settlements.

2. It did not succeed in building public consent and both regional plans and the eco-towns proved vulnerable to the allegation that they were 'top down' Whitehall impositions but without the benefit of the levels of funding or Development Corporations of the New Towns programme. The important lessons about the complex but fruitful relationship between central and local government in the New Towns programme had, in general, been forgotten. While many of the eco-towns remained good ideas, there was little time for them to emerge through a genuine local process.

3. The final issue is the bizarre inability of the government to recognise the value of the New Towns programme in driving housing delivery. We have already made clear that this almost wilful failure to grasp the obvious solution was framed by a fear that central government would appear 'Stalinist'. Although this is a complete misreading of the new towns' experience, it proved an unshakeable article of faith. The government did use Urban Development Corporations for regeneration purposes and notably for some growth areas, but did not designate a New Town Development Corporation nor seek to set out a national approach to housing needs.

2010 to 2018: slums or garden cities?

The 2010 general election resulted in a new coalition government with radically different approaches to planning, approaches that reflected the anxiety in many Conservative local authorities about the scale of growth contained in regional plans. The Secretary of State for Communities and Local Government, Eric Pickles, seized upon the notion of 'localism' to sweep away any strategic approach to housing growth. Neighbourhood planning was seen as a new approach to building bottom-up planning. A whole series of technical bodies that provided evidence on housing and planning were abolished. This was a ground-zero approach to planning for place based on a simplistic call for a 'bonfire of the quangos' and clearly identifying planning as the enemy of enterprise. The government announced that the eco-towns PPS would be revoked as part of a streamlining of planning guidance.[8] In retrospect, the period after 2010 represented a new low point in the fortunes of town planning, often fuelled by the sort of mythology that this book has set out to challenge. While the deregulation and underfunding of planning has been well documented, its zenith came with the removal of the need to seek planning permission to change office and commercial buildings to residential use. This expansion of permitted development has led to a well-documented and staggering fall in the quality of homes, but it has been justified by the government as contributing to housing delivery numbers.

The aftermath of 2010 left an intellectual, moral and practical vacuum about how to deal with housing growth in England. It assumed, without any evidential basis, that the housing market unleashed from regulation could meet the complex housing needs of society at the right rate and to sufficient quality. It took some time for the consequences of these changes to become apparent and Chapter 13 explores how, at their worst, they are leading to a new generation of slum housing.

'Locally led' garden cities

It can only be described as ironic that having abolished all notions of strategic planning for new homes, the coalition government began the slow road to reinventing it. By April 2014, two years after Prime Minister David Cameron first announced his support for a new wave of garden cities in Britain, a long-awaited Locally-led Garden Cities prospectus was launched.[9] This echoed the reference in the 2012 National Planning Policy Framework to the Garden City Principles. The language of garden cities is important because it was considered to be much safer than talking about new towns, even though it implied much more radical outcomes, not least the mutualisation of development profits. The prospectus invited expressions of interest for proposals for new communities with 15,000 or more homes that demonstrate 'local support', 'scale', 'connectivity', 'robust delivery arrangements', 'commercial viability' and a 'high proportion of brownfield land'.[10] Subsequent rounds of this programme have seen the scale of this ambition reduced to include places of 1,500 homes (Figure 3.9).

Much of the supporting text of the prospectus said the right things about being ambitious, innovative and 'delivering inspirational new garden cities fit for the 21st century'.[11] But the prospectus could not square the circle between its commitment to localism and defining the right level of national policy and financial support. There were no locational criteria or any forms of strategic approach, no requirement for expressions of interest to demonstrate how the project will apply the Garden City Principles, no new funding and a lack of clarity on how the programme would work with existing planning processes. In short, the identification of major new

3.9
CHILMINGTON GREEN, IN ASHFORD, KENT. PART OF THE GOVERNMENT'S 'GARDEN COMMUNITIES' PROGRAMME, CHILMINGTON GREEN IS DEVELOPING INNOVATIVE APPROACHES TO STEWARDSHIP AND DESIGN-QUALITY STANDARDS AND WILL EVENTUALLY INCLUDE UP TO 5,750 HOMES.

settlements would need to come forward through the existing local plan process, rather than using the New Towns legislation which was designed specifically to deliver them.

2016 onwards – from 'garden cities' to 'garden communities'

By August 2016, the Locally-led Garden Cities prospectus had led to Cherwell District Council (Bicester), Wellingborough, Kettering and Corby Borough Councils (North Northamptonshire), Basingstoke and Deane Borough Council (Manydown), Braintree, Colchester, Tendring Districts and Essex County Councils (North Essex) and Shepway District Council (Otterpool Park) receiving support from the government (Figure 3.10). Many of these schemes were not new and some were part of the eco-towns programme. At Ebbsfleet, an Urban Development Corporation was established to drive delivery of existing identified growth and to knit together a new community. This was an immensely complex and sensitive job given that virtually all the land was in the hands of private developers and much of it already had planning permission.

The 2016 budget made clear that the government supported the construction of a new wave of garden towns and cities across the country, with the potential to deliver over 100,000 homes. There were three main elements to this. Firstly, the provision of capacity support, assisted by

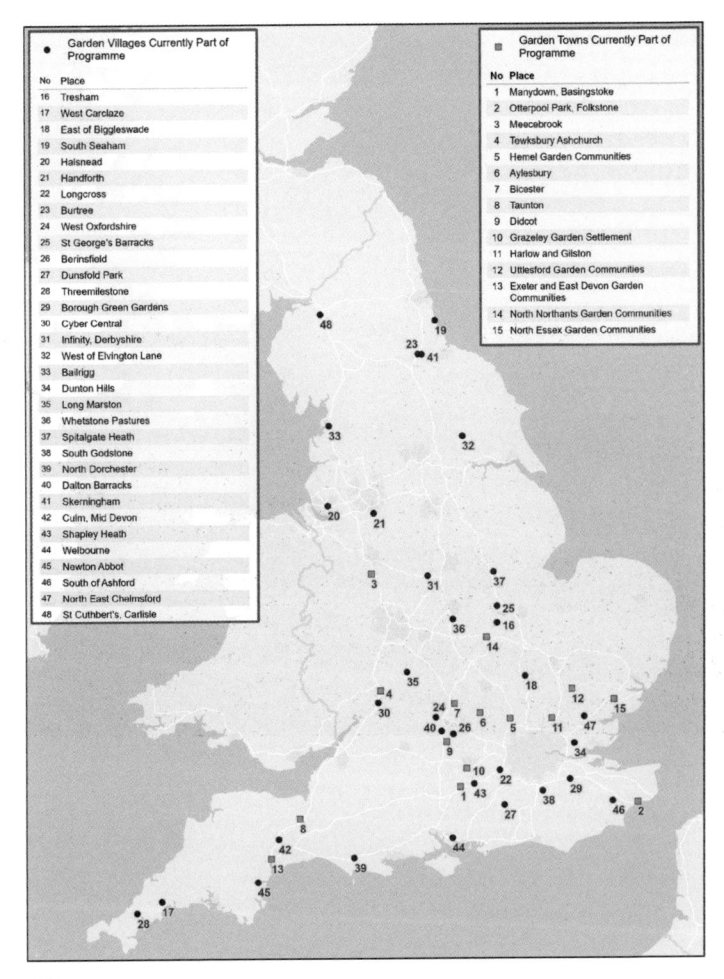

3.10
A MAP OF PROJECTS RECEIVING SUPPORT UNDER THE 'GARDEN COMMUNITIES' PROGRAMME BY AUGUST 2019.

a new prospectus; secondly, a commitment to update legislation to 'speed up and simplify the process for delivering new settlements'; and thirdly, that 'incentives' would be introduced for places willing to commit to higher housing numbers.[12] Further details were provided in a new prospectus launched by the Department for Communities and Local Government (DCLG).[13] The new prospectus included an offer of support for 'Garden Villages' of 1,500–10,000 homes, but while the ambition may have been there for larger-scale new places, in practice nothing on the scale of new towns has been proposed.

After much advocacy of the new towns model by the TCPA, the government amended the New Towns Act 1981 to create a new, parallel route for the creation of 'locally led New Town Development Corporations'[14] passed successfully through the House of Commons, providing a new opportunity for ambitious councils planning new communities to have a leading role in their delivery. Updating the New Towns legislation appeared to be a totemic moment in the debate about new communities, but its contents ignored some of the key lessons of the New Towns programme.

Rather than modernising the primary route, the government instead decided to create a new, parallel route, through secondary legislation. The New Towns Act 1981 (Local Authority Oversight) Regulations enable a local authority, or group of local authorities, to take on some of the Secretary of State's role, including acting as Oversight Authority for the 'locally led New Town Development Corporation'.[15] This shifts the core responsibility for the new town's Development Corporation outside of national government and places the full weight of financial responsibility on the local authority. This has significant implications for the take-up of these measures, making them attractive mainly to high-value areas where development values can provide the confidence for local action. It also removes the responsibility of national government to frame the right support package and to force a dialogue with other key government departments on things like transport and health infrastructure.

Despite these challenges, it is significant that the new towns approach has been recognised and that there have been attempts to strengthen the requirements for long-term stewardship of a Development Corporation's assets. However, taken as a whole, the locally led approach will be of limited utility unless it is backed by the right financial offers and strategic support from the government and unless such a designation can command public confidence. The removal of the requirement for a public inquiry before designation for a locally led new town is not going to help build trust. It is becoming increasingly clear that the architecture of original New Towns legislation represents the most effective way of securing delivery. In a small nation, national government has to play an active role in supporting local action.

Given the political uncertainty that confronts the nation in 2020, it is not easy to pass a definitive judgment on the last decade, but two things are apparent. Firstly, the stop-start nature of national policy illustrates a collective failure to build a consensus about the value of long-term democratic planning. The abrupt abolition of strategic planning in 2012 has been followed by the rapid reinvention of ad hoc strategic cooperation around England. The reluctance of national government to set out an evidence-based approach to our national housing and development needs has resulted in a fragmented policy approach to housing delivery. There are signs that this is beginning to change, with a more active role for Homes England and local government. Capacity and skills remain a major problem, however, and rebuilding the capacity and confidence of local authorities will take time.

Secondly, the powerful policy assumption that markets alone can deliver housing needs has crowded out more creative thinking about effective delivery models. These models include a more fruitful relationship between the market and public sector, and the building of trust and a genuine partnership between local and central government. They would certainly include a much more open and honest national conversation with the public on how to solve the housing crisis. While any number of the many government initiatives in the last decade might be welcome in their own right, there has been little policy coherence on how to manage housing growth strategically. This lack of a development narrative for England remains a striking feature of our recent history. The last decade has been one thrown away on a deregulatory experiment which has failed, while the obvious opportunity of the new towns model has not been seized. On some issues, such as poverty and climate change, this time we could ill afford to waste.

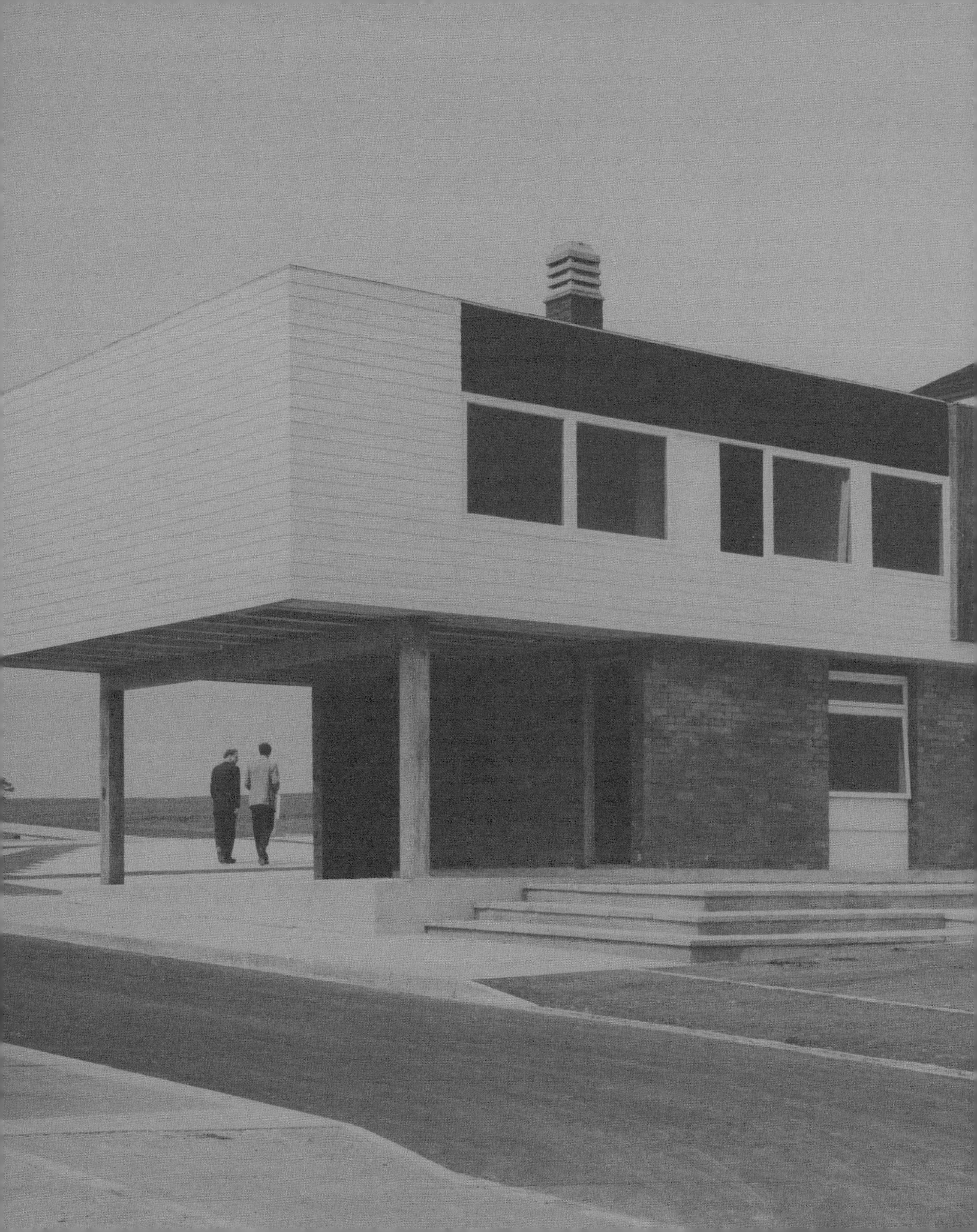

PART II

THE NEW TOWNS AT MIDDLE AGE

04 THE NEW TOWNS TODAY   05 CASE STUDY: HARLOW
06 CASE STUDY: PETERLEE, COUNTY DURHAM
07 CASE STUDY: CWBRAN, TORFAEN COUNTY (MONMOUTHSHIRE)
08 CASE STUDY: CUMBERNAULD, NORTH LANARKSHIRE
09 CASE STUDY: SKELMERSDALE, WEST LANCASHIRE
10 CASE STUDY: CRAIGAVON, COUNTY ARMAGH
11 CASE STUDY: MILTON KEYNES, BUCKINGHAMSHIRE

04

THE NEW TOWNS TODAY

Introduction

In 2021 it will be 75 years since the New Towns Act was passed and many of the new towns are now celebrating milestone designation anniversaries (Figure 4.1). The new towns are in fact no longer 'new', but established places which currently provide homes for 2.8 million people.[1] But as the Act's Diamond anniversary approaches, how are the new towns themselves faring today?

As a set of places, the 32 new towns created through the New Towns Act exhibit a range of successes and failures – including, as they do, both the fastest-growing and most successful places in the UK yet also some of the most deprived. The new towns were always 'new communities', but in fact varied from the creation of a whole new city combining existing villages (e.g. Milton Keynes), expansion of historical towns (e.g. Peterborough), provision of housing for existing industry (e.g. Peterlee and Cwmbran) and the regeneration of whole subregions (e.g. Central Lancashire). Each place has had its own experience which cannot be divorced from the wider economic and social context in which it sits. However, they all have in common both an approach to delivery through the New Towns Act, and the legacy, particularly in the later new towns, of a dramatically abandoned programme of support. Understanding their individual and collective experiences is essential to learn lessons – not only for their growth and renewal (Figure 4.2), but to understand what we can learn about tackling our current housing crisis. Part 2 of this book looks at those individual and collective experiences of the places created through the New Towns Act to help understand the lessons for today.

NEW TOWNS: THE RISE, FALL AND REBIRTH

(a)

(b)

4.1
IN 2017 MILTON KEYNES CELEBRATED ITS 50TH BIRTHDAY WITH A PROGRAMME OF CULTURAL EVENTS, INCLUDING THE 'FESTIVAL OF FIRE' (A) AND A PARTY AT BLETCHLEY PARK (B).

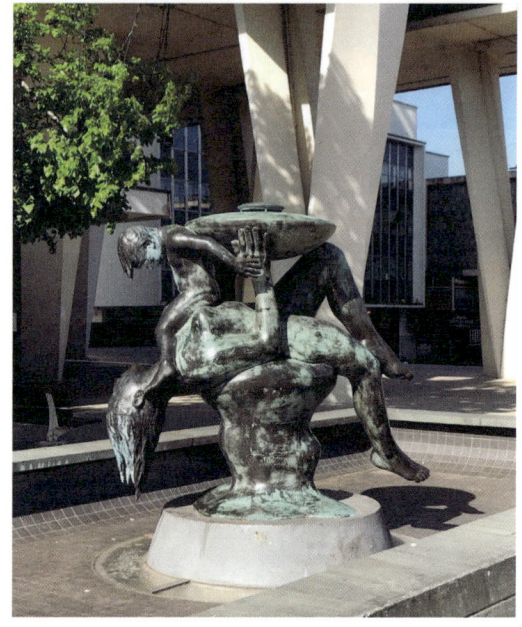

4.2
MOTHER AND CHILD, BY MAURICE LAMBERT, 1962. THE SCULPTURE WAS DESIGNED FOR BASILDON DEVELOPMENT CORPORATION AND IS TODAY A SYMBOL OF THE REBIRTH OF NEW TOWNS.

Recognising and understanding the new towns' legacy

Just as national government and wider civil society has adopted a negative mythology about the new towns, so those in control of the new towns today have an equivocal relationship with the legacy. For many years, 'new town authorities' (the 'host' local authorities where the new towns are located) were keen to distance themselves from the 'new town' label, considering themselves to be no longer 'new' and keen to secure whatever support was available from a government not interested in the new town story. In recent years this appears to have changed. Perhaps fuelled by the submission of evidence to the Select Committees on the New Towns in the 2000s, many places are now realising that while they share many issues with other towns of a similar age, they are, in fact, a 'special case'.[2] Their history, design and built heritage provides them with opportunities to address urban challenges in a way not available to other places.

The Town and Country Planning Association's New Towns Network[3] and ongoing research into lessons from the new towns[4] has sought to bring authorities together to understand these unique attributes and shared experiences. In 2014, the second stage of this research included a survey of chief planners in each of the new town authorities, which sought to understand the legacy of the Development Corporations in their new towns, and the challenges and opportunities they are facing today. This was combined with analysis of 2011 Census data (and equivalents for Scotland, Wales and Northern Ireland) to gather headline statistics on key socio-economic information.[5] That information is used in this chapter, along with information gathered from countless conversations, visits and meetings with the new town authorities and through the work of the New Towns All-Party Parliamentary Group (see page 158), to give a picture of how the new towns are faring today, and what is needed to secure their growth and renewal. It does not claim to be definitive, but offers a well-informed portrait of these places.

Key statistics

Population

The New Town Designation Orders specified target population numbers rather than housing numbers, which enabled some flexibility in the way homes were delivered and proved a useful approach as projected populations fluctuated over time. Overall, the 32 new towns were planned to provide homes for a population of approximately 3.3 million (2.6 million in England, 330,500 in Scotland, 68,000 in Wales and 364,500 in Northern Ireland). These figures included projections which looked forward 40–50 years, to as late as 2006 for the first wave new towns, and of course the reality of this has fluctuated over time, but in 2011 the new towns were home to 2,761,272 people:

- 2,227,627 in England
- 268,702 in Scotland
- 205,051 in Northern Ireland
- 59,892 in Wales.[6]

Housing

The nearly 2.8 million new town residents live in 1,150,226 households, representing 4.3% of the 26.4 million households across the UK.[7] A high proportion of homes for social rent was a characteristic of the New Towns programme. While the new towns were far from immune to the impact of the 'Right to Buy', they have retained a high proportion of socially rented housing, with 23% of all households in the new towns being socially rented – 4.9 percentage points higher than the UK average.[8] This equates to 5.5% of the UK's socially rented housing stock, a significant contribution. The new towns also provide 4.3% of the UK's owner-occupied housing, but the average number of households in owner-occupation in the new towns is 4.9 percentage points lower than the UK's average, while the proportion of privately rented homes in the new towns is 3.4 percentage points lower than the UK average.[9] This simply reflects their new town heritage and the focus on the provision of socially rented homes.

Deprivation

Deprivation statistics reflect the very mixed fortunes of the new towns today. Overall the new towns perform close to the national average, but several of the new towns – for example Runcorn (Halton ranked 32nd most deprived), Washington (Sunderland ranked 38th most deprived) and Corby (Corby, ranked 51st most deprived) – are located in some of the lowest-ranking authorities in England for deprivation (ranking 1–327, where 1 is the most deprived). The picture is far starker in Scotland, where new town authorities all feature at or above middle ranking for deprivation (out of Scotland's 32 unitary authorities, where 1 is the most deprived):

1. Cumbernauld: 5
2. East Kilbride: 12
3. Glenrothes: 16
4. Irvine: 3
5. Livingston: 11.

For Northern Ireland, the four new town authorities rank at 20 or below (out of 26, where 1 is the most deprived):

- Antrim: 20
- Ballymena: 11
- Craigavon: 4
- Derry-Londonderry: 3.[10]

Employment

Taken as a whole, the employment statistics for the new towns show a positive picture (Figure 4.3), with the average percentage of the population that is economically active for all the new towns being 71.7%, which is 2.2 percentage points higher than the UK average of 69.5%, and average employment across all the new towns being at 63.4%, 1.8 percentage points higher than the UK average of 61.6%.

04 THE NEW TOWNS TODAY

4.3
WARRINGTON TOWN CENTRE. NEW TOWNS SUCH AS WARRINGTON ARE AMONG THE FASTEST-GROWING PLACES IN THE UK.

Of course, the reality is more nuanced, and the economically active rates range between 59.2% (Derry/Londonderry) and 78.4% (Bracknell). Predictably, the Southeast England new towns contain the highest percentages of economically active populations: Bracknell (78.4%), Crawley (76.9%), Milton Keynes (75.9%), Stevenage (75.7%) and Hemel Hempstead (75.3%). Three quarters of the new towns (24 out of 32) have an economically active percentage above the average for their region (those below the regional average are: Peterlee, Hatfield, Basildon, Runcorn, Glenrothes, Irvine, Craigavon and Derry/Londonderry). Only three new towns have a figure more than 2.5 percentage points below their regional average: Peterlee (62.2%), Hatfield (65.2%) and Derry/Londonderry (59.2%). Hatfield's statistics are misleading due to the high proportion of students (33.7% of the working-age population in the town is made up of students, of which 12.8% are economically active). Bracknell has the biggest positive difference, with an economically active percentage that is 6.3 percentage points higher than the average for the Southeast region. Derry/Londonderry has the biggest negative difference, with an economically active percentage that is 7.1% lower than the average for the Northern Ireland region. As well as highlighting the overall positive performance of the new towns in terms of economic activity, counterbalanced by the pockets of deprivation highlighted above, the statistics reinforce the fact that the economic performance cannot be separated from its wider subregional/regional economic context.

The new towns' legacy today – challenges and opportunities

While every new town is unique, the core design characteristics and the fact that many Development Corporation employees moved between corporations mean that there are some common legacies – both positive and negative. There are clear positive legacies of green infrastructure, accessibility, social housing, community development, built heritage, innovation and a spirit of 'going for growth'.

Conversely, speed of delivery and use of cheap and poor-quality materials in some of the new towns mean they are facing the need for 'whole-estate' renewal. The sale of new town assets to the private sector is making the renewal of town centres a challenge, and claw-back mechanisms set by HM Treasury on new town land are in many cases preventing their development. Tight administrative boundaries restrict growth for many new towns and their green-space assets are not properly used. All of these legacies have implications for how the new towns are managed today.

The renewal of town centres and reimagining civic space

The key issues facing the commercial centres of many of the new towns would be familiar to many places – the lack of a night-time economy, the need to improve competitiveness with other centres and the impact of online shopping.[11] But the design approaches and delivery of the new towns' centres has created specific challenges for how they are managed today.

Movement and public realm

Many of the new towns built in the 1960s were designed to provide for all forms of transport but reflect the dominant needs of the private car, with many town centres offering abundant and free parking to welcome the auto-age. This remains a key positive for many people but a real challenge for sustainable transport patterns and people's health and wellbeing. The new towns' – often pedestrianised – town centres have poor pedestrian connectivity to surrounding neighbourhoods and an aging public realm. For example, some key elements, such as pedestrian underpasses that connected town centres to parks and gardens, are in some new towns now a positive deterrent to walkability because of poor maintenance and fear of crime. Dealing with the legacy – resulting sometimes from design, sometimes from delivery, sometimes both – that put the needs of cars above the pedestrian is a common challenge for new towns and existing cities. Creative solutions, beyond using art to make underpasses more inviting (see Figure 4.13), have yet to be found.

Land ownership

The often monolithic design of shopping centres in the new towns made them easy assets to sell off to the private sector when the corporations were wound up, but also hard to adapt to changing retail and development needs. In many places this has proved a challenge for local authorities who have little control over land they do not own, making comprehensive town centre renewal difficult. It has also resulted in a renewal focused on larger retailers who may previously have been suited to out-of-town shopping centres. Covered markets, filled with small independent retailers, in new towns as varied as Newton Aycliffe (Figure 4.4), Cwmbran and Milton Keynes, are considered no longer viable.

Some places are working hard to overcome the common challenge of fragmented land ownership resulting from the sale of the corporation's assets. In Stevenage, the £1-billion regeneration scheme aims to transform the town over the next 20 years through residential-led, mixed-use developments to revitalise the town centre and provide transport and public realm improvements. Stevenage Borough Council, as well as working with political and commercial partners, has been buying back some of the vacant retail units in its iconic town square to enable it to have more control over its renewal.

04 THE NEW TOWNS TODAY

4.4
NEWTON AYCLIFFE TOWN CENTRE. FOR PLACES SUCH AS NEWTON AYCLIFFE, COVERED MARKETS FILLED WITH INDEPENDENT RETAILERS ARE UNDER THREAT FROM REDEVELOPMENT, TO BE REPLACED BY LARGER AND EDGE-OF-CENTRE STORES.

Not all town centres are owned by pension funds, however – in Hatfield, Welwyn Hatfield Borough Council is working closely with local landowner Gascoyne Cecil Estates, who have developed a master plan for the renewal of Old Hatfield, including strategic projects such as improvements to the railway station and public realm. This ongoing partnership has formed part of the Hatfield 2030+ Renewal Partnership, which was established in 2015 to devise a long-term plan for the future renewal of Hatfield to 2030 and beyond.[12] In February 2019, Welwyn Hatfield Borough Council became the first local authority to secure funding through the government's local authority accelerated construction programme. The council will use the £10.6 million funding from Homes England to prepare three sites to build 670 new homes, and deliver new retail and leisure.[13] In Milton Keynes, local business leaders are keen to influence change in the city centre through the country's first Business Neighbourhood Plan. At the time of writing, this remains the only Business Neighbourhood Plan in the country and has encountered its own challenges.

Central Milton Keynes Business Neighbourhood Plan

In Milton Keynes, an alliance of Central Milton Keynes Town Council and local business leaders, working in partnership with Milton Keynes Council, has sought to shape change in the town centre through a pioneering Business Neighbourhood Plan. The Central Milton Keynes (CMK) Alliance Plan 2026, adopted in 2015 following a hugely successful referendum, sets out plans for the renewal, expansion and diversification of CMK's commercial, retail and housing offer. It intends to celebrate CMK's distinct design and heritage, which it recognises are fundamental to the commercial attractiveness and quality of life in the town centre. However, despite this plan, some recent development proposals, including the extension of the shopping centre, caused local tension. The Town Council and a local community organisation felt the shopping centre proposals were in direct conflict with the plan and the application was called in by the Secretary of State (who subsequently ruled in favour of the extension).[14]

Design and built heritage

Renewal challenges – in town centres and beyond – extend to maintaining the unique architectural detailing and design in many of the new towns. For many new towns, the importance of their built heritage is only just being realised and at the same time has never been more under threat. There are, however, some interesting responses emerging.

Writing in a 2018 special edition of the TCPA's journal, Sharon Taylor, leader of Stevenage Borough Council, explained how one of the key principles of the regeneration scheme is to make sure that Stevenage is still recognisable. The aims of the scheme (Figure 4.5) include: '*Treasuring and protecting the historic landmarks and countryside that make Stevenage unique … Inspiration for many of the new buildings and developments draws from Stevenage's rich culture and heritage and we will make sure there will be no unsightly juxtaposition between the old and new.*'[15]

Harlow Council included a heritage assessment in preparation for its Town Centre Area Action Plan. The assessment noted the negative impact of the loss of new town heritage assets such as the former town hall, built in 1959 and demolished in 2002, as a 'cautionary tale for future assessment of new development options and the buildings they may replace' (Figure 4.6).[16]

Meanwhile, Hemel Hempstead has used the restoration of its iconic Water Gardens, created by renowned landscape designer Sir Geoffrey Jellicoe and completed in 1962, to provide an award-winning focus for the renewal of the town centre (Figure 4.7).

4.5
STEVENAGE'S PROPOSED REGENERATION SCHEME. THE BOROUGH COUNCIL IS KEEN TO MAINTAIN THE TOWN'S CHARACTER THROUGH THE TOWN CENTRE RENEWAL PROCESS.

04 THE NEW TOWNS TODAY

4.6
HARLOW'S WATER GARDENS, DESIGNED BY FREDERICK GIBBERD AND BUILT 1960–63. THE GARDENS WERE DESIGNED AS THE CENTREPIECE OF THE TOWN'S CIVIC CENTRE, KNOWN AS 'THE HIGH'. THEY WERE MOVED WHEN THE TOWN CENTRE WAS REDEVELOPED IN THE EARLY 2000S AND GIBBERD'S TOWN HALL WAS DEMOLISHED. THEY ARE AN IMPORTANT AMENITY BUT ASDA AND CHAIN RESTAURANTS PROVIDE A LESS-THAN-IDEAL SETTING (*SEE* ALSO FIGURE 5.5).

4.7
HEMEL HEMPSTEAD WATER GARDENS. IN 1957 SIR GEOFFREY JELLICOE, ONE OF THE GREATEST 20TH-CENTURY LANDSCAPE ARCHITECTS, WAS ASKED TO DESIGN A NEW TOWN CENTRE PARK FOR HEMEL HEMPSTEAD. IN 2017 IT REOPENED FOLLOWING A MULTIMILLION-POUND RESTORATION FUNDED BY THE NATIONAL LOTTERY AND DACORUM COUNCIL. THE RENOVATION HAS WON A CIVIC TRUST AWARD AND PROVIDES AN IMPORTANT ANCHOR FOR THE RENEWAL OF THE REST OF THE TOWN CENTRE.

Cultural regeneration

In many new town centres, cultural facilities are both under threat and acting as a catalyst for renewal. In 1985, The Point in Milton Keynes provided the city centre with the UK's first multiplex cinema (Figure 4.8). Despite its iconic design, this local landmark is soon to be demolished as its owners are opening a new cinema in an out-of-centre location. Addressing head-on the challenge that new towns lack the cultural offer of more 'traditional' towns, Milton Keynes recently opened a new extension to its gallery, located in the 'theatre district'. Milton Keynes Council has also recently employed a New Town Heritage Officer to promote the new town's built and cultural heritage to schools and visitors. For other new towns, such as Basildon, new or updated cinemas in the town centre are proving to be an important means to diversify the retail offer to leisure and encourage a night-time economy. Culturally based regeneration provides a huge opportunity for new town centres, but seizing that opportunity requires leadership and resources, which are clearly absent in the complex governance of some of the new towns. One fact remains undeniable, many of the people who live in new towns feel a strong affection for their places, and this civic pride is a vital asset in their future regeneration.

NEW TOWNS: THE RISE, FALL AND REBIRTH

Permitted development rights

Encouraging more people to live in town centres can be an obvious way to provide accessible homes and encourage a more diverse and night-time economy. In many of the new towns, the deregulation of planning is leading to the conversion of huge office spaces to residential use. In places such as Basildon, the conversion of units above shops in the town centre could provide much-needed revitalisation and homes. But any positive change resulting from such conversions can be overshadowed by the very poor quality of units created. The conversion of Terminus House, in Harlow, to tiny residential homes without play space or any contribution to affordable housing marks a low point in English planning practice (see Figure 4.12). It is also deeply ironic that such development, which is about storage for human beings and not about creating homes, should take place in the very places that demonstrate the value of comprehensive planning to meet human needs.

Housing estate renewal

While for many people the image of new towns is one of social housing in low-rise blocks surrounded by wide grass verges, in fact housing provision in the new towns varies widely within and between places and phases of the New Towns programme. New towns are, of course, also living places which continue to evolve and change in line with wider economic and political forces. Towns like Stevenage and Harlow, for example, are dealing with the wider growth pressures in the South of England. Despite this diversity, the need for whole-estate renewal is one of the overriding challenges facing new town authorities today, with most identifying at least two or three specific problematic estates.

4.8
THE POINT, MILTON KEYNES. DESPITE BEING THE UK'S FIRST MULTIPLEX CINEMA, THE ICONIC STRUCTURE IS DUE TO BE DEMOLISHED.

4.9
MODERN HOUSING IN GRANGE FARM, MILTON KEYNES. MANY OF THE LATER HOMES DELIVERED BY THE PRIVATE SECTOR ARE LESS DISTINCTIVE IN STYLE THAN EARLY DEVELOPMENT CORPORATION HOUSING, BUT HAVE REMAINED POPULAR, SUCH AS THE MANY 'EXECUTIVE' HOMES IN MILTON KEYNES.

Build quality

Early housing estates in 'Mark One' new towns were built in a postwar period where materials were cheap but often of poor quality, and when the pressure to deliver at speed meant that many homes of the same age are now in need of renewal at the same time.

The push for the new – in all phases of the New Towns programme – resulted in experimental housing designs. While this led to some exciting and innovative results in some places, in many cases designs that would look great in a coffee-table book have not stood the test of time. Several factors have contributed to this fate. From the outset, flat or mono-pitched roofs were never suited to the climate of the Welsh Valleys or Scottish Lowlands. In some cases, this was evident early on as residents struggled with leaking roofs and poorly insulated walls, issues that persist today where renovation has not taken place. The debate about the extent to which people's day-to-day lives were considered in the design of homes in some of the new town estates divides opinion but is significant when we consider the delivery of new homes at speed today. Even the best designs were at the mercy of those building them. Builders using unfamiliar materials, such as concrete, and structures, under pressure to deliver at speed, meant that poor build quality was inevitable – this was an issue for Cumbernauld's megastructure town centre. As with many such issues, the problem is as much to do with maintenance and stewardship as design. If Victor Pasmore's housing in Peterlee (see page 90) had been afforded the same maintenance charge as the Barbican, would it have stood the test of time? Possibly, but it would almost certainly now be in private ownership.

But this is not a universal story, and while there are real challenges on some new town estates, a lot of housing delivered by the corporations has in fact stood the test of time and is only just being recognised as important modern architectural heritage by councils such as Milton Keynes and Harlow and organisations such as the Twentieth Century Society and Historic England. The homes delivered by the corporations to Parker Morris design standards continue to provide well-designed, usable and desirable homes. Later development in some new towns by the private sector was always less ambitious, reflecting the monotype 'anywhereville' red-brick boxes that have dominated housing delivery in the UK (Figure 4.9).

4.10
THE LAKES ESTATE, MILTON KEYNES. THIS ESTATE IS ONE OF THE COUNCIL'S PRIORITY RENEWAL AREAS.

Community facilities – from play areas and public art to community hubs – were also an essential part of the estates' design success but in many cases assets – such as the play facilities in Basildon highlighted in the documentary film *New Town Utopia* (*see* page 75) – have not been maintained because of a combination of austerity and the absence of a stewardship model.

Continuous maintenance of these estates is expensive (Figure 4.10), and represents a significant financial burden for new town authorities who, with the asset stripping of the new towns in 1980, were left without the financial resources to carry out the necessary work. Some of the problematic estates were also those which were transferred to the authorities as assets when the corporations were wound up. Such a high proportion of socially rented homes enabled a broad social mix but made the new towns particularly vulnerable to changing policies, such as the introduction of the 'Right to Buy' scheme (Figure 4.11). This has contributed, in part, to the estates becoming liabilities, and the resulting piecemeal owner occupation has inhibited the comprehensive renewal of housing estates. Where estates were transferred to housing associations, such as in Cwmbran, renewal depends on the actions of those providers, with varied results. More recent pressures result from changing policy (Figure 4.12), such as the deregulation of planning and permitted development and houses of multiple occupation, in new towns such as Milton Keynes.[17]

04 THE NEW TOWNS TODAY

4.11
NETHERFIELD, MILTON KEYNES. THE PERSONALISATION OF MANY HOMES IS THE VISUAL EVIDENCE OF THE 'RIGHT TO BUY' PROCESS BUT IT ALSO REFLECTS A REACTION TO A DELIVERY MODEL WHERE COUNCIL HOUSING DESIGN WAS SEEN AS REPETITIVE AND TIGHT RESTRICTIONS WERE PLACED ON SIMPLE THINGS SUCH AS PAINTING YOUR OWN FRONT DOOR.

4.12
TERMINUS HOUSE, HARLOW. TODAY CHALLENGES SUCH AS OVERCROWDING IN HOUSES OF MULTIPLE OCCUPATION ARE PROMINENT IN MANY NEW TOWNS, PARTICULARLY IN THE SOUTH OF ENGLAND.

Meeting modern housing standards is also a renewal challenge, with some authorities stating that they can only keep retro-insulating homes so far before the entire fabric needs changing. This has sparked debate about renovation versus demolition, and the potential desire for densification in several new towns, such as Milton Keynes.

Strategically, housing offer does not always meet the needs of the workforce, resulting in inward commuting in some new towns, such as Stevenage and Harlow.

Infrastructure and accessibility

Most new towns are well connected by rail and road, albeit to systems that are often at capacity. For places like Milton Keynes and Warrington, their strategic location on key transport routes has made a direct contribution to their success. But accessibility is not universal, and other new towns, like Peterlee and Skelmersdale, have never secured a rail link despite, in Peterlee's case, the proximity of a rail line 1km from the town centre which could link the town to Newcastle.

One of the key strengths of the new town approach was the ability to plan holistically for the infrastructure and movement in each new town, and they were designed to accommodate all modes of transport. The accessibility of new towns by bicycle, and to local centres and green infrastructure on foot, remains an important positive legacy in many of the new towns. Just as important in the first-wave new towns, such as Harlow and Stevenage, as it was in Milton Keynes, these cycle networks mean you can still travel from one side of the town to another without ever having to cross a road.

For planners in many new town authorities today, planned transport networks are recognised as providing good accessibility and delaying the rise of congestion in their new towns compared with towns of a similar age. However, the wider need for the renewal and development of infrastructure and improved transport networks is among their top priorities.

Maintenance issues and perceptions of safety are a key contributor to underused infrastructure, highlighting that good planning does not always equate to good usage.[18] Milton Keynes' cycle 'redways', while well used on some routes, are in many places not in great condition, and are considered by some to feel unsafe as they are set back from main roads and the vegetation around them has matured to the point where they are no longer overlooked. Underpasses enable pedestrians and cyclists to avoid main roads and are an important characteristic of new towns. However, some of these have not been maintained and are perceived as unsafe locations. A number of projects have looked specifically at underpasses and how to make them more inviting (Figure 4.13) – through art, better lighting or, in the case of Stevenage and Craigavon, inviting local school children to 'adopt an underpass'.[19] In some places the response has been to fill in the underpasses, abandoning transport segregation completely and replacing underpasses with 'at grade' crossings. These require the introduction of traffic lights and the related street clutter – and sometimes traffic jams – that accompany them.

While the design of new towns provided a framework for all forms of transport, including public transport, some aspects of their design and layout, combined with the failure of public transport services, made cars the most convenient way to travel.

In 2008 the Communities and Local Government Select Committee found that the segregation of uses and the low density of development in some of the new towns had left residents needing to travel further to some services than in many towns and cities. While some services had been provided within walking distance at local centres, access to town centres relied heavily on cars – a situation exacerbated by inadequate bus services in many of the new towns. When it comes to travelling to work, the number of journeys made by people driving a car or van (45%) or as a passenger in a car or van (5%) are higher than the national averages by 6.5 and 3.5 percentage points respectively. Other modes (walking, cycling and public transport) are broadly in line with UK averages.[20]

Debate on infrastructure in the new towns, like elsewhere, remains stubbornly focused on accommodating cars, which can prevent a more comprehensive conversation about how to enable the renewal of new town cycleways, green space and aspects of accessibility which could help to make new towns more climate resilient and people-friendly in the long term. The accessibility by road within the new towns should make them easy for viable public transport services. Later new towns, like Milton Keynes, were designed specifically with flexibility for future unknown transport needs, for example by allowing additional width along some grid roads. Looking forward, it seems a combination of behaviour change, better maintenance and interventions to encourage people to use existing foot and cycle paths, combined with a rebalancing of priorities for public transport, is required.

04 THE NEW TOWNS TODAY

4.13
AN UNDERPASS NEAR THE CRAIGLINN ROUNDABOUT IN CUMBERNAULD, BEFORE, DURING AND AFTER ITS TRANSFORMATION. THE COUNCIL HAS USED PUBLIC ART AND WORKED WITH LOCAL SCHOOL CHILDREN TO CHANGE THE PHYSICAL APPEARANCE AND PERCEPTIONS OF ITS UNDERPASSES.

Stewardship - green spaces and public realm

One of the most visible legacies of the corporations in the new towns is their green infrastructure. For many who pass through new towns, green infrastructure is limited to wide grass verges on the side of road networks and housing estates, but for those who live and work in them, the emphasis on green infrastructure that was a feature of the new town master plans remains an important element of the towns today. Landscaping on the grid roads in Milton Keynes has now matured to the point visualised by its designers. These assets also provide important resources for renewal and climate resilience. Milton Keynes and Peterborough show what is possible when a stewardship body is set up to manage the green space and endowed with the resources to maintain and enhance green infrastructure without ever requiring a service fee (Figure 4.14), something which is proving a challenge for many new housing developments, including in Milton Keynes itself.[21] For the rest of the new towns, this fantastic resource has become a maintenance burden. In Peterlee, confusion over land ownership and a lack of resources have meant that some of the former crowning-glory town parks have now become no-go areas at night. This challenge is echoed in the wider public realm of many new town centres and estates. For those places where expensive regeneration schemes are yet to be secured, a lack of stewardship of the public realm contributes to negative perceptions from residents and visitors alike.

NEW TOWNS: THE RISE, FALL AND REBIRTH

4.14
CAMPBELL PARK, MILTON KEYNES. DUE TO THE PARKS TRUST'S MANAGEMENT, MILTON KEYNES HAS SOME OF THE BEST-MAINTAINED GREEN INFRASTRUCTURE IN THE COUNTRY, IN CONTRAST TO MANY OTHER NEW TOWNS, WHICH LACK THE RESOURCES TO ADEQUATELY MAINTAIN THEIR GREEN SPACES.

The new town art and design heritage

Another standout characteristic of the new towns is the legacy of the artists and town architects who were involved in their delivery. There was a clear sense of pride in the role of design and designers in the new towns, with recognition of their part in establishing local character and a sense of place. The legacy of the artists employed by the Development Corporations remains visible in many town centres, through sculptures and murals on buildings and tucked away, and often loved but sometimes uncared for, in residential estates. This approach was about more than sculptures and murals – learning from the garden city movement, creativity and the arts were integral to the new town idea. These assets are also proving to be important catalysts for renewal. In 2010, Harlow declared itself to be the world's first 'sculpture town', building on the legacy of Harlow Art Trust, established in the 1950s, promoting these assets as a visitor attraction (Figure 4.15).

Milton Keynes is also home to the City Discovery Centre, which was set up in 1987 to increase understanding and appreciation of Milton Keynes' unique urban geography and rich history. With Milton Keynes Council and other partners, the City Discovery Centre is working on a project celebrating new town heritage, and at the time of writing had recruited a post that would develop a toolkit for identifying and celebrating new town heritage in Milton Keynes. In Skelmersdale, Glassball, an interdisciplinary arts practice, is celebrating the town's heritage.[22] In Northern Ireland, the 'Capturing Craigavon' project has gathered stories and images from residents and archives to help document the people's history of the new town.[23]

A resurgence in interest in postwar architecture and design, and in council housing, provides a huge opportunity for the new towns. In 2016, an exhibition at Somerset House, London, on postwar public art included the story of Harlow and its sculptures.[24] Books by John Grindrod and John Boughton, independent documentary films, and journals and study tours by the Modernist Society and Twentieth Century Society, and of course the TCPA, have brought the new towns story to life. *New Town Utopia*, a documentary released in 2018 and directed by Christopher Ian Smith, tells the story of Basildon new town through the stories of its artists. Its general release in UK cinemas brought the new town story to the attention of a new audience. New town anniversaries provide an ideal opportunity to capture the imagination of those within and beyond the built environment profession.

Accommodating future growth

The new towns allowed for rapid growth but as many have reached their intended populations, and in the face of the wider housing crisis, housing land supply and the challenge of accommodating housing growth were the most commonly cited development issues in planning officer surveys[25] and were also notable issues in Local Plan evidence documents. In several cases, the tight administrative boundary was noted as an issue, with housing needs having to be accommodated in the green belt or in neighbouring authorities, which is an issue when the Duty to Cooperate is the only means of strategic planning. A particular problem was noted where local authority boundaries were drawn close to the new town boundary (for example at Stevenage). Where the boundary is not tightly drawn, the green belts around those new towns that have them have prevented development at their edges, fulfilling one of their original objectives. It is likely that such constraints on growth would not be an issue if a strategic planning system that promoted consideration of 'larger than local' housing needs were in place.

Where authorities are forced to deal with housing needs within the town's boundaries, and even where they are not, there is a live debate about whether growth and renewal should include the densification of the new towns. This includes 'infilling' in residential areas – building on some of the grass areas mentioned above, a practice which is proving popular in London's suburbs, which in many cases are of a similar density to new town estates. Some argue that this would facilitate different, and more sustainable, transport modes and energy systems. Others argue that such development would destroy the legacy of green infrastructure which was so key to the new town design ethos.

While change is necessary to reflect the challenges and to secure renewal, there is need for a great deal of sensitivity to and respect of the powerful vision that residents bought into when they moved to the new town. The brochures sold a lifestyle, amenities and culture which new residents, particularly early new town pioneers, invested in, even when they may have moved into a building site. Former Milton Keynes Development Corporation planners spoke with passion and excitement about the unique experience of building a new town. They also reflected on the pioneering spirit of the first generation of residents. David Lock, who lives and works in the town and worked at MK Development Corporation, said, 'The story of the new town was a book to be written and we (the residents) were to be its joint authors.'[26] Ignoring this powerful identity and the ideas that created it would be grave mistake.

Many new towns have also been looking strategically at how to deal with growth needs. In Milton Keynes, the 2050 Futures Commission looked at a range of growth and renewal scenarios for the authority area.[27] Basildon recently completed its Breakthrough Basildon Borough Commission process, which sought to consider how to rebalance the borough, including the new town (Figure 4.16). Joining them, Dacorum and West Lancashire councils are considering the role of new communities to deal with housing growth needs in Hemel Hempstead and Skelmersdale respectively, for which they are seeking support through the government's 'garden communities' programme. At Harlow, a proposed new community of 10,000 people provides an opportunity to secure renewal for the town, but only if the right partnerships are in place. In Warrington and Runcorn, continued growth and renewal within the areas of the original new town designations have led them to feel they are simply 'finishing the job'.

Employment and industry

The new towns perform well when it comes to employment statistics (*see* page 62) and councils are keen to ensure this is protected and evolved. Improving and protecting employment land and improving access to employment were also common issues raised in the planning officer survey responses and found in Local Plans. Retaining and building upon balanced employment as part of wider economic growth and competitiveness is also a key issue, particularly for those new towns that have suffered from the loss of big employers and industry.

4.15
HARLOW DECLARED ITSELF A SCULPTURE TOWN TO CELEBRATE ITS CULTURAL HERITAGE AND PROVIDE A MEANS TO ATTRACT VISITORS AND INVESTMENT.

04 THE NEW TOWNS TODAY

4.16
A RECEPTION TO LAUNCH THE BREAKTHROUGH BASILDON BOROUGH COMMISSION, HELD AT THE HOUSE OF COMMONS IN DECEMBER 2017, HOSTED BY BARONESS SMITH OF BASILDON (PICTURED HERE). THE COMMISSION PROCESS WAS USED TO GATHER INFORMATION FROM RESIDENTS AND EXPERTS TO PROVIDE A VISION AND STRATEGY FOR A FUTURE OF 'INCLUSIVE GROWTH' IN THE BOROUGH AS A WHOLE, INCLUDING ITS NEW TOWN.

4.17
STEVENAGE BIOSCIENCE CATALYST. STEVENAGE HAS BECOME A HUB FOR BIOSCIENCE AND TECH RESEARCH; THE BIOSCIENCE CATALYST WAS ATTRACTED TO THE TOWN DUE TO ITS LOCATION, ACCESSIBILITY AND FACILITIES.

The ownership and control of some of the assets in the new towns was noted as an issue – particularly where covenants imposed by the Commission for the New Towns or its successors have restricted the ability of the local authority to redevelop. Many of the new towns benefit from large industrial areas, with Hemel Hempstead having the largest business park in the East of England. Harlow is about to benefit from the relocation of Public Health England. Stevenage is home to some of the world's largest pharmaceutical, aerospace and defence companies (Figure 4.17). Accessibility of places like Warrington make them ideal for logistics, and large areas for research and development. In the same vein as the Development Corporations that preceded them, many new town authorities are tackling new town image stigmas head-on and rebranding to attract new investment and industry.

What next?

In many of the new towns, programmes of ambitious renewal are now under way. There are opportunities to harness the adaptive capacity built into the original designs to meet modern challenges – for example, reimagining the use of green infrastructure in new towns for renewable energy, biodiversity and local food, or harnessing the legacy of road infrastructure to deploy driverless electric cars (Figures 4.18 and 4.19). Throughout, the message when considering all these issues is threefold: new towns can thrive again with the right management and stewardship of remaining assets; unique heritage is an asset that should be a core catalyst to enable this; most importantly, people must be involved in growth and renewal processes to make them a success.

Whether these opportunities are seized still rests on familiar issues of leadership and good governance. For some new towns, it is hard to see how progress can be made when they have no dedicated local authority that can represent and champion the town (i.e. they are one of several towns in a large local authority). For some, the stigma of being a new town is still hard to overcome. For all of them, the lack of interest from central government is unhelpful.

NEW TOWNS: THE RISE, FALL AND REBIRTH

Despite these common issues and opportunities, every new town tells its own unique story and the following chapters illustrate how the general issues raised above have played out in specific circumstances. The locations have been selected to represent a range of dates of designation and geographical locations across the UK. Emerging from the case studies are a series of crucial lessons. These lessons – good and bad – are set out in Chapter 12 and are essential to enable us not only to understand how best to renew and grow existing new towns but also to understand the implications for contemporary housing delivery.

4.18
A DRIVERLESS CAR IN MILTON KEYNES. NEW TOWNS SUCH AS MILTON KEYNES ARE MAINTAINING THEIR SPIRIT OF INNOVATION THROUGH INITIATIVES SUCH AS THE PILOTING OF DRIVERLESS CARS.

4.19
AN, INCREDIBLE EDIBLE, PLOT IN TODMORDEN, WHERE THE MOVEMENT BEGAN. INCREDIBLE EDIBLE IS A GRASSROOTS MOVEMENT THAT HAS SEEN COMMUNITIES ACROSS THE WORLD PLANT FOOD IN UNDERUSED PUBLIC SPACES. CREATIVE USE OF GREEN INFRASTRUCTURE IN THE NEW TOWNS, PARTICULARLY IN GRASSED AREAS IN SOME NEW TOWN ESTATES, COULD TRANSFORM THEIR FUTURE

05

CASE STUDY:
HARLOW, ESSEX

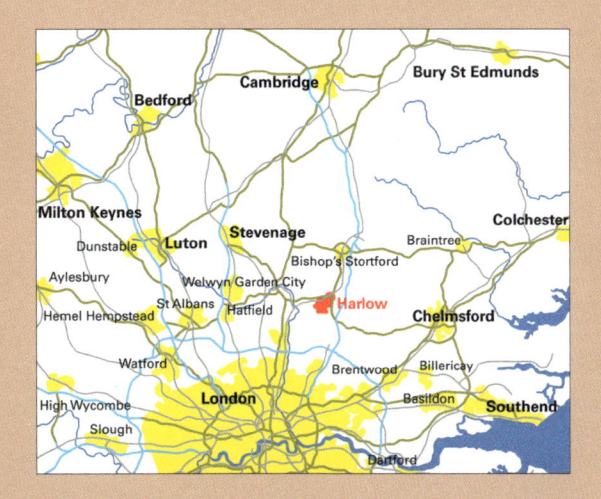

5.1
HARLOW IS IN ESSEX, NORTHEAST OF LONDON.

Key facts

Location: 37km northeast of London (Figure 5.1). Harlow District is a small, predominately urban district with a tight administrative boundary.

2011 Census population: 81,944, in 34,620 households.[1]

Local authority: Harlow Council.

Local Plan status: Saved policies from Harlow Local Plan 2006 are in place. The Harlow Local Development Plan was submitted to the Secretary of State for examination in public on 19 October 2018 and was scheduled for adoption at the end of 2019.[2]

New Town designation

Designated: 25 March 1947.

Designated area: 2,558 hectares.

Intended population: 60,000, revised to 80,000 (in the second master plan, approved in 1952) (population at designation: 4,500).

Development Corporation: A key design feature was higher-density housing, with the majority of the town's open space provided within 'green wedges'. Expansion proposals between the 1950s and 1970s put forward a population of up to 150,000, which was turned down in 1977. The Development Corporation was wound up on 30 September 1980.

NEW TOWNS: THE RISE, FALL AND REBIRTH

Introduction

Identified as the location for one of eight London 'ring towns' in Patrick Abercrombie's Greater London Plan, 1944 (see Figure 1.6), Harlow's existing connections to road and rail networks and the quality of its landscape influenced its designation. Conceived through Sir Frederick Gibberd's master plan, Harlow's 'green wedges' give the town a distinctive character and connect residential neighbourhoods with open spaces and the countryside beyond; although today they present their own management challenges. Harlow's population increased significantly in the 1950s and 1960s, but numbers declined in the 1970s and 1980s. Today, supporting the town's regeneration aspirations, there are proposals for around 12,000 new dwellings by 2031. Harlow's recent extension at Newhall has won several architecture and design accolades.

Background

As well as its connectivity and landscape character, Harlow was attractive to Abercrombie as it was 'relatively close to the East End and therefore should prove for that reason to be an attractive one to develop'.[3] So promising was the area for potential growth, that proposals for a town of 30,000 people had already been prepared by Essex County Council. In 1946 Lewis Silkin called for Frederick Gibberd to prepare an 'unofficial' plan for Harlow, ahead of an 'official' master plan to be prepared by the Development Corporation. Gibberd's appointment was significant given the lively debate at the time between the garden city enthusiasts and those influenced by the modern movement about the extent to which the garden city model was 'urban' and how new towns might be influenced by it, yet different from it. A draft design was required by 1 April 1947. The designation was made on 25 March 1947, Gibberd's initial plan was approved by the advisory committee on 8 May and Harlow Development Corporation came into existence on 16 May, just six weeks after the order was passed. The master plan – subsequently evolved by Gibberd for the Development Corporation – received ministerial approval in March 1949; a second edition was published in 1952.

Harlow master plan

Frederick Gibberd's vision and master plan for Harlow New Town reflected the new town ethos of the 1940s, drawing inspiration from the earlier garden city movement and the drive to provide high-quality, spacious homes with access to clean air and open space. The 1952 master plan (Figure 5.2) was based on three fundamental principles – an essentially human environment (that the design should be based on the pedestrian); an urban atmosphere; and the principle of evolution. According to Gibberd, 'The third predicted a flexible approach. The first two were basic to the concept of new towns.'[4]

The master plan was influenced by the area's distinctive landscape and environmental features, such as the River Stort in the north, and the valley ridges and wooded areas in the south. The new town was built around a series of neighbourhoods, dissected by large areas of natural and semi-natural spaces, now known as 'green wedges'. These key physical features of Harlow have shaped its subsequent growth.

05 CASE STUDY: HARLOW, ESSEX

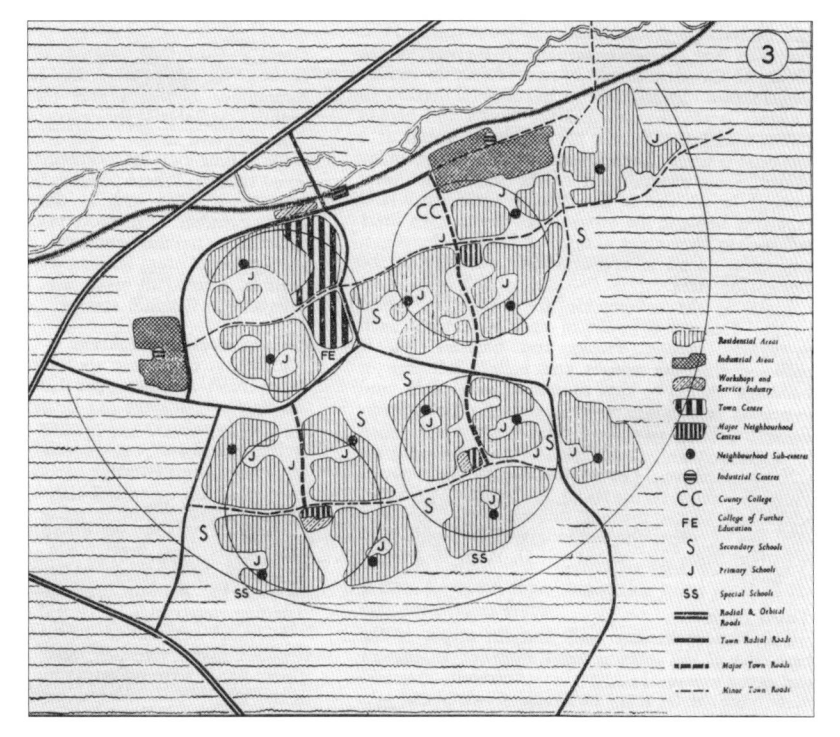

5.2
HARLOW MASTER PLAN, 1952.

The neighbourhoods were focused around a shopping centre with easy access to social and educational facilities, connected by a series of distributor roads together with a network of cycleways and footpaths. The 'green wedges' which separate them continue to provide amenity= space for residents, habitats for wildlife, transport corridors, locations for schools and sport and community facilities. Two industrial sites, Templefields and Pinnacles, were located in the north and west of the district, relatively close to the railway line. The Town Park was provided to the northeast of the town centre and was designed around existing landscape features and a hamlet. Harlow became home to the first residential point block tower in Britain – *The Lawn* was designed by Sir Frederick Gibberd and built in 1951 to coincide with the Festival of Britain.

In 1952 it received a Ministry of Health housing medal and it was one of the first postwar buildings to be Grade II listed by English Heritage; it still stands today.[5] The Harlow Art Trust was established in the 1950s and acquired works by up-and-coming sculptors and assisted them by providing a permanent, public exhibition of their works. Today a collection of sculptures of national significance are sited throughout the town, including Henry Moore's *Family Group* (see Figure 0.1) and Auguste Rodin (see Figure 5.3).

Harlow's delivery was rapid; the first residents moved in just four months after the Masterplan was approved. By 1956 the Corporation had built over 70 factories and 7,000 dwellings and by 1959 was the first British town with a health centre. Within 15 years the Corporation was generating enough surplus income to become a lender to other public bodies such as Thames Water. By 1977 it has been agreed that the Corporation should be wound up as there would be no more developable land available without expansion. The Corporation was dissolved in 1980.[6]

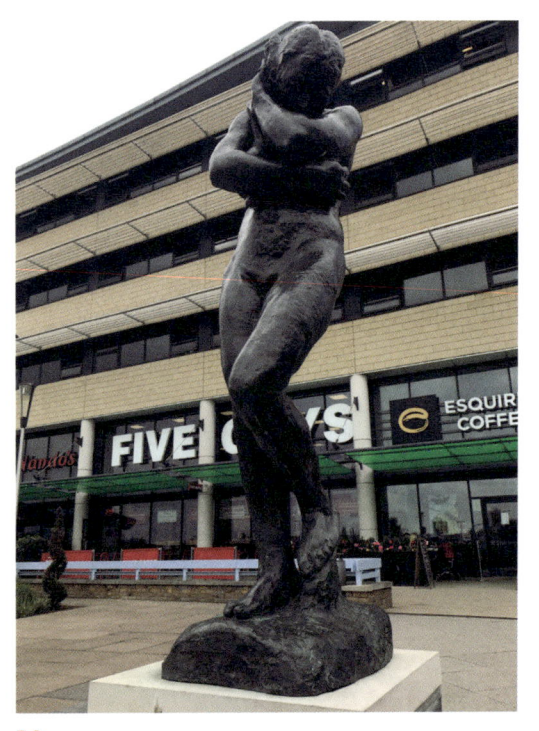

5.3
EVE BY AUGUSTE RODIN (1882), IN ITS UNCONVENTIONAL SETTING IN HARLOW TOWN CENTRE.

5.4
THE MULTI-AWARD-WINNING *NEWHALL BE* BY ALISON BROOKS ARCHITECTS, FOR LINDEN HOMES AND GALLIFORD TRY PLC.

Harlow today – challenges and opportunities

In 2017 Harlow celebrated the 70th anniversary of its designation. In addition to celebrating its past and present, the council took the opportunity to look to the future and launch new initiatives to start the 'renaissance' of the new town.

Since its inception, Harlow has been subject to distinct phases of growth and change. The district still faces significant challenges, including a shortage of affordable housing and the need for a range of good-quality housing stock; a highway network which is severely congested at peak times; an aging physical environment; localised deprivation; and a skills shortage. Harlow performs poorly against comparator towns on a range of measures, including employment growth, gross value added (GVA) per worker, knowledge-based businesses, skills base and retail ranking. This, along with the district's tight administrative boundaries, means that Harlow's ability to meet its long-term needs are inhibited, which can hinder the district's regeneration and long-term economic prospects.[7]

The council has recognised that addressing these issues – and the resulting image and perception problems for the town – requires investment and sustained renewal of the town centre, a broader mix of housing, infrastructure upgrade and investment, and a broader economic base.

Some progress is already being made to address these issues through development and change already proposed in Harlow. This includes approximately 4,000 dwellings at Newhall (Figure 5.4) and land north of Gilden Way and the creation of up to 5,000 new jobs at the Harlow Enterprise Zone. There are also a number of infrastructure improvements that are proposed across Harlow or have been completed recently, including a new junction at the M11. Projects such as Newhall have already been recognised for their creative approach to design and layout, setting a standard for residential development elsewhere in the town.

The council is also planning for the creation of between 8,000 and 12,000 new jobs and will be supporting investment from new businesses to broaden the town's employment base and to provide opportunities for the town's growing workforce. The plan will also build on Harlow's status as one of 24 Enterprise Zones set up across England to drive job creation and business growth.

Town centre

The town centre went through dramatic changes following the dissolution of the Development Corporation in 1980, with the privately owned shopping centre – the Harvey Centre – growing to dominate the town centre. More recently, the Water Gardens development, completed in 2004 in a public-private partnership with Harlow Council and English Partnerships, provided a retail extension to the centre of Harlow, new civic offices for Harlow Council and the relocation of the existing Water Gardens (see Figure 4.6).

Harlow Town Centre, neighbourhood centres and many of the town's Hatches (small neighbourhood centres) are outdated, with a risk of long-term decline; issues include the quality of the retail offer and the physical environment (Figure 5.5). The council has recognised the need to upgrade the level of retail provision, encourage a broader mix of uses (including residential), introduce a high-quality public realm and consider restructuring centres to increase passing traffic and overcome accessibility issues.

Harlow town centre has excellent transport connections to the wider subregion and a comparatively large shopping population, but the 2018 Area Action Plan Preferred Options Report notes that there are high vacancy rates, a lack of high-end retailers and a lack of a night-time economy, as well as poor connectivity to adjacent residential areas.[8]

A lack of council-owned land in the centre restricts opportunities for redevelopment. However, there continues to be significant private-sector investment in the centre, with plans for the redevelopment of an area to the north of the Harvey Centre to create a mixed-use development comprising 468 residential units, enhanced retail provision, car parking, cycle parking and landscape enhancements to the vicinity of the site. Public Health England (PHE) is also investing in the town. In 2017 PHE received planning permission to build a £400-million world-leading home for public health science, choosing the former GlaxoSmithKline site in Harlow due to its size, existing facilities and strategic location.[9] PHE plans to have up to 2,750 staff based at the site by 2024, following a phased opening from 2021.

Housing

Like all new towns, Harlow has a varied housing stock. This includes neighbourhoods which are showing signs of deterioration and localised deprivation, particularly in the southern, central and western parts of the town. Renewing these areas is a key priority for the council, with specific requirements including the need to increase and diversify housing provision and the replacement

NEW TOWNS: THE RISE, FALL AND REBIRTH

5.5
AN AERIAL VIEW OF HARLOW TOWN CENTRE (A), SHOWING THE CIVIC CENTRE IN THE CENTRE, WITH THE RELOCATED WATER GARDENS IN FRONT OF IT; BROAD WALK, IN THE PEDESTRIANISED ZONE (B); AND THE DISTINCTIVE CLOCK (C) IN HARLOW'S MARKET SQUARE. HARLOW TOWN CENTRE CONTAINS MANY FEATURES OF ARCHITECTURAL SIGNIFICANCE, SUCH AS THE MARKET SQUARE FAÇADE AND CLOCK (CURRENTLY UNLISTED).

(a)

(b)

(c)

of obsolete housing, as well as improving public spaces within and around residential areas. Population forecasts and affordability issues with Harlow's current housing stock mean that a minimum of 7,500 new dwellings is required by 2031 to meet Harlow's population growth alone. In 2013, Harlow Council launched a five-year council housing investment programme, funded by rents and grants secured by the council. By 2017, the £100-million Modern Homes Programme had led to 48,200 improvements to its 10,000 council homes.[10]

Priority estates

Harlow Council is working in partnership with Countryside Properties plc and Home Group on transforming The Briars, Copshall Close and Aylets Field (known as BCA estate) in Staple Tye. The scheme, costing £71 million, will replace postwar bungalows that have become dated and do not meet Decent Homes standards (Figure 5.6). A total of 343 homes will be constructed, after the old homes are demolished, including around 200 affordable homes. The project has three stages so as to be able to rehouse current residents – who will eventually move back onto the estate once the new homes are completed. Residents are also given the option to permanently move to alternative council or housing association accommodation elsewhere in the town.

5.6
POSTWAR BUNGALOWS IN HARLOW, BEFORE DEMOLITION. REDEVELOPMENT OF THE BUNGALOWS IN HARLOW'S PRIORITY ESTATES BEGAN IN 2016.

Prentice Place

Harlow Council is also investing £3 million in the regeneration of the 1950s neighbourhood shopping centre, Prentice Place, in the southeast of the town; work began in January 2018. The project aims to give a sense of openness and safety for residents, retailers and customers alike, by removing unused bin stores to open up walkways and by investing in better lighting.

Harlow and Gilston Garden Town

Harlow Council and neighbouring authorities East Hertfordshire District Council, Epping Forest District Council, Hertfordshire County Council and Essex County Council are working in partnership with Hertfordshire Local Enterprise Partnership (LEP) and South East LEP and with site promoters Places for People to bring forward transformational growth at the site of the new Harlow and Gilston Garden Town. The site, the Gilston Area of the Metropolitan Green Belt, was allocated for development in the emerging East Hertfordshire District Plan, to deliver 10,000 homes. The development was awarded a £500,000 'Garden Town grant' from the government in January 2017 to support the transformational strategic proposals, fund research and provide specialist support using Garden City Principles to ensure local communities are involved in the development of master plans for the sites.

Sculpture and new town heritage assets

Harlow Sculpture Town

True to its pioneering ethos, Harlow offers a diverse and unique range of arts, cultural and heritage assets. In 2010 Harlow rebranded itself as 'Harlow Sculpture Town' in recognition of the town's publicly accessible sculpture collection. Arts and culture is an important feature embedded throughout the town (Figure 5.7). This not only celebrates the sculptures owned by Harlow Art Trust but other sculpture collections in Harlow, including those of the council, the Gibberd Garden and Parndon Mill. The Harlow Art Trust recently commissioned a major new work to be sited at Newhall to commemorate the life of Lady Patricia Gibberd.[11]

NEW TOWNS: THE RISE, FALL AND REBIRTH

Next steps for Harlow

Frederick Gibberd described Harlow as 'an organism which would go on changing and being rebuilt as the needs of the people alter'.[12] That has certainly been true, and Harlow is now on the brink of significant change. The integrity of its master plan means it remains a unique place with significant arts and environmental assets but faces issues of aging infrastructure and the legacy of 21st-century private-sector redevelopment, which has destroyed some of its design heritage. Recent developments, such as Newhall, show the town is able to deliver high-quality design. The challenge for the council now is to ensure the full benefits are harnessed from the new garden town status and investment from Public Health England to secure the renewal of the town centre and surrounding estates. One of the primary challenges is the lack of council-owned land in the centre. Harlow is suffering from the relaxation of permitted development rights, with a significant number of conversions of office to residential on former industrial estates (Figure 5.8), without contributions made to affordable housing or public amenities. The council's challenge is to harness the forthcoming opportunities to enable the right kind of renewal that will last another 70 years or more.

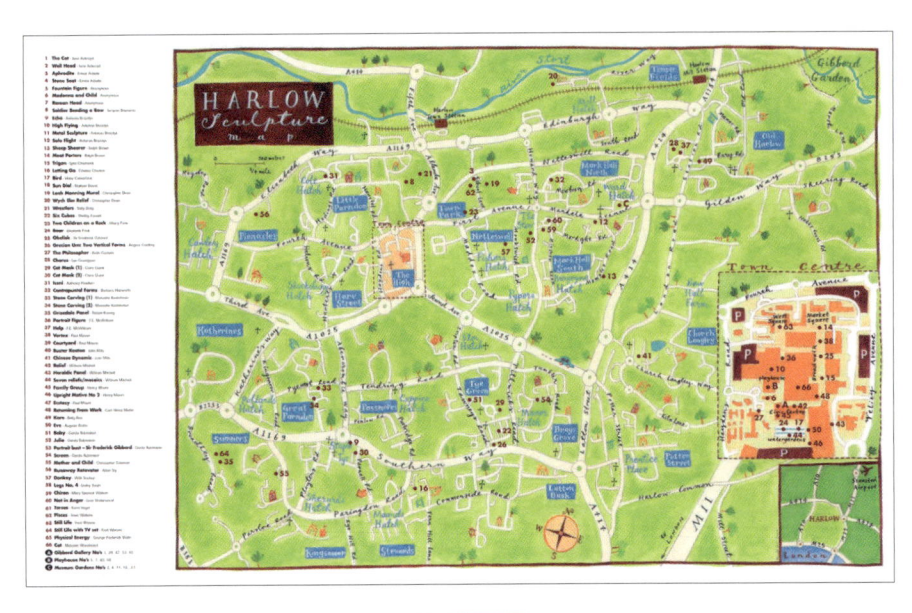

5.7
HARLOW SCULPTURE MAP, SHOWING THE TOWN'S PUBLICLY ACCESSIBLE SCULPTURE COLLECTION.

5.8
TEMPLEFIELDS HOUSE, HARLOW. FORMERLY AN OFFICE BUILDING, IT WAS CONVERTED TO RESIDENTIAL USE THROUGH PERMITTED DEVELOPMENT.

06

CASE STUDY:
PETERLEE, COUNTY DURHAM

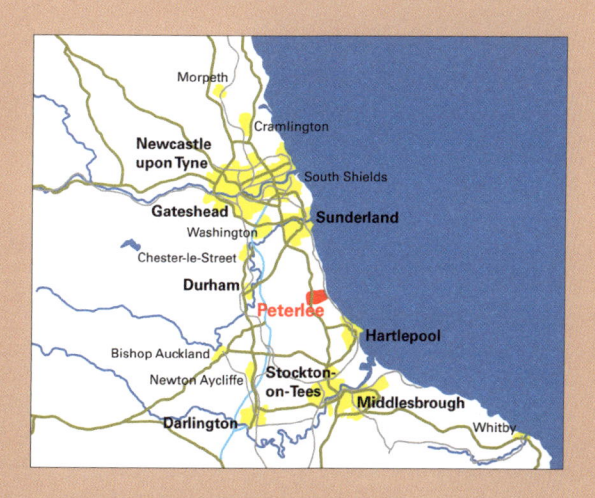

6.1
PETERLEE IS IN COUNTY DURHAM, BETWEEN HARTLEPOOL AND SUNDERLAND.

Key facts

Location: 14km east of Durham, 16km south of Sunderland, 19km south of Newcastle (Figure 6.1).

2011 Census population: 20,164, in 8,514 households.[1]

Local authority: Durham County Council.

Local Plan status: Peterlee has been part of the unitary Durham County Council area since 2009. The Development Plan is the forthcoming County Durham Plan, currently due for adoption in July 2020. Saved policies from Easington Local Plan (adopted in 2001) are a material consideration.[2]

New Town designation

Designated: 10 March 1948.

Designated area: 950 hectares, revised several times up to 12,000 hectares.

Intended population: 30,000 (population at designation: 200).

Development Corporation: The corporation aimed to provide homes and services for poor-quality and badly served settlements; to provide a recreational and commercial centre; and to develop a balanced community and provide employment for female workers and those not employed in the colliery. The Development Corporation was wound up on 31 March 1988.

Introduction

Situated on what was the richest seam of the Durham coalfield, Peterlee was conceived to provide housing and a better living environment for the local scattered rural population and for colliery workers, and to provide a centre offering commercial, social and cultural facilities. The town was named after a former colliery worker, Peter Lee, who later became a councillor campaigning for better living conditions for colliery workers. Peterlee was the Northeast's second new town, following nearby Newton Aycliffe, designated in 1947. The two towns shared a Development Corporation from 1963 until its dissolution in 1988.

Located in the A19 corridor, today Peterlee is a town with a strong manufacturing base, constituting the third-largest economy in County Durham. It is tightly constrained to the south, east and west and is adjacent to the Durham Coast Line, which served the area until the railway station closed in 1964.

Background

Though many of the postwar new towns resulted from local-authority-led campaigns, Peterlee is perhaps the most extreme example. Its designation was championed by C.W. Clarke, Easington Rural District Council's engineer and surveyor, who responded to the government's 1943 call to assess postwar housing needs by producing a report called *Farewell Squalor*, which called for planned new developments, including a new town in the district, to provide mining communities with a new future.[3] Receiving overwhelming support from local authorities, and fitting well with the ambition of Lewis Silkin, Minister of Town and Country Planning, for a new town for the Northeast, Peterlee was designated in 1948 and its Development Corporation constituted shortly after. Soviet émigré architect Berthold Lubetkin (Figure 6.2) produced the first master plan, but the town's growth was restricted by a ten-year running battle with the National Coal Board regarding the existing coal resources under the site, leading eventually to Lubetkin's resignation.

Following its designation in 1948, the new town grew through phased migration from the neighbouring colliery and former colliery villages, with 79% of the original housing stock available for social rent. The decline of the coal industry stimulated a major and sustained campaign for new employment and industry, which continues today. This change, along with changing government policy, such as the 'Right to Buy', also saw a shift in tenure and a broader resident population. Peterlee's Town Council was created in 1974 and responsibility for housing matters in Peterlee transferred to Easington District Council on 1 May 1978, which itself became part of Durham County Council in 2009. Peterlee Development Corporation was finally wound up on 31 March 1988.

Peterlee master plan

Following Lubetkin's resignation, Preston-born architect George Grenfell-Baines was appointed to create a master plan for Peterlee, and by 1952, under considerable pressure, he had created a scheme that was not only accepted by the corporation, the minister and the Coal Board, but was noted for reflecting Peterlee's special conditions in its design (Figure 6.3). This included integrating the new housing areas closely with the topography and landscape of the site, including Castle Eden Dene, an area now recognised as having significant biodiversity and landscape value.

Peterlee was planned around the concept of a tightly defined retail/commercial centre with five outlying residential neighbourhoods, and industrial estates to the north of the town. Later this included the industrial area immediately west of the A19 trunk road at Shotton Colliery. As with all the new towns, housing in Peterlee reflects the changes in housing methods and layout but also changes in the socio-economic character of the different estates and the intake of population when they were built, as well as changes in the Development Corporation and ministerial policy. While early housing in Peterlee was built to space standards that exceeded the minimum at the time, the Parker Morris report of 1961 had a significant impact on the higher standards of kitchen and electrical fittings, central heating and car parking spaces. Early housing at Peterlee was a vast improvement on the living conditions at the mining villages the residents had left, but was also built at speed and often cheaply to save money on materials.

6.2
BERTHOLD LUBETKIN CHATS WITH MINERS OF THE EAST DURHAM COALFIELD, IN 1948.

6.3
PETERLEE'S MASTER PLAN, CREATED BY GEORGE GRENFELL-BAINES IN 1952.

Victor Pasmore at Peterlee

By the mid-1950s, and coinciding with pressure from Ministry of Town and Country Planning, the Development Corporation was worried that the new town's housing areas would become increasingly monotonous. With the view that Lubetkin's departure had 'involved the departure from the spectacular to the non-descript',[4] they employed artist Victor Pasmore as consultant advisor on housing design and layout, including landscape. Pasmore was given a whole southwest area of the town to work on.[5] Subsidence issues, and the legacy of the conflict over the Lubetkin plan, meant that the designs produced by Pasmore's team were limited to two storeys in height. While innovative, the designs took time to get through the authorities and were equally celebrated and criticised at different levels (Figure 6.4). Functionally, the flat roofs did not suit the Northeast climate and, combined with the inexperience of the engineers, meant the developments have not stood the test of time.

6.4
A CANTILEVERED HOUSE WITH A CAR PORT AT GROUND LEVEL AND MAISONETTES ABOVE, ON AVON ROAD, PETERLEE, PHOTOGRAPHED IN 1961. R.J.A. GAZZARD WAS THE CHIEF ARCHITECT RESPONSIBLE FOR THIS PHASE OF THE DEVELOPMENT, WHILE PETER DANIEL AND F.J. DIXON WERE RESPONSIBLE FOR THE DESIGN OF THE HOUSING AND VICTOR PASMORE FOR THE LANDSCAPING.

Apollo Pavilion

Pasmore's most famous intervention in Peterlee was his Apollo Pavilion (Figure 6.5). In 1969 the artist decided to create 'an architecture and sculpture of purely abstract form through which to walk, in which to linger, and on which to play; a free and anonymous monument which, because of its independence, can lift the activity and psychology of an urban housing community on to a universal plane.'[6]

Pasmore's vision materialised as a structure made of reinforced concrete, cast on the site. The design comprises large geometric planes of concrete with the only decoration being two painted murals. In its original form, the Pavilion provided a pedestrian link between the two halves of the Sunny Blunts Estate. From the late 1970s onwards, the pavilion attracted graffiti and became a meeting place for teenagers, promoting complaints from residents who suggested that the Territorial Army should be invited to blow up the sculpture. In response, Pasmore visited the site and joked with residents that, instead, the neighbouring homes could be bombed and the graffiti had 'humanised [the sculpture] and improved it more than I ever could have done'. The lively meeting with the artist ended amicably and trouble subsided when, in 1982, at the suggestion of one local resident, the Pavilion was retained and the steps to it removed by Easington District Council.[7]

Since 2002, the Pavilion has received renewed recognition as an important cultural heritage feature for Peterlee. The Apollo Pavilion Community Association secured the future of the Pavilion by instigating an application to the Heritage Lottery Fund, who awarded a grant of £336,000 towards the costs of restoring the structure. The approved scheme, completed in 2009 (see Figure 6.9), involved restoring the Pavilion and surrounding site back to its original condition (with some minor agreed changes).[8] This controversial piece of art is a rare example of a large-scale experiment in the synthesis of art and architecture in the UK and is now Grade II listed.

6.5
THE APOLLO PAVILION, COMPLETED IN 1970. VICTOR PASMORE ENVISAGED A SCULPTURE 'OF PURELY ABSTRACT FORM THROUGH WHICH TO WALK, IN WHICH TO LINGER, AND ON WHICH TO PLAY'.

6.6
CASTLE DENE SHOPPING CENTRE, IN PETERLEE TOWN CENTRE.

Peterlee today – challenges and opportunities

Today Peterlee is the main town in East Durham, occupying a strategic location between the Northeast's two conurbations, with good road links to surrounding towns but poor connections to some adjacent villages, including neighbouring Horden. Despite its lack of a train station, the town's immediate access to the A19, one of County Durham's principal roads and economic corridors, means Peterlee has become a major employment centre for manufacturing and heavy industry, acting as a service centre for East Durham's surrounding settlements. To the east, the Durham coast is recognised for its high-quality landscape and seascape and is of growing importance as a visitor destination, resulting from campaigns and promotion by the Heritage Coast Partnership and associated agencies.

While investment in strategic infrastructure has enabled Peterlee to continue to attract and sustain business and industry, this success is not consistently reflected throughout the town. As with many of the new towns, there are pockets of deprivation in Peterlee, with levels of deprivation higher than both the UK and new town averages, and within County Durham itself. The proportion of economically active residents is lower than the UK average, unemployment is slightly higher than the national average and the town is among the lowest performing in the county in terms of public health indicators such as life expectancy and long-term illness. There is a significant amount of in and out commuting, with 10,000 commuters travelling in to Peterlee from outside the local area to work in its industrial estates every day. Like many new towns, this suggests that skilled workers choose not to live in Peterlee, and that suitable employment is not available locally for the resident population.

Town centre

Peterlee town centre is contained and defined within the existing ring road and has suffered the fate of many town centres of the era. The pedestrianised shopping centre contains a mix of national retailers (Argos, Wilkinsons), independent retailers and high-street services, with the retail offer dominated by ASDA. The privately owned Castle Dene Shopping Centre is a covered mall providing 28,430sq m of retail and office space (Figure 6.6). Much of the town centre suffers from poor build quality and inadequate pedestrian access from surrounding residential areas and is noted for lacking sufficient cultural amenities or a night-time economy. Office space in the centre is low quality and underused, and the main centre for jobs in the town is the industrial estate by the A19.

Durham County Council is seeking to address these challenges through a series of initiatives, guided by its regeneration master plan. This includes key strategic aims to improve quality, attractiveness and marketability of town centre office accommodation, diversify the retail offer in the town centre and address issues of cultural amenity and night-time economy.

Progress on these initiatives is challenged by complicated ownership throughout the town centre. A new leisure centre development is aimed at bringing in more local choice and potentially could serve as an opportunity to improve infrastructure and linkages. Large employment allocations at the North West and South West Industrial Estates have been made to enable the town to grow and play a stronger role in the county and region. A rail halt is also proposed to the east of Peterlee at Horden, which will have regular passenger services on the Durham Coast Line and will improve access between the area and Sunderland, Hartlepool and further afield. However, there is growing concern among some residents that the new edge-of-centre retail park at East Durham College will threaten the viability of Caste Dene Shopping Centre and the town centre as a whole.[9]

Housing

Peterlee's housing offer has changed since its original provision of 79% socially rented housing and now includes extensive private housing estates. The proportion of households which are socially rented is now 24% (a huge reduction from 79%, but still 6 percentage points higher than the UK average and 3 percentage points higher than the UK new town average).[10] The legacy of designing estates with consideration for landscape means there are characteristic wide green verges along residential access roads, and many estates appear to be in fairly good condition. In contrast, there are also pockets of deprivation in some residential areas, and the build quality of some early estates has not stood the test of time. Council documents also highlight the 'Radburn' style layouts (*see page 17*), the separation of vehicle and pedestrian movement and the low-density areas as a challenge.

As well as estate renewal, Peterlee is planning for growth and the need to accommodate 1,830 additional homes by 2030. Durham County Council has overall objectives to secure new homes at a range of tenures, better housing standards and better provision for vulnerable populations. For Peterlee this includes objectives to stabilise and expand its population, recognising its role as a key service centre. Housing Land Availability Assessments have concluded that there is insufficient land available within the current boundaries, requiring parts of the North East Industrial Estate to be earmarked for housing. Peterlee is a main focus for new housing in East Durham and has a significant number of commitments, including a large site at Low Hills and a further site allocated at North Blunts. The opportunity for regeneration at North East Industrial Estate will also be pursued.

Green infrastructure and public realm

Peterlee's landscape character has been recognised as an important feature for the town. In addition to Pasmore's influence on the landscape of the Sunny Blunts housing area, the original landscape features of the town's area were incorporated into the design of the early estates. The planned structure of Peterlee has created a core of landscape corridors and avenues besides principal access roads. Castle Eden Dene nature reserve forms an important natural resource close to the town and woodlands link it to the town centre. Peterlee Town Council and Durham County Council recognise these assets but also that the extent of open space and a shortage of resources will put significant pressure on the councils to ensure their maintenance.

Governance and stewardship

What Durham County Council's reports do not share is the reality of some of these spaces or the lived experience of residents – both positive and negative. Castle Dene Park, once a celebrated asset for the town centre (Figure 6.7), has now become a significant management challenge for the council and authorities. The once landmark hotel is now a nightclub and the park, used by drug-users alongside dog-walkers, is a 'no-go' area at night for many residents (Figure 6.8).[11]

Significant efforts are under way to address these issues. For Castle Dene Park, local police are working with Groundwork North East and Peterlee Town Council to improve street lighting and visibility and to increase patrols around hotspot times.

At a wider scale, alongside the regeneration master plan, the East Durham Trust was created in 2007 to promote the renewal of former mining communities in East Durham. A programme of arts and health and wellbeing initiatives, such as East Durham Creates, Community Coaches and Active Minds, is designed to address some of Peterlee's deprivation issues.[12]

Next steps for Peterlee

While many of the issues facing Peterlee are common to ex-industrial communities, its new town heritage provides a specific set of conditions which present both opportunities and challenges for its future. The piecemeal division and sale of land and assets when the Development Corporation was dissolved, coupled with the existence of both a town council and a unitary authority, had led to challenges such as confusion over land ownership. This makes even the simplest problem a governance challenge when no one knows who is responsible for cutting which patch of grass. Peterlee contains some fantastic assets – from its artistic built heritage (Figure 6.9) to the internationally recognised resources in Castle Eden Dene and the heritage coast beyond. The challenge going forward is to enable a coordinated approach across the various tiers of governance, but importantly one which embeds people in the process.

6.7
CASTLE DENE PARK IN THE 1970S. THE PARK WAS A POPULAR FEATURE IN THE TOWN CENTRE, CONTAINING A LAKE AND THE NORSEMAN HOTEL.

6.8
(LEFT) CASTLE DENE PARK TODAY. THE NORSEMAN HOTEL IS NOW A PUB AND NIGHTCLUB AND THE PARK IS A LOCATION FOR ANTISOCIAL BEHAVIOUR, WHICH THE COUNCIL IS WORKING IN PARTNERSHIP WITH LOCAL STAKEHOLDERS TO ADDRESS.

6.9
THE APOLLO PAVILION. LOCAL CHILDREN ENJOY THE RESTORED PAVILION AT ITS LAUNCH EVENT IN 2009.

07

CASE STUDY:
CWMBRAN, TORFAEN COUNTY (MONMOUTHSHIRE)

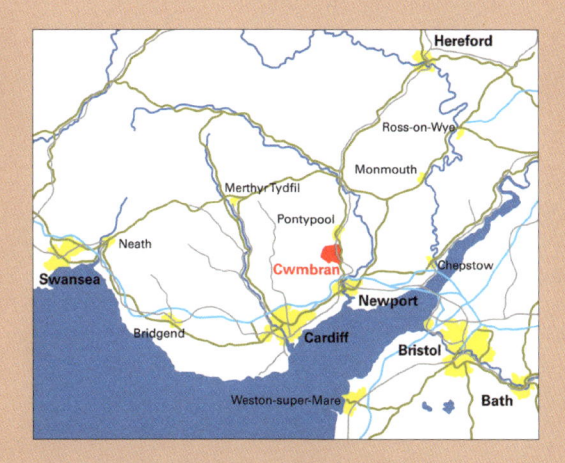

7.1
CWMBRAN IS IN WALES, 21KM NORTHEAST OF CARDIFF.

Key facts

Location: Southeast Wales, 8km north of Newport and 21km northeast of Cardiff (Figure 7.1).

2011 Census population: 48,535, in 20,495 households.[1]

Local authority: Torfaen County Borough Council.

Local Plan status: Torfaen County Borough Local Development Plan (to 2021), (adopted 2013).[2] Replacement Torfaen Local Development Plan is currently in production, with adoption scheduled for December 2021.[3]

New Town designation

Designated: 4 November 1949.

Designated area: 1,279 hectares.

Intended population: 30,000, raised to 55,000 in 1969 (population at designation: 13,000).

Development Corporation: Created 24 November 1949 to provide houses for existing industry. The original master plan was prepared by Anthony Minoprio, with Hugh G.C. Spencely and Peter Macfarlane. The Development Corporation was wound up on 31 March 1988.

Introduction

Cwmbran was the first new town to be designated in Wales and followed proposals made by the Minister of Town and Country Planning, Lewis Silkin, in 1948 for two Welsh new towns. Cwmbran included existing housing and industry and was partly constrained by existing railway lines and a canal. It was designed to provide housing for those employed in existing industry who travelled from the South Wales Valleys. It was thus an unusual 'Mark One' new town in that it was designed to provide homes and not employment and was intended to correct an existing imbalance rather than create a new 'balanced community'. Today, Cwmbran is the largest settlement in Torfaen County Borough and is well located, with good access to the M4 and the city coastal zone (Figure 7.2). It is considered by its current planners to be successful and popular.

Background

The designation of Cwmbran New Town in 1949 provided a welcome solution to the challenge of addressing the impact of the decline in the coal industry, which had blighted the South Wales region. The designation was almost unanimously welcomed by surrounding local authorities.[4] The chosen valley had already been a focus for a broad range of industry and the existing towns of Cwmbran and Pontnewyd had an existing population of approximately 13,000. Osborn and Whittick note that 'it was not an ideal site for a new town' due to the close proximity of existing town centres, which could be compromised, therefore a green belt for Cwmbran 'should be regarded as imperative'.[5]

Ministerial committees set up to explore the applicability of the New Towns Act 1946 in Wales concentrated on opportunities to designate areas of housing to support existing industries. County councils were asked to nominate suitable sites. Sites in the Cwmbran area had been identified as potential new town locations in the 1949 'Outline Plan' for the South Wales region.[6] The South Wales Outline Plan proposed that the population of the Cwmbran area should be expanded through the creation of three new residential neighbourhoods, each housing 10,000 people. The minister felt that neighbourhoods of such scale must be 'accompanied by the provision of proper social and other facilities ... entailing a heavier financial and administrative responsibility than the local authorities concerned could be expected to carry' and therefore that it was in the national interest that a Development Corporation should be used for the task.[7]

In 1949 the minister consulted with all the local authorities that appeared to him to be concerned. Except for Newport Borough Council, all the local authorities welcomed and supported the proposal. However, there was some difference of opinion over the most suitable site, and some concerns that the rights, responsibilities and operations of the local authorities might be affected by the designation and that the New Town Development Corporation might be given exceptional priority and special facilities.[8] Newport Borough Council expressed 'no opinion' on the necessity for the establishment of a new town, but suggested as a possible alternative the expansion of Newport and Pontypool. Industrial interests were also concerned that the designation of land and the preservation of the green belt would prevent them from

07 CASE STUDY: CWMBRAN, TORFAEN COUNTY (MONMOUTHSHIRE)

7.2
CWMBRAN FROM THE AIR.

obtaining land for expansion. Cwmbran Development Corporation obtained 133 acres of land via a Compulsory Purchase Order. The first Annual Report of Cwmbran Development Corporation states that 'none of the land owners objected to the order'.

Cwmbran Development Corporation came into existence on 24 November 1949, aiming to 'set a standard of what a modern Industrial Town should be' and 'to create a happy, friendly and pleasing town'.[9] Officials wrote to all local authorities near the designated area asking for nominations for board members. Most simply nominated their chairs, with only Newport nominating one from each political party. The board met fortnightly (later monthly), with a site visit in between. Some of the staff also worked for Mid-Wales Development Corporation, which was delivering Newtown.

The fact that Cwmbran Development Corporation was an undemocratic body caused some resentment among the district councils, who felt that the Development Corporation got more money from the government (in fact, this was not the case) and preferential treatment. The strength and nature of relationships between Cwmbran Development Corporation and the district and county councils varied between individual functions in the corporation. While there were positive relationships between Development Corporation planners and the county architect, there was some tension between Cwmbran Urban District Council and the Development Corporation, which improved in 1970 when Lord Raglan, a local landowner and politician, became the corporation's chairman.

Cwmbran master plan

Master-planners Anthony Minoprio, Hugh G.C. Spencley and Peter Macfarlane, who were also master planners for Crawley New Town in 1947, were appointed in 1950 to create a survey of the area and prepare an outline plan. Following submission to the minister, it received only three objections at its public inquiry and was approved in December 1951 (Figure 7.3).

A green belt was allocated for Cwmbran, which was controlled jointly by the Development Corporation and Monmouthshire County Council. The town centre was located in the middle of the industrial area and seven residential neighbourhoods were included, grouped around the town centre and industries.

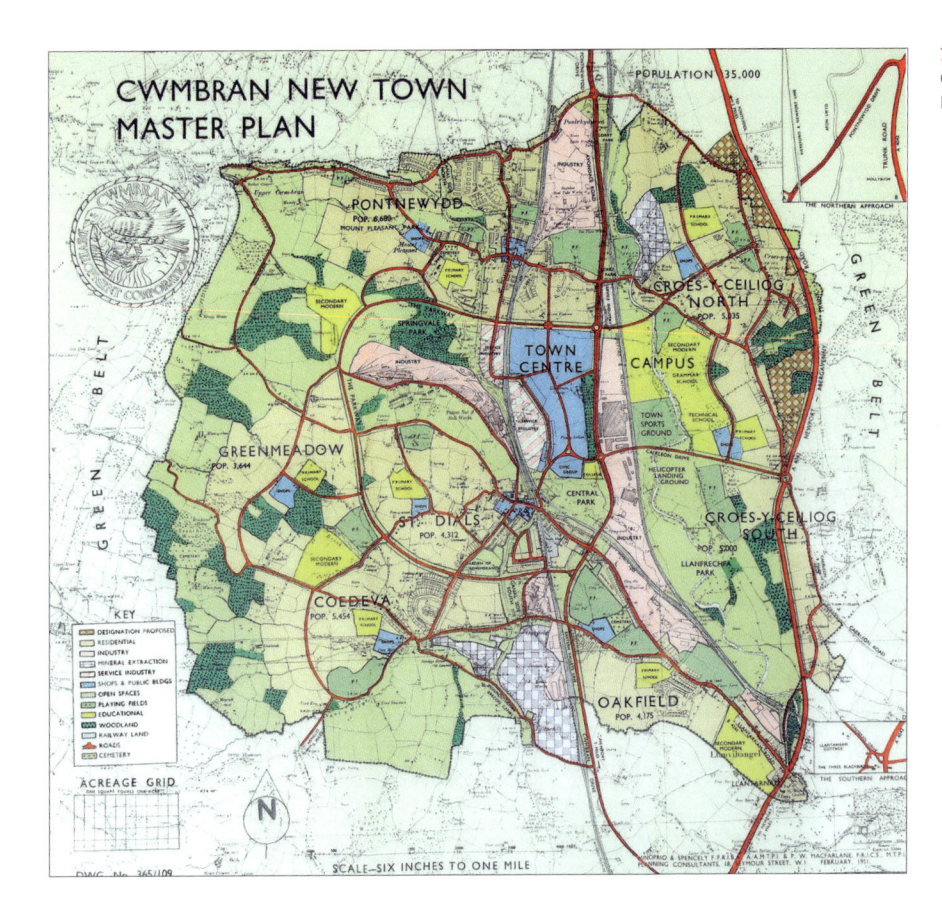

7.3
CWMBRAN NEW TOWN MASTER PLAN, 1951.

Each neighbourhood was planned with a small shopping centre and primary school, with a population of approximately 5,000 people in each neighbourhood, enough to sustain a centre of approximately 20 shops, a bank and post office, junior and infant school and 'certain community buildings such as a hall, clinic and branch library'.[10] The population target was raised to 45,000 in 1962.

However, the earlier stages of development were not without their problems. For example, the aesthetic qualities and design ambitions were often not being met due to the fast pace of development (Figure 7.4). The contemporary mono-pitched housing in Coed Eva won many awards for its original design but has not stood the test of time.[11] At Greenmeadow it was noted that 'a particularly unfortunate feature of some of the corporation's housing schemes of the early sixties was the decision to use flat roofs'.[12] The motivation behind this idea was to break away from the 'dull, "council estate" appearance of the older developments'. However, this resulted in 'a legacy of damp penetration that lasted years after ideas of this sort were abandoned'.[13]

Following consultants' reports, flats were limited to 10% of housing stock, with it viewed that 'terraced housing following the contours will prove to be the most useful for development on the steep slopes'.[14] Flats were located near the town centre to 'add architectural interest'.

Notable attention was given to the detailing of homes – evident in roof shapes and cladding choice, for example – and to the planting of a range of trees to create early visual interest.

In later neighbourhoods the houses consisted mainly of two-storey terraced blocks with 'roads branching in and garages or car parking arranged in rows'.[15] Most had small fenced gardens and were grouped to form pedestrian courts, some of which had boulders for children's play. Roofing was mainly low or mono pitched.

In 1966, a 22-storey block of flats was constructed in the town centre as a 'prominent landmark for many miles around'. It also provided 61m chimneys for the district heating system.

Delivery at Cwmbran was fast – by 1967 the population had nearly reached the revised intended population of 45,000 and by 1969 there was discussion of raising the target population to 75,000–90,000, but a new figure of 55,000 was eventually settled on.

Winding up the Development Corporation was first mooted in 1982 and this took place in 1988. By this time, the corporation had built 10,199, mainly rented, dwellings. It sold some prior to 1976 and many more from 1980 onwards.

Cwmbran today – challenges and opportunities

Cwmbran has adapted to many changes that the Development Corporation never anticipated, such as those in the housing market. Its retail offer owes much to the town's accessibility and convenience (helped by free parking), although its impact on retailing in surrounding towns is also something that was not anticipated by the corporation.

7.4
A HOUSE WITH BRICKWORK AND WEATHERBOARDING AT LLANFRECHFA, CWMBRAN, BY RHYS-DAVIES AND MIALL, 1950 (PHOTOGRAPH TAKEN 1959). FLAT ROOFS WERE NOT SUITED TO THE CLIMATE OF THE WELSH VALLEYS.

Town centre

Today, Cwmbran has a thriving town centre, one of the key legacies of the Development Corporation (alongside the provision of housing, a comprehensive green space network, a community farm, and the provision of extensive employment land). Torfaen County Borough Council is aiming to improve the town centre by linking the retail area with the Monmouthshire and Brecon Canal to create a more accessible and pleasant environment, and by renewing the night-time economy. In April 2018, a planning application was approved to redevelop parts of the town centre, including Monmouth Square.[16] While this provides a new public space, it involves flattening the former water gardens, one of the town centre's few district architectural heritage features (Figure 7.5).

Green infrastructure and public realm

The provision of public open spaces, woodlands and a linear park as part of the new town design have made Cwmbran an attractive place to live. However, the council notes the significant revenue implications for maintenance. A proportion of open space was transferred to Bron Afon (a registered housing provider) as part of the 2008 housing stock transfer; Bron Afon is now considering using this space for the provision of new affordable housing. Across Cwmbran, the open space provision planned as part of the new town, and the older employment areas constructed by the Development Corporation, are coming under increasing pressure for development for higher-value uses. The Monmouthshire and Brecon Canal runs

7.5
MONMOUTH SQUARE (A), WITH THE WATER GARDENS IN THE FOREGROUND. THE WATER GARDENS (B) WILL BE LOST IN THE SQUARE'S REDEVELOPMENT, APPROVED IN 2018.

07 CASE STUDY: CWMBRAN, TORFAEN COUNTY (MONMOUTHSHIRE)

7.6
A CYCLE PATH ALONGSIDE THE MONMOUTHSHIRE AND BRECON CANAL (A) AND A SCENIC STRETCH OF THE WATERWAY (B). THE CANAL IS AN IMPORTANT GREEN INFRASTRUCTURE ASSET WHICH COULD PROVIDE MULTIPLE BENEFITS IF PROPERLY LINKED TO CWMBRAN TOWN CENTRE.

(a) (b)

through Cwmbran and provides both a challenge, but, as recognised by the council, also a huge opportunity in terms of health, social, economic and environmental benefits, and the council is seeking to create a new mixed-use quarter based around the canal, adjacent to the town centre (Figure 7.6). To complement these initiatives and to maximise opportunities for renewal, Cwmbran would benefit from a town-wide green infrastructure strategy that includes measures for greening the shopping centre.

Housing

Despite some difficulties of the challenges of flat or mono-pitched roofs in the Welsh climate, many of the original housing design and layout principles remain intact, such as the high level of open and recreational space, and the provision of community and retail facilities at the core of each of the original neighbourhoods.[17] Bron Afon took on the social housing stock, with an initial focus to ensure that housing met the Welsh Housing Quality Standard (Figure 7.7). More strategically, Cwmbran is identified as a growth hub for the borough, with plans for 2,275 homes in five 'Action Areas' (Figure 7.8). Cwmbran is now part of a City Deal agreement, which seeks to improve the economic profile of the region over the next 20 years, which will include further housebuilding in the region.

Governance and stewardship

There were no specific 'stewardship' bodies set up to manage Cwmbran's assets after the Development Corporation was wound up. That task fell mainly to Torfaen County Borough Council. However, there are two major landowners in the town today, who in their own way provide important stewardship functions. Cwmbran Shopping owns most of the shopping centre, which is thriving, with zero vacancy rates. Single ownership provides opportunities for the centre to be managed in a holistic way, but Torfaen County Borough Council has less control over the public realm in the centre, which presents its own challenges. Bron Afon, the housing association that took on ownership of Cwmbran's social housing following asset transfer, also plays an important stewardship role in the town.

Next steps for Cwmbran

The new Local Development Plan (2018–33) provides opportunity to consider the town's future. In a 2018 article on growth and renewal in Cwmbran, written for the Town and Country Planning Association's journal, Torfean County Borough Council demonstrated its awareness of the opportunities and challenges presented by Cwmbran's new town legacy, including the need to ensure that regeneration is undertaken while retaining the best of the new town design in terms of the provision of neighbourhoods, green spaces and employment sites.[18] The threat to green spaces from new development is clearly high on the council's list of concerns, but this recognition provides an important foundation to ensure that future growth from the City Deal and regional initiatives can help to secure a positive future for the town.

7.7
ASHTON HOUSE, CWMBRAN. BRON AFON COMMUNITY HOUSING SPENT £1 MILLION RETROFITTING THE INSULATION OF THE PROPERTY IN 2015.

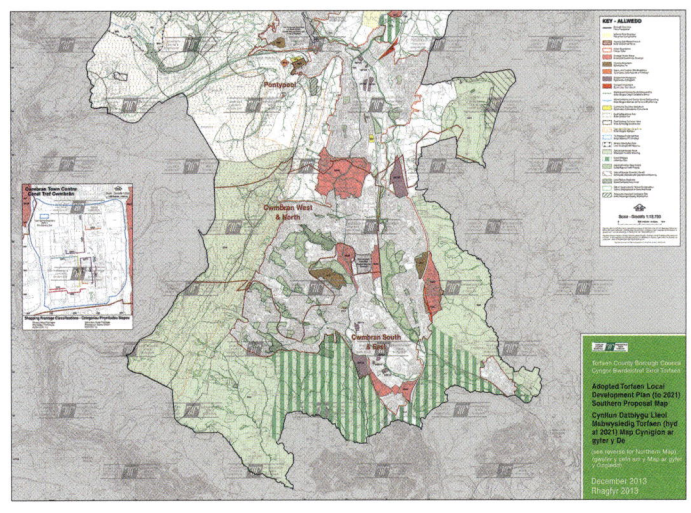

7.8
ADOPTED TORFEAN LOCAL PLAN TO 2021 (SOUTHERN PROPOSALS MAP) 2013. STRATEGIC ACTION AREAS ARE SHOWN IN PINK.

08

CASE STUDY:
CUMBERNAULD, NORTH LANARKSHIRE

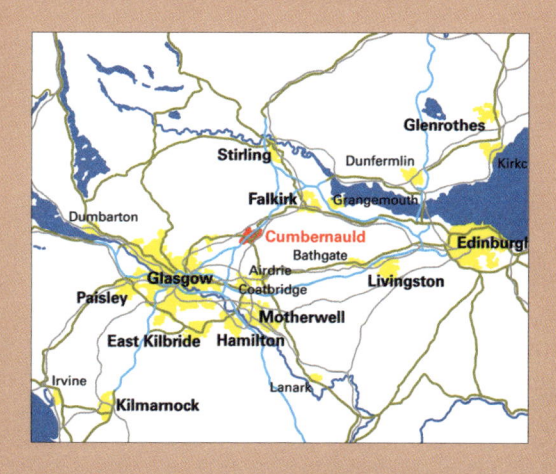

8.1 CUMBERNAULD IS IN NORTH LANARKSHIRE, 21KM NORTHEAST OF GLASGOW.

Key facts

Location: 21km northeast of Glasgow, in North Lanarkshire, Scotland (Figure 8.1). Cumbernauld is located in the northeast of the Greater Glasgow conurbation.

2011 Census population: 52,270, in 22,105 households.[1]

Local authority: North Lanarkshire Council.

Local Plan status: North Lanarkshire Local Plan (adopted 2012). Work on a new Local Development Plan is under way, with consultation on the Modified Local Plan Policy Document taking place in 2019. The Clydeplan Strategic Development Plan covers North Lanarkshire and seven other authorities in and surrounding Glasgow.[2]

New Town designation

Designated: 9 December 1955.

Designated area: 1,680 hectares, revised later to 3,152 hectares.

Intended population: 50,000, revised to 70,000 in 1961 (population at designation: 3,000).

Development Corporation: Designated to accommodate Glasgow overspill population. The Development Corporation was wound up on 31 December 1996.

Introduction

Designed to help manage Glasgow's housing needs and today an important regional town for Lanarkshire, Cumbernauld offers far more than its iconic megastructure. Consciously designed to depart from the 'neighbourhood' principle adopted in the previous new towns, Cumbernauld's designers applied higher densities within fewer urban areas and a single town centre on the hilltop (Figure 8.2). The town was designed to be more 'urban' than its predecessors[3] and contains some of the best examples of Modernist architecture in the UK. It is a town of two halves, bisected by a motorway. The southern half was built in a Modernist low-rise style in a Radburn layout (see page 17) by the Development Corporation, while the majority of the northern half was developed by the private sector, with the Development Corporation as facilitator. By the 1990s, Cumbernauld had grown to be North Lanarkshire's biggest town. It occupies a strategic location at the junction of the M73/M80 motorway network and is in close proximity to the M8 and M9. This provides good access links east/west to Edinburgh and Glasgow and north/south throughout Scotland and beyond. There is no train station in the town but there is one 20 minutes' walk from it.

Background

Cumbernauld was included in Patrick Abercrombie's Clyde Valley Regional Plan of 1946 (see page 22 and 28), to complement the earlier new town at East Kilbride and accommodate some of Glasgow's population, but was not designated until nine years later.[4] The delay in designation was due to HM Treasury's concern that the new towns were costing a lot of money and its consequent reluctance to agree to further designations. Meanwhile, Glasgow Corporation was hesitant about making financial contributions to housing outside the city. However, the 1952 Glasgow Plan demonstrated that Glasgow could not solve its housing supply problems inside its own boundaries. The Clyde Valley Regional Planning Advisory Committee was reconstituted in 1953 and recommended that Cumbernauld should be the first large-scale housing development outside the city.[5] The changes in Britain's economic climate in the mid-1950s reversed government concerns over the cost of the new towns, which were now generating profit that HM Treasury wanted to retain. In 1955, Glasgow Corporation eventually came to an agreement with the Secretary of State over contributions to the cost of Cumbernauld.

The Draft Designation Order was published in July 1955. However, the proposed designated area overlapped the counties of Lanarkshire and Dunbartonshire. Lanarkshire was prepared to accept industry but not the new town project as a whole. To avoid delay, the Scottish Office decided to proceed with a designation which covered just the land in Dunbartonshire, with two important consequences: 'First, it meant that the railway line to Glasgow was now peripheral rather than central to the designated area. Secondly, the Dunbartonshire land was poor quality.'[6] During a public inquiry held in October, most of the objections raised related to the demand by local councillors and several residents for a continuing role for Dunbarton County Council in providing new housing for Cumbernauld village. The inquiry was completed in one day as 'there were no serious objections to the principle of the New Town designation'.[7] Cumbernauld was designated on 9 December 1955.

08 CASE STUDY: CUMBERNAULD, NORTH LANARKSHIRE

8.2
AN AERIAL VIEW OF CUMBERNAULD, SHOWING ITS HILLTOP LOCATION AND LANDSCAPE SETTING.

Cumbernauld Development Corporation was established in February 1956 and was accountable to the Secretary of State for Scotland through the Scottish Office Industry Department. From the first meeting, the corporation knew that Cumbernauld would be different from the new towns that had been designated to date. This was partially in reflection of the need to fit 50,000 people into a small and challenging site, requiring densities to be 60% higher than in the older new towns. It was also a reaction to what by then was perceived as a lack of 'urban' feel to the older, lower-density new towns.

Multidisciplinary design teams were assembled from the best talent across the UK. David Cowling, an architect and town planner who worked for Cumbernauld Development Corporation in the 1960s and 1970s, wrote: 'There was a rare atmosphere of pioneering adventure. Those involved believed themselves to be engaged upon something new, something unique.'[8] However, they were facing extremely challenging rates of delivery. By the mid-1960s, the momentum of the housebuilding programme had increased to average 1,000 houses per annum.[9] Senior Cumbernauld Development Corporation employees knew even then that this build-out rate meant compromising on things such as the quality of materials, but they had deadlines to meet. Nevertheless, the architects were keen to work with the contours of the site in the housing areas and deliver the vision of a balanced community in an expression of modern urbanism.

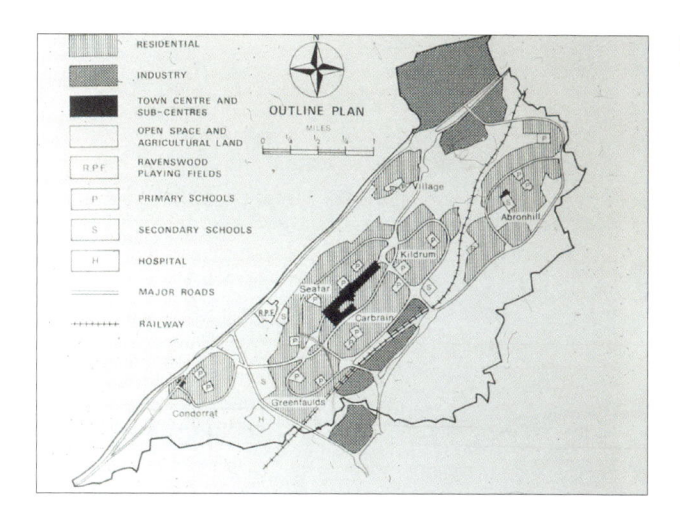

8.3
1962 CUMBERNAULD MASTER PLAN.

105

8.4
HOUSING AT SEAFAR, CUMBERNAULD, 1967. TOWER BLOCKS LIKE THESE, BUILT IN 1966 AND DESIGNED BY LEAKER AND WILSON FOR CUMBERNAULD DEVELOPMENT CORPORATION, WERE USED TO ACCOMMODATE AN INCREASING TARGET POPULATION.

Cumbernauld master plan

The master plan for Cumbernauld New Town (Figure 8.3) envisaged it as 'a tight urban place, suitable for a hilltop' with a 'single multi-purpose town centre'.[10] The presence of this town centre meant that the housing areas contained only small shops, in contrast to the previous new towns, which had largely taken the form of multiple satellite neighbourhoods with their own individual centres. In 1961, 'the Scottish Office lifted the target population to 70,000', meaning that the plan had to be adapted to accommodate an extra 20,000 residents.[11] Initially, plans sought to cater for this extra population by adding additional tower blocks. However, after some tower blocks were built, this method was found to be infeasible for achieving the target population and was negatively 'distorting the design of the housing areas' (Figure 8.4).[12] To fix the population problem, in 1973 'the Secretary of State virtually doubled the designated area to the north of the A80 trunk road', to provide housing for the extra 20,000 people.[13]

08 CASE STUDY: CUMBERNAULD, NORTH LANARKSHIRE

The original master plan was amended to accommodate these changes, detailing that 'in addition to the main hilltop site, developments are proposed at four villages – Condorrat, Cumbernauld Village, Wardpark and Abronhill, each complete with local shops and other minor facilities but depending on the main town centre for the principal shopping, entertainment and cultural activities'.[14] The plan also sought to ensure that these changes would not be of detriment to the original vision for the settlement, as 'the general picture of the form of the town on the hilltop – the most important comprehensive scene at Cumbernauld – has not altered materially since the issue of the First Addendum Report'.[15]

Due to the addition of the extended designated area, the plan for Cumbernauld became a town of 'two halves'; the first being 'the high-density urban cluster on its exposed hilltop with its associated tight satellites' and the second being 'an extended "suburb" across the valley, filling the open space which was once thought of as the essential lung for those living in tight urban form'.[16] The two halves of the town were bisected by the A80 road, which later became the M80 motorway.

Copcutt's megastructure

The jewel in the crown of the hilltop town was Geoffrey Copcutt's town centre megastructure. Designed to realise Le Corbusier's ideas of the Radiant City (see Figure 1.11), this eight-storey structure was intended to provide all the facilities needed in a town within a single structure (Figure 8.5).[17]

8.5
CUMBERNAULD'S TOWN CENTRE MEGASTRUCTURE, PHOTOGRAPHED DURING ITS CONSTRUCTION IN 1966. IT WAS COMPLETED IN 1967 AND OCCUPIED A PROMINENT HILLTOP POSITION.

8.6
A 1963 DEPICTION OF GEOFFREY COPCUTT'S PROPOSED MEGASTRUCTURE, DRAWN BY MICHAEL EVANS. THE ICONIC STRUCTURE WAS DESIGNED TO PROVIDE A RANGE OF FACILITIES FOR RESIDENTS.

This included penthouses for executives, shops, a hotel, an ice rink, a police station and other amenities (Figure 8.6). It tackled the separation of pedestrians and vehicles several years before the 'Traffic in towns' report.[18]

The building was widely anticipated and visited by students from across the globe. The engineering company contracted to deliver the centre went bankrupt, leaving sparse engineering plans for the site – which led to problems with structural integrity during build-out and the early degradation of the structure. The centre was opened in 1967, winning an international award for Community Architecture, and by 1971 had the largest supermarket in Scotland. Later phases were built by the Development Corporation and the sites sold directly to the private sector. A shopping management group purchased the Phase 1 megastructure building when the corporation was wound up in 1996. Phases 3 and 4 were subsequently demolished and the site is currently owned by Belgate Estates.

It seems a combination of design and delivery proved a challenge to achieving Copcutt's vision. The location (on a Scottish hilltop and on a smaller site than intended, on poorer quality land than intended), a failure to construct windbreaks, the quality of the build, and changing economic circumstances all seem to have contributed to it challenging history.[19] The structure continues to divide opinion and in the past two decades was famously awarded 'carbuncle' awards for most dismal town centre – it has been compared a 'rabbit warren on stilts'. Beyond the architectural observations of critics who have no doubt never lived or worked in the town (along with some unhappy residents), despite its lack of maintenance it remains an important social and economic focus. Its role in creating a sense of identity for Cumbernauld's residents was reflected in 2012 when it won a public vote for civic pride, winning 'Best Town' at the Scottish design awards.[20]

Community development

From the early days of development there was an active community arts scene in Cumbernauld. Members of the Development Corporation met in each other's houses for talks, record recitals, poetry readings and organised visits to theatres in Glasgow. By 1961 they had formed the Cumbernauld Theatre Group and persuaded the Development Corporation to let them have a block of two ancient farm cottages. In 1973 the Theatre Group produced development proposals for what is now the Cumbernauld Theatre. The Cumbernauld Theatre Trust was set up in 1977, but today the theatre is run by North Lanarkshire Council. There are a large number of active community groups in Cumbernauld today, but not enough affordable spaces for them to use.[21]

An extension to the designated area was granted in 1973. The extended area lies to the north of the town centre and its designation coincided with increased interest from the private sector in delivering housing in the new town. Today, around 80% of the housing in the extended area is private-sector housing.

The dissolution of the New Towns programme in Scotland was somewhat different from the procedure in England in that no statutory residuary bodies were created. In the main, the new unitary authorities inherited all the functions of the former Development Corporations. One exception to this was that industrial land was transferred to Scottish Enterprise to market and develop. As noted in Chapter 2, a memorandum by North Lanarkshire Council stated, 'We would not appear to have suffered the same problems as the English New Towns have experienced when dealing with English Partnerships in this regard.'[22]

Cumbernauld today – challenges and opportunities

Today Cumbernauld is still famous for its 'megastructure' town centre and hilltop location but it has suffered from a challenging reputation in the media, including once being voted Britain's most hated building in a poll for Channel 4 television.[23] It is true that the town centre is in urgent need of maintenance to improve its accessibility and visual aesthetic, but that does not make its form any less impressive. Beyond the town centre, the housing areas in Cumbernauld demonstrate the sense of ambition and enthusiasm of Cumbernauld Development Corporation's young architects, who worked hard to create high-quality homes in a challenging physical environment (and at great speed). North Lanarkshire Council is working to renew and unify the 'town of two halves'. (Cumbernauld now sits in North Lanarkshire, a new single-tier authority created in 1996 as one of 32 council areas for Scotland. It covers parts of the traditional counties of Dunbartonshire, Lanarkshire and Stirlingshire.)

Town centre

Today Cumbernauld town centre remains an important regional centre for Lanarkshire. The health check and action plan created for the town centre by North Lanarkshire Council recognises that its megastructure and subsequent phases of demolition and construction make it a special case but are far from proposing drastic measures such as demolition. Familiar challenges of attracting a diverse and competitive retail offer and night-time economy are accompanied by the challenges of a need for public realm improvements and a more diverse cultural offer, and accessibility challenges resulting from its design.[24] An overriding challenge of public perception – affecting the public's use of space as well as attracting retailers – is to be addressed through a series of actions including a rebranding of the town centre, improvements to accessibility and the cultural offer, and a greening policy linked to the Cumbernauld Living Landscape project. Ongoing town centre regeneration, including provision of a hub building for community activities and start-up businesses, is planned to address these issues (Figure 8.7).

NEW TOWNS: THE RISE, FALL AND REBIRTH

8.7
CUMBERNAULD TOWN CENTRE TODAY. THE TOWN CENTRE IS SOME WAY FROM THE VISION OF ITS ORIGINAL DESIGNERS, BUT ONGOING REGENERATION IS PLANNED.

08 CASE STUDY: CUMBERNAULD, NORTH LANARKSHIRE

8.8
ESTATE HOUSING IN CUMBERNAULD TODAY IS SURROUNDED BY A MATURING LANDSCAPE AND HAS RETAINED ITS INNOVATIVE DESIGN BUT ESTATE MAINTENANCE IS A CHALLENGE (A). IN OTHER AREAS HOMES HAVE BEEN BOUGHT AND RENOVATED BY DESIGN-CONSCIOUS RESIDENTS ATTRACTED BY THE TOWN'S ACCESSIBILITY AND GREEN SPACE (B).

Housing

Regeneration plans for Cumbernauld include improvements to former public-sector houses sold under the 'Right to Buy' (Figure 8.8), and investment in homes for affordable rent, including plans to retrofit homes for low-carbon energy efficiency.[25]

North Lanarkshire Council has ambitious plans for growth in Cumbernauld (Figure 8.9), focused primarily in two urban extensions to the south of the town. As the council owns the land at these two sites, there are huge opportunities to create new developments that reflect the pride and ambitions of the town, using innovative approaches to land value capture and long-term stewardship, not least by using Cumbernauld's extensive green infrastructure networks and ecological assets as a catalyst. The town's housing growth plans will require amendment to the green belt boundary, as identified in the green belt review.

Green infrastructure and public realm

Landscape setting and quality were important features of the town's early development and remain so in many areas today. The town centre environment is a harsh contrast, with initial emphasis on the concrete megastructure and more recently with extensive surface car parking,

8.9
NORTH LANARKSHIRE COUNCIL IS PLANNING FOR A RANGE OF NEW HOUSING PROVISION IN AND AROUND CUMBERNAULD.

and limited landscape treatment and maintenance. The town centre has had a lack of high-quality civic spaces since its development, with the emphasis from the outset on developing the megastructure building as the centre of civic and community life.

Governance and stewardship

No specific stewardship bodies were set up when the Development Corporation was wound up. Today, housing associations play an important stewardship role, as does the Scottish Wildlife Trust. Over 50% of Cumbernauld town centre is made up of green spaces: parks, woodlands and gardens. However, these areas are often disconnected from one another and many are not as good for people – or wildlife – as they could be. The Scottish Wildlife Trust runs an initiative called Cumbernauld Living Landscape, which aims to maximise the benefits of this important asset in improving health, wellbeing and access to nature within the town.[26]

Next steps for Cumbernauld

Cumbernauld remains an important economic centre and manufacturing base for North Lanarkshire. The council's ambitious plans for housing growth and renewal reflect the town's strategic location and after 60 years it remains a place which can help deal with Glasgow's housing needs. Its town centre and significant green infrastructure provide simultaneously the biggest challenges and perhaps the greatest opportunities for the town's future. Can a model for renewing the town centre be found which respects its design heritage but makes it fit for purpose for residents and businesses in the 21st century? Its ownership may make this a challenge but renewing the town centre could transform the opportunities presented in the town. New development provides an opportunity to secure resources to support existing stewardship partnerships for Cumbernauld's green spaces and to create new stewardship models related to the renewal of existing estates, while imaginative reuse of green space in existing housing estates could help make their retrofitting for climate resilience even more effective. In a challenging economic climate, this will require both ambition and a long-term view from all involved.

09

CASE STUDY:
SKELMERSDALE, WEST LANCASHIRE

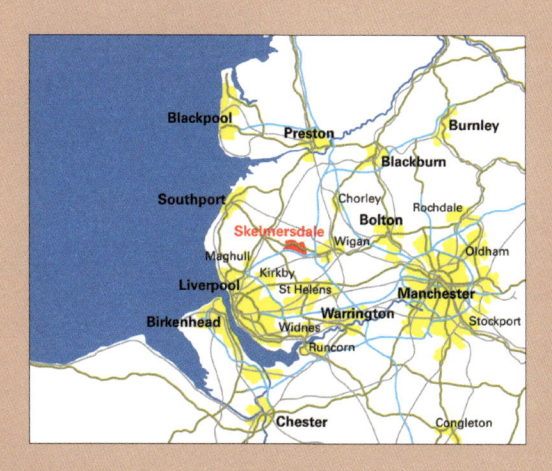

9.1
SKELMERSDALE IS IN WEST LANCASHIRE, 21KM NORTHEAST OF LIVERPOOL AND 26KM NORTHWEST OF MANCHESTER.

Key facts

Location: 21km northeast of Liverpool, 26km northwest of Manchester (Figure 9.1). It is the second-largest town in the Northwest without a railway station, but Preston, Liverpool and Manchester are all within a 30-minute drive.

2011 Census population: 40,710, in 16,769 households (6,175 of which, in 2,597 households, are in adjoining Up Holland).[1]

Local authority: West Lancashire Borough Council.

Local Plan status: West Lancashire Local Plan 2012–2027 (adopted 2013). A Local Plan review began in 2016 and was halted in 2019. Work on a new plan is to start soon.

New Town designation

Designated: 9 October 1961.

Designated area: 1,630 hectares, revised to 1,670 hectares.

Intended population: 80,000, later reduced to 61,000 (population at designation: 8,500).

Development Corporation: The 'Basic Plan' adopted in 1966 was based on a need to plan for: the car; integrated industrial and residential sites; green belt and a clear limit to development to avoid sprawl; a well-balanced population; and a staged development approach with a full range of facilities provided at each stage. The Development Corporation was wound up on 31 March 1985.

Introduction

Skelmersdale was the forerunner of the 'Mark Two' new towns and the first in the Northwest. Formerly a small mining town, it was designated as a new town to accommodate some of the rapidly expanding population of Liverpool and the wider Merseyside area. Today, it is the largest and most densely populated settlement in the West Lancashire Borough and is adjoined to the east by the more traditional settlement of Up Holland. Clearly defined industrial and residential areas and a significant green space network are legacies of its master plan. Skelmersdale rail station was closed to passengers in 1956 and the station and line closed completely in 1963. The town is well placed for haulage as it is located midway between Wigan and Liverpool. A significant proportion of residents are employed in the town, particularly in retail and manual work in the manufacturing industries, suggesting that the skills base in the town is low. There is limited knowledge-based employment available in the town.[2] Some of the new town estates and the town centre are in urgent need of regeneration but a programme of town centre renewal, urban extensions and a new rail link are planned to address this.

Background

Authorities in the Northwest of England had recognised for some time before Skelmersdale's designation that a new settlement was necessary to accommodate the populations being rehoused from the extensive slum clearance programmes in Liverpool. A new community at Skelmersdale was identified in the 1956 Lancashire Development Plan. Local authorities planned for its delivery under the Town Development Act 1952 as, although sympathetic to the proposals, the Ministry did not at that point approve of its development under the New Towns Act. By 1960 there was a recognition that the current approach was putting a strain on local authorities and was unlikely to ensure development on a scale and at the speed required to satisfy urgent housing needs. In 1961, Skelmersdale became the first new town to be designated in England for 11 years.[3]

Skelmersdale master plan

Sir Hugh Wilson was appointed in 1962 to prepare a master plan for the new town. Interim proposals were approved in 1963 and the basic plan was submitted to the Ministry and approved in 1966 (Figure 9.2). Following the approach Wilson took when designing Cumbernauld some years earlier, the plan for Skelmersdale departed from the neighbourhood principle applied at the earlier new towns and instead included concentrated pockets of residential development close to the town centre.

Recognising the Tawd Valley as an asset, the town centre was located in the geographical centre of the site, to the east of the river (Figure 9.3). The majority of housing, for around 61,000 people, was provided to the east of the centre with a second residential area to the west, including the existing town of Skelmersdale, earmarked to accommodate around 14,000 people. Up Holland, to the southeast of the designated area, was an existing small town proposed to accommodate around 5,000 people.

09 CASE STUDY: SKELMERSDALE, WEST LANCASHIRE

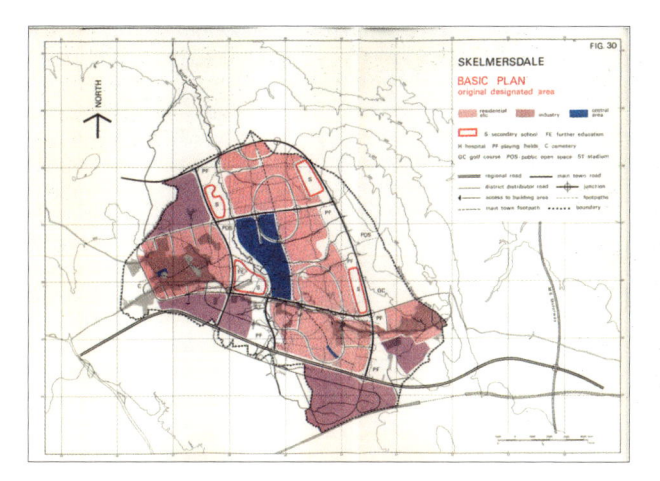

9.2
SKELMERSDALE BASIC PLAN, 1966. THE PLAN SHOWS RESIDENTIAL AREAS STRADDLING THE TAWD VALLEY AND SURROUNDING THE TOWN CENTRE.

9.3
GREENERY AND WILD FLOWERS IN THE TAWD VALLEY. THE VALLEY WAS RECOGNISED AS AN IMPORTANT ECOLOGICAL ASSET BY MASTER-PLANNERS.

Early analysis of the plan from Osborn and Whittick noted that most of the residential areas were to be within 1 mile of the town centre and 50% within half a mile of it.[4] The majority of residential areas were planned at a fairly high density for the new towns, of 148–172 to the hectare (60–70 to the acre). Early plans for high rise near the town centre – reducing to low rise at the edge – were dismissed as the higher densities were considered unacceptable.[5]

Skelmersdale aimed to be self-sufficient and provide up to 36,000 jobs. Three principal industrial areas were identified to accommodate this, to the north and south of old Skelmersdale and to the south of Up Holland. The majority of industrial provision was for manufacturing (Figure 9.4), a lack of diversification that would later contribute to the town's decline. Skelmersdale grew rapidly as an overspill town for Liverpool, but its target population was revised down to 61,000 in 1978 following Government's review of the New Towns Programme. The Corporation was dissolved in 1985.

Skelmersdale today – challenges and opportunities

Despite its new town heritage, Skelmersdale was not immune to the forces facing many Northern industrial towns and today suffers from acute problems of multiple deprivation – in particular, the Digmoor area of the town is ranked among the top 1% most deprived areas in the country. No less than 14 of Skelmersdale's 23 Lower Super Output Areas feature in the top 20% most deprived areas of the country. This is in contrast to the rest of the borough, which has relatively low levels of deprivation. Some of the more severe problems are linked with low income, high unemployment, poor health and low educational attainment. The resulting poor image means that for many, Skelmersdale optimises pre-conceived ideas of new towns and why they failed, and it is often used as a default reference point for the media and commentators wanting to highlight why new towns are a bad idea.[6] Apart from the wider subregional economic influences on the

9.4
BY THE END OF 1969, MORE THAN 60 COMPANIES WERE ESTABLISHED IN THE TOWN, MAINLY ON SITES LEASED BY THE DEVELOPMENT CORPORATION.

9.5
THE SKELMERSDALE STORY, A BOOK PUBLISHED AS PART OF THE SKELMERSDALE PLACE INITIATIVE, WHICH WAS LAUNCHED IN 2016. THE BRANDING INITIATIVE AIMS TO GET PEOPLE TO THINK DIFFERENTLY ABOUT THE TOWN AND TO ENCOURAGE INVESTMENT.

town, the recurring new town issue of fragmented land ownership is making strategic renewal of the town centre and some housing estates more challenging. The Tawd Valley provides a resource with immense potential, but one whose full potential was not recognised by those who designed a town centre to turn its back on the spaces. The stripping of the town's assets have, like may new towns, left the council without the resources to maintain some of its public realm.

West Lancashire Borough Council is honest and upfront about these challenges, and in recent years has set in motion a series of initiatives to tackle this issue head-on, and has sought to re-brand the town and address deprivation through wellbeing initiatives.

A key moment for this was in 2016 when the Skelmersdale Place brand was launched (Figure 9.5). West Lancashire Borough Council worked to create a brand for Skelmersdale with consultants Thinkingplace and Place Board partners Hotter Shoes, the Homes and Communities Agency (HCA), that is now Homes England, West Lancashire College, Edge Hill University and Fairbanks Environmental Ltd. This rebranding included establishment of a Place Board made up of key Skelmersdale leaders, from business and public-sector organisations, who provide a strategic view, approach and leadership for the promotion and development of Skelmersdale. These 'ambassadors' work to promote business in the town.

Complementing this initiative, in January 2016 the 'Well Skelmersdale' initiative was established as one of 10 'pathfinder' projects of Well North, an NHS England funded programme designed to support local authorities in the North to tackle health inequalities.[7] By building partnerships between the community and local voluntary, faith, charitable, business, enterprise and public sectors, Well Skelmersdale aims to create healthy living environments in which the people of Skelmersdale can flourish. So far this has led to a number of activities along the themes of 'education, skills and learning' and 'making the most of the local environment', as well as specific action to improve respiratory health (Figure 9.6). Pursuits such as sewing, working out and singing form part of the 'social prescribing' activities, an enterprise hub has been established and a blog provides accessible updates.[8]

Town centre

Skelmersdale's town centre consists of a number of isolated buildings with poor connections, including the Concourse Centre, a shopping centre that provides a relatively limited range of services and, as once observed by local MP Rosie Cooper, 'pretends to be the town centre'.[9] The town centre lacks an entertainment and night-time economy and is effectively closed off in the evenings. Consequently, many residents travel further afield, to Wigan, Liverpool, Southport and Ormskirk.[10] There are also a number of existing civic spaces within the town centre. These are generally characterised as areas of featureless hardstanding with sporadic shrub and tree planting which, as noted by West Lancashire Borough Council, 'are in general poorly maintained and poorly valued pieces of land which do very little to improve the visual amenity of the town centre' (Figure 9.7).[11]

To address these challenges, plans for a £20-million redevelopment of Skelmersdale town centre, creating 500 new jobs, were formulated as part of a partnership between the council, Homes England and St Modwen Developments. The partnership formed in 2007, and a planning application was submitted in August 2012 after a comprehensive public consultation that showed over 80% of respondents in favour of the proposals. Planning consent was granted in March 2015 for 50,000sq ft of retail and 50,000sq ft of leisure (including a cinema, restaurants and bars) to encourage night-time leisure opportunities. However, years of legal rows with Skelmersdale Limited Partnership (SLP), the owner of nearby Concourse Shopping Centre, slowed the scheme's progression. Rosie Cooper MP said, 'When the local council attempted to build a genuine town centre and a modern high street, the owners of the Concourse took out High Court injunctions and made appeals to block it.'[12] In March 2017 an update showed better progress, with some level of interest from potential occupiers for the scheme. The project will also include a link between West Lancashire College and the Concourse Centre, as well as new public spaces with improved light and pedestrian surfaces (Figure 9.8).

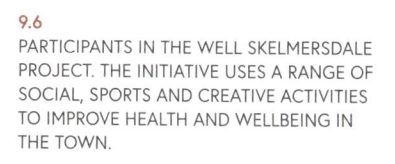

9.6
PARTICIPANTS IN THE WELL SKELMERSDALE PROJECT. THE INITIATIVE USES A RANGE OF SOCIAL, SPORTS AND CREATIVE ACTIVITIES TO IMPROVE HEALTH AND WELLBEING IN THE TOWN.

9.7
SKELMERSDALE'S TOWN CENTRE. KEY BUILDINGS SUCH AS THE LIBRARY TURN THEIR BACK ON THE BEAUTIFUL TAWD VALLEY AND THE SPACE IS DOMINATED BY A SHOPPING CENTRE.

Housing

The new town housing areas, several of which have Radburn layouts (see page 17), have left a legacy of varying housing quality (Figure 9.9). Footpaths, underpasses and footbridges, initially designed to segregate pedestrians from traffic and provide safe and healthy routes, are now noted by the council as areas which many people do not feel comfortable using due to the perceived risks of crime. Just under half of all homes in Skelmersdale are rented, mainly from West Lancashire Borough Council. In Birch Green, this amounts to 41% of homes being rented from the council.[13] The highest proportions of privately rented homes in the town are in Moorside, Digmoor and Skelmersdale South. The council has also undertaken housing revival projects at Elmstead and Firbeck in the town and will shortly be starting a further project at Beechtrees in Digmoor.

West Lancashire Council is also planning for housing growth. Following a slow period of completions in the first five years of the Plan (2012–2017), the latest Local Plan Review Preferred Options document is planning to meet demand for housing by developing three new garden villages to the southeast of the town, which will complement land already allocated within the town itself.[14] This suggests that the housing market in Skelmersdale is growing alongside the economic performance of the town, demonstrating the positive outlook for Skelmersdale going forward.

Green infrastructure and public realm

Notably, Skelmersdale scores badly in all of the individual deprivation domains except for environment, where it performs better than other areas of West Lancashire.[15] The Tawd Valley Park, approximately 65 hectares of green open spaces, runs through the centre of Skelmersdale following the line of the River Tawd and is an integral part of the character of the town. At present the town centre, though strategically located on the valley corridor, appears to turn its back to this asset.

In November 2017, a master plan for the Tawd Valley was approved which includes: new cycle paths – a BMX and mountain bike track included; wetland habitat areas; an amphitheatre for an informal event space; creation of a heritage trail; picnic spaces (close to the town centre); and access/improvement work to footpaths and landscapes. The project aims to bring significant recreational and environmental benefits to the surrounding area. Partners working together on the scheme are Groundwork, the Environment Agency, the River Douglas Catchment Partnership, SHARES and West Lancashire Council for Voluntary Services.[16] The plans also propose to reuse assets such as the concrete signage to retain some of the new town design heritage. If fully implemented, the plans would also transform the town centre and provide opportunities for prolonged partnerships which might create resources for long-term stewardship throughout the town. Governance, as always, will be a core challenge.

Movement and transport

A new rail station will provide an important link for Skelmersdale, and a new infrastructure interchange has been proposed. This should have a transformational impact on movement in the town, as its current car-based approach is challenging in an area of deprivation where car ownership is comparatively low. The council is also aiming to turn the underpasses which people are scared to use into an asset, supporting, for example, 'wildlife corridors, fitness use, specific leisure'.[17] It is an interesting idea which at the time of writing had not yet been further developed.

09 CASE STUDY: SKELMERSDALE, WEST LANCASHIRE

However, the implication that these are 'redundant' suggests changes to at-grade crossings – a significant departure from the original new town design, and one which could challenge its future.

Governance and stewardship

One of the positive legacies of Skelmersdale's new town heritage is the strength of community spirit in the town.[18] People are proud of their distinct neighbourhoods. This appears to manifest itself positively, in the strength of community-led action to tackle health and deprivation issues. But it was also suggested that this can present a challenge when planning strategically for growth and renewal in the town, with some areas not wanting to accommodate homes for those from adjacent neighbourhoods. Initiatives such as Incredible Edible Skelmersdale demonstrate what might be possible. The challenge with the shopping centre and estate renewal demonstrates the challenges for renewal when ownership is so fragmented.

9.8
REGENERATION PLANS FOR SKELMERSDALE TOWN CENTRE. PARTS OF THE TOWN CENTRE ARE ALREADY GOING THROUGH SIGNIFICANT RENEWAL.

Next steps for Skelmersdale

Like many post-industrial towns, Skelmersdale lacks a strong economic narrative, including on its role in the subregional economy. While existing opportunities related to road distribution have been recognised, the town suffers from its former reliance on single, large manufacturers, a situation not exclusive to new towns. The council is being creative about housing growth options for the town and a new rail link could make a significant strategic regional difference. Support from central government could also help to make renewal a reality and balance the employment offer. There is also a need to look after the public realm in a way that will reassert pride of place. While there are clear governance and ownership issues to overcome in the town centre and for estate renewal, there are equally important opportunities related to the town's green infrastructure assets, including repurposing some of the expanses of grassed areas to improve deprivation through local food initiatives. Addressing these issues requires addressing connectivity, resources and governance.

9.9
A TYPICAL ESTATE IN SKELMERSDALE (A), WITH EXPANSES OF GRASSLAND AND OFF-STREET PARKING (B) AND A NEIGHBOURHOOD CENTRE AND POCKET PARK.

10

CASE STUDY:
CRAIGAVON, COUNTY ARMAGH

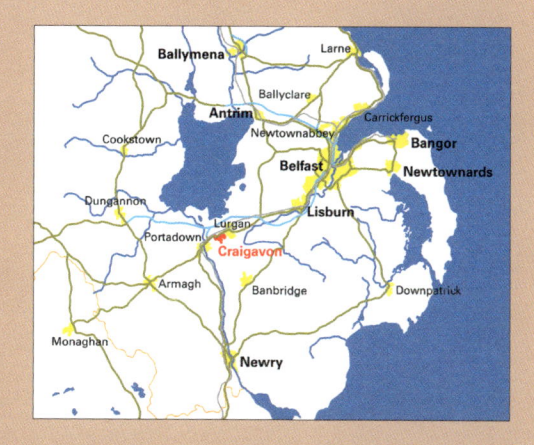

10.1
CRAIGAVON IS IN COUNTY ARMAGH, NORTHERN IRELAND, 34KM SOUTHWEST OF BELFAST.

Key facts

Location: 34km southwest of Belfast (Figure 10.1).

2011 Census population: 61,056 in 24,778 households (of the 61,056, 16,792 live within central Craigavon, the residential area between Lurgan and Portadown).

Local authority: Armagh City, Banbridge and Craigavon Borough Council under Northern Ireland's new local government arrangements.

Local Plan status: Craigavon Area Plan 2010 (adopted 2004).[1] The Craigavon Integrated Development Framework (2010) provides a framework for the Craigavon urban area. Armagh City, Banbridge and Craigavon Borough Council is currently in the process of producing its first Local Development Plan. As such, recent information is drawn from the Preferred Options Paper 2018 and may be subject to change as the Local Plan progresses.[2]

New Town designation

Designated: 26 July 1965.

Designated area: 2,456 hectares.

Intended population: 120,000 by 1981, and 180,000 by 2000 (population at designation: 61,700).

Development Commission: Designated to provide a new major base for industry, a new residential settlement to reduce housing and traffic pressures in Belfast, and a service centre to contribute to the regeneration of the south and west of Northern Ireland. The master plan envisaged Craigavon as a single linked regional city, including Portadown, Lurgan and the new town to be developed between them at Brownlow. The Development Commission was wound up on 1 October 1973.

Introduction

The first of four new towns in Northern Ireland, Craigavon was conceived in response to the 1962 plan for the Greater Belfast region as a linear regional city that included the existing towns of Lurgan and Portadown, with a new city centre to be built in between. Today, Craigavon is one of the largest urban centres in Northern Ireland, with around 70% of Craigavon Borough's population living within the Craigavon urban area (which includes Lurgan, Portadown and central Craigavon). Its designation as a new town has been a major influence on the scale and nature of its development and has contributed to the emergence of a strong industrial base (Figure 10.2). A number of political issues, demographic changes, some resistance to planning, and over-provision of housing have attracted some criticism and have led to undeveloped areas within the central area. With the devolution of planning responsibilities in Northern Ireland that occurred in April 2015, for the first time since the Development Commission was in operation Craigavon now has a single body responsible for all aspects of planning and development (except highways).

Background

By the mid-1950s problems of unemployment and housing shortages in Belfast were so acute that the government decided direct intervention and centralisation of power was necessary. The Belfast Regional Survey and Plan, 1962 (the Matthew Report), was commissioned to explore the wider future of the Belfast region, bearing in mind the geographic, economic and cultural pattern of Northern Ireland as a whole. The plan included a proposal for the existing towns of Lurgan and Portadown to become the focus of a substantial new 'regional city' for approximately 100,000 people.[3]

With the passage of the New Towns Act (Northern Ireland) 1965, the Minister of Development was empowered to designate an area as a new town and to constitute a New Town Commission to carry out both development and municipal functions. Craigavon was designated the same year, with the intention to 'create a modern environment of the highest standards, embracing all aspects of living – urban, village, rural. All this must be developed in accordance with a single unified plan.'[4]

Craigavon, like all the Northern Ireland new towns, had a very large designated area (105 square miles – approximately 67,000 acres or 27,114 hectares). The aims of the Craigavon Development Commission were: 'Firstly, to provide a new major base for industry, attracting British, European and American firms to the Province; secondly, to create a new residential settlement which would alleviate housing and traffic pressures in Belfast; thirdly, to form a service centre that could contribute to the regeneration of the south and west of the Province.'[5]

The legislation gave New Town Commissions and the Ministry of Development powers beyond those which applied in the rest of the UK (a New Town Commission was able to take on municipal functions and operate in designated areas, which included surrounding villages, and development was to follow very detailed plans set out by the Commission).[6]

10.2
AN AERIAL VIEW OF CRAIGAVON'S CIVIC CENTRE AND LAKE. CRAIGAVON HAS VERY FEW NATURAL LANDSCAPE FEATURES – THE RECREATIONAL LAKE IN THE CENTRE IS AN IMPORTANT, ALBEIT ARTIFICIAL, FEATURE.

Craigavon master plan

The original 1967 master plan for Craigavon (Figure 10.3) envisioned the new town as a settlement with a linear structure that would link the existing neighbouring towns of Lurgan and Portadown to form a distinct new urban area. It stated that 'the Craigavon plan incorporates an urban core or Inner Area and a rural envelope or Outer Area', with it being planned that by the year 2000, the Inner Area would be a 'linear structure some 10 miles long and 1.5 miles wide comprising up to six residential sectors including the two existing towns, a city centre and park located to the north of the sector chain, and supplementary district centres in the existing towns'.[7]

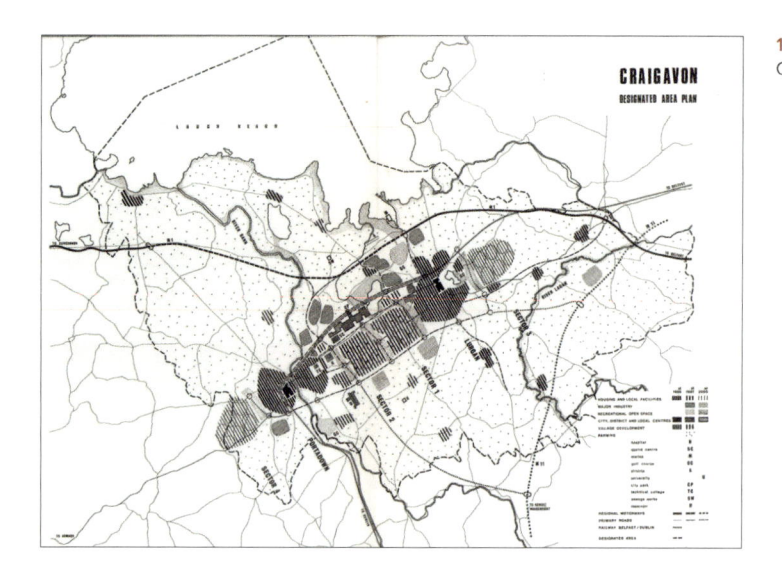

10.3
CRAIGAVON MASTER PLAN, 1967.

The importance of the countryside featured heavily in the original plans, with the master plan stating that 'this whole core area is related physically and functionally to a defined rural hinterland' and recommending that Craigavon should be given an entirely new settlement classification, termed 'The Rural City'.[8] This also helped to inform the decision to give the town a linear structure, as it was hoped that this layout would 'allow every inhabitant of the city to be virtually within walking distance of the countryside' and would mean that 'many houses in the city could have views out to farmland and open landscape'.[9] The master plan also determined that 'the notion of an urban area protected by a green belt is considered inapplicable in this instance' as 'the close inter-relationship of urban and rural elements, each of which is given space and a population base, should promote a rich and varied environment'.[10] Cycle and pedestrian routes were separated from a road network which today cannot cope with the volume of cars.

The new city was also provided with many local amenities (Figure 10.4), including a leisure centre, shopping centre, civic centre, artificial lakes, playing fields and even a petting zoo and gardens at Tannaghmore. However, the first sign of problems appeared when it emerged that some large-scale housing areas had been built with materials and techniques that had not been fully tested, meaning the homes were not fit for use, no doubt a consequence of pressure to build at speed but a responsibility ultimately of the Commission.

The outbreak of the Troubles in the late 1960s only made matters worse, with increasing levels of emigration, and investment into Northern Ireland drying up. Consequently around 50% of what was planned was never built, with some of what was built having to be demolished after becoming empty and derelict.

The area's main employer was Goodyear, which had a large fan-belt factory in the Silverwood industrial estate, which, at the time, was one of Europe's largest factories. The vision took a major blow when the plant, which had failed to make money on a consistent basis, closed down in 1983. It also emerged that the population projections for Northern Ireland upon which the project was based were wildly inaccurate.

10.4
CRAIGAVON'S DESIGN INCORPORATED PUBLIC TRANSPORT AND CYCLE PATHS.

The area designated in the plan as Craigavon 'city centre' contained the municipal authority, the court buildings and a shopping mall. Surrounded by housing estates and greenfield land, it became a source of much derision by local residents and the media. In recent years, with an increasing population, the end of the Troubles and high property prices in Belfast, new housing has been built around the shopping centre, creating a situation where Central Craigavon once again has a future.

The extent of the Troubles or the resulting levels of emigration were not anticipated by the government and until this time there was great pressure on the New Towns programme in Northern Ireland to deliver at speed. The full force of the legislation was used to assemble land quickly, much to the dismay of local farmers, some of whom were furious at the prospect of losing land that had been in their family's ownership for generations. For some, that dismay turned to resentment when parts of that land were subsequently left undeveloped.

Craigavon Development Commission was wound up in 1973 with the same speed with which it had been established. No specific stewardship bodies were established on wind-up. Today, Craigavon, as with the rest of Northern Ireland, benefits from policy approaches that recognise the role of long-term stewardship in good place-making.

Craigavon today – challenges and opportunities

Craigavon still feels like a town in three parts – a disconnection that is felt by many of its residents (many of Craigavon's residents recognise themselves as being from Lurgan or Portadown, but not Craigavon). Nevertheless, Craigavon has recently been lauded as being among the most desirable postcode areas in the UK in a survey that considered green spaces, commuting and affordable housing.[11]

Today, Armagh City, Banbridge and Craigavon Borough Council is putting great emphasis on community engagement in delivering a positive future for Craigavon, and there are a number of active community groups working on proposals to make the Brownlow area an 'urban village'. Beyond Craigavon there is still a stigma attached to the name of the 'New City'.

Even the Northern Ireland Executive's stewardship guidance includes a picture of Craigavon in its 'bad places' chapter,[12] perhaps reinforcing the stigma of the town despite the recent identification of it being one of the UK's most desirable postcodes. The council and the area's communities are working hard to address this, with future investment in the town centre and leisure developments designed to attract further private-sector investment. A number of local community initiatives are also seeking to celebrate the town's heritage. 'Capturing Craigavon' is a community-based project that aims to explore and document the history of the New Town of Craigavon (Figure 10.5).[13]

Town centre

As acknowledged by the council's own master-plan report, Craigavon centre feels, at present, like an out-of-town retail park (Figure 10.6). The predominant buildings are a large shopping mall, large warehouse buildings with a single customer entrance and large blank frontages. Vast surface car parks dominate substantial areas of the site. There are no functional public spaces and the whole area is a car-dominated environment with two pedestrian footbridges and no

10.5
THE CAPTURING CRAIGAVON PROJECT, WHICH AIMS TO EXPLORE AND DOCUMENT THE HISTORY OF CRAIGAVON. AS PART OF THE PROJECT, LOCAL PEOPLE HAVE BEEN ASKED TO RECORD THEIR MEMORIES AND EXPERIENCES OF THE TOWN.

10 CASE STUDY: CRAIGAVON, COUNTY ARMAGH

10.6
CRAIGAVON TOWN CENTRE TODAY. THE CENTRE FEELS MORE LIKE A RETAIL PARK AND HAS POOR PEDESTRIAN CONNECTIONS TO SURROUNDING RESIDENTIAL AREAS.

(a)

(b)

10.7
THE CONDITION OF HOUSING IN CRAIGAVON VARIES, BUT SOME BUILDINGS ARE IN NEED OF URGENT RENOVATION.

footpaths. The positive green and natural features are concentrated on the eastern area of the site but are not integrated into the centre. The site, at present, 'does not offer the experience of a town centre; not even within the "modernist" 1960s vision that created it'.[14] There is a desire to retrofit the central area to make it more like a traditional town centre by including a mix of uses, and by maximising the benefits of the strategic location to create a gateway and destination. The extent of private-ownership land within the boundary means there is a unique opportunity, as well as a reliance on private-sector investment to achieve this.

Housing

Among residents today there is a recognition that the New Towns programme at Craigavon produced both 'good' and 'bad' housing design (Figure 10.7), but the best-designed housing has stood the test of time. Despite dereliction in some places, there is a recognition that the designers were trying to implement something visionary, and there remains a sense of civic pride in the town (Figure 10.8). Many of the older housing estates have now been demolished and privately redeveloped. The introduction of these new estates has brought many new people into the area.

NEW TOWNS: THE RISE, FALL AND REBIRTH

Green infrastructure and public realm

The central area is just one of the elements of Craigavon's impressive green infrastructure network (Craigavon is home to the Northern Ireland branch of the Landscape Institute). This green network could be an important tool for the renewal of the town (Figure 10.9), helping to improve accessibility and sense of place. There is an opportunity for the new administration to use its land ownership in the town to promote innovative models of stewardship and land value capture.

Next steps for Craigavon

The reorganised local government arrangements in Northern Ireland provide an opportunity for the new Armagh City, Banbridge and Craigavon Borough Council to plan more strategically for the future of Craigavon. For example, plans to develop the leisure offerings around the lake in Central Craigavon will no doubt encourage further private investment in the town and help to draw Craigavon's three 'parts' together. This includes harnessing the opportunity to use land ownership in the town to promote innovative models of stewardship and land value capture to pay for the renewal of estates and ongoing maintenance of green infrastructure.

10.8
THE BROWNLOW COMMUNITY HUB, BUILT IN 2012. THE STATE-OF-THE-ART COMMUNITY FACILITY WAS AWARDED THE RICS AWARD FOR COMMUNITY BENEFIT 2012.

10.9
AN ARTIST'S IMPRESSION OF THE NEW MULTIMILLION-POUND LEISURE DEVELOPMENT BEING BUILT AT SOUTH LAKE. THE CENTRE WILL DELIVER FIRST-CLASS FACILITIES FROM 2020.

11

CASE STUDY:
MILTON KEYNES, BUCKINGHAMSHIRE

11.1
MILTON KEYNES IS IN BUCKINGHAMSHIRE, 72KM NORTHWEST OF LONDON.

Key facts

Location: 72km northwest of London, 92km southwest of Birmingham (Figure 11.1), on the West Coast Main Line and M1 motorway.

2011 Census population: 211,062, in 82,175 households.[1]

Local authority: Milton Keynes Council, a unitary authority.

Local Plan status: Plan:MK 2016–2031 was adopted March 2019.[2]

New Town designation

Designated: 23 January 1967.

Designated area: 8,870 hectares.

Intended population: 250,000 (population at designation: 40,000).

Development Corporation: The plan for Milton Keynes emphasised social and economic development, framed within a gentle grid of transport corridors on which local centres also served nearby neighborhoods. A new city centre was to serve the whole of MK, and was all set in a comprehensive green infrastructure network The Development Corporation was wound up on 31 March 1992.

Introduction

Since its designation, Milton Keynes (MK) has been a centre for innovation on matters ranging from recycling and low-carbon housing to community stewardship and the arts.[3] Designated to accommodate overspill from Greater London (the first new town with this purpose since Bracknell was designated in 1949), Milton Keynes is the UK's largest and fastest-growing new town (Figure 11.2). Its strategic location has been key to its success in attracting industry and investment. Its iconic grid master plan and supporting policy provided a framework intended to be flexible enough to accommodate future change and support high social and environmental ambitions. Despite financial struggles in the 1970s due to inflation, affecting the cost of borrowing from the government, Milton Keynes has grown to be one of the UK's most successful towns and cities in terms of high employment levels and residents' satisfaction. National Infrastructure Commission proposals to double MK to 500,000 by 2050 have been embraced by MK Council and joint city-regional studies of possible spatial concepts have begun to emerge.

Background

By the early 1960s, Buckinghamshire County Council had become concerned about the pressure for development in its southern area and was examining the possibility of promoting a 'North Bucks New Town', with the intention of diverting this pressure to this less favoured part of the county. Between 1962 and 1964, detailed studies were undertaken by the County's chief architect and planning officer, Fred Pooley, culminating in proposals for a high-density monorail city for 250,000 people focused on the West Coast Main Line railway between industrial Bletchley and Wolverton railway town. The County sought government support for the scheme. Housing Minister Richard Crossman instead decided, following the South East Study (1964) and Northampton, Bedford and North Bucks Study (1965), that it should become a government scheme under the New Towns Act, and given a wider regional role in accommodating growth.

An inquiry was held into the designation of the new town in July 1966 and the Designation Order was confirmed in January 1967. An interim masterplan report produced in 1967 was used as the basis of a consultation process that aimed to involve all 40,000 inhabitants of the designated area, as well as all relevant official bodies such as the local authorities in the area. The proposals for Milton Keynes were amended in light of the responses.

Milton Keynes master plan

Llewelyn-Davies, Weeks, Forestier-Walker and Bor, appointed as master-planners, in 1967 just as Llewelyn-Davies had finished their masterplan for Washington New Town, set about collecting two years worth of information on urban form in a study that was without precedent in British town planning. Pooley's monorail idea was discarded and their iconic grid master plan (Figure 11.3) became one of the most distinctive of the 20th century and, with its visionary landscaping and capacity to accommodate change, it is one of the Development Corporation's most important legacies.

11 CASE STUDY: MILTON KEYNES, BUCKINGHAMSHIRE

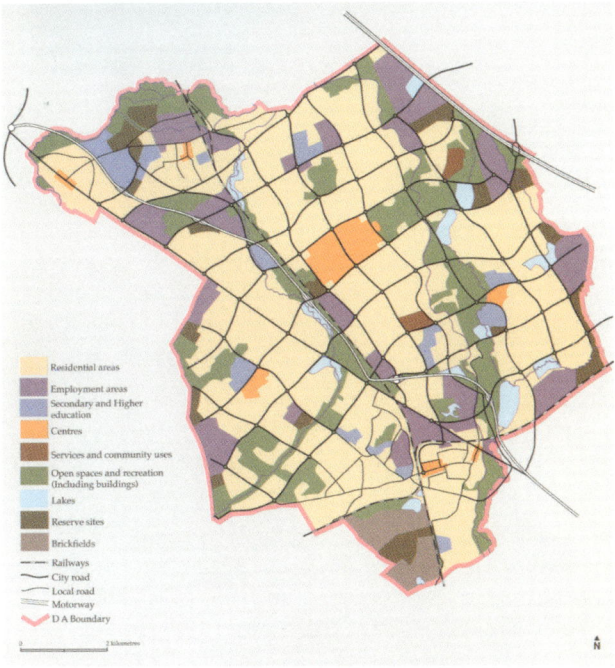

11.2
MIDSUMMER BOULEVARD IN CENTRAL MILTON KEYNES. A 2019 SURVEY FOUND MILTON KEYNES TO BE THE UK'S FASTEST-GROWING 'CITY', BASED ON A COMBINATION OF POPULATION, GROWTH IN ECONOMIC OUTPUT AND COMMERCIAL PROPERTY RENTAL DATA.

11.3
THE MILTON KEYNES MASTER PLAN, 1967. THE 'LAZY' GRID AND EXTENSIVE GREEN INFRASTRUCTURE ARE APPARENT.

131

The master plan, approved in 1969, provided for a city of 250,000 people, with employment to serve a wider population drawn from the surrounding countryside. It proposed a 'lazy' grid of cross-city transport corridors which gently followed the landscape and created pockets of development land roughly 1km by 1km in size. The founding principles were beautifully simple and brief:

- opportunity and freedom of choice
- easy movement and access, and good communications
- balance and variety
- an attractive city
- public awareness and participation
- efficient and imaginative use of resources.

11.4
A 1970S ADVERT FOR MILTON KEYNES. THE DEVELOPMENT CORPORATION UNDERSTOOD FROM THE OUTSET THAT THE NEW TOWN'S LOCATION GAVE IT 'UNPARALLELED ADVANTAGES', AND SPENT UP TO £20 MILLION A YEAR PROMOTING MILTON KEYNES INTERNATIONALLY AS EUROPE'S TOP DESTINATION FOR DOING BUSINESS, AS WELL AS A GREAT PLACE TO RAISE A FAMILY.

Delivery

Milton Keynes Development Corporation had the autonomy and powers necessary to deliver at speed – in the late 1970s over 3,500 homes per annum were being delivered by the Corporation. Between 1967 and 1992, the Development Corporation enabled the creation of 83,000 jobs and the construction of 44,000 houses and planted more than 14 million trees and shrubs in what was conceived as 'the City of Trees' (Figure 11.4).[4]

The Development Corporation put great effort into creating a 'balanced community', through arrivals workers, Community Development Officers, community meeting places, artists in residence, and annual surveys monitoring the views of new residents on everything from housing design to jobs for 'housewives'.

By the late 1970s, the Corporation began to switch its efforts to home ownership and other Conservative policies in anticipation of the incoming Thatcher Government.[5] At the beginning of the 1980s, public housing programmes were stopped and shared ownership was invented by the Corporation to give some access to those with less income. Rising interest rates and costs of construction in the 1970s resulted in Government writing off £510 million of MK's public housing borrowing. Labour and Conservative political leaders nationally had turned towards urban regeneration as a priority, and 1981 the Thatcher Government announced that the Corporation was to be dissolved in 1992. This was only 30 years from commencement, and its land and property was required to be sold when immature. Continuing sales by successor Government agencies enabled all non-housing borrowing to be repaid the Government, with interest, and have yielded several billion pounds for spending elsewhere.

Milton Keynes today – challenges and opportunities

Today, Milton Keynes is one of the fastest-growing towns and cities in the UK. It is extremely successful economically, but also contains some pockets of severe deprivation in areas that are now a focus for urban renewal. MK's population profile is changing, which has implications for future housing, facilities and community infrastructure. The population has gone from a very young one (typical 'new town') to an aging one, and there has been a sharp increase in black, Asian and minority ethnic (BAME) residents (in 2001, 13.2% of the population was from a BAME group; in 2011 this had risen to 26.1%). Milton Keynes is now more ethnically diverse than the England average.[6] The community development legacy of Milton Keynes Development Corporation still lives on, and a huge interest in neighbourhood planning is helping to inform growth rather than prevent it.

Milton Keynes' continuing growth has resulted in some tension with the original vision for the new town, and there has been some misunderstanding about how to grow a place using the grid structure, no doubt a symptom of the new towns moving in and out of favour – and therefore being part of learning processes – over the decades. Some wish to make MK look and feel like ordinary towns. Others wish to sustain its distinctiveness. As the city grows and interest moves between these perspectives, MK has become a living exhibition of different urban design cultures. This is a challenge for Milton Keynes Council, facing great commercial and cultural potential, yet handicapped by deep cuts in public spending. At least the council has a major opportunity to continue the legacy of innovation in Milton Keynes, particularly as it has purchased the last remaining new town assets from Homes England and laced them in a company formed for the purpose called the Milton Keynes Development Partnership[7] The council is exploring different ways to fund its growth and plan strategically for the future – a characteristic it attributes to its new town heritage.

In 2015 the MK Futures 2050 Commission was set up as a way of thinking about the future of Milton Keynes and with an aim to create a long-term vision for the way MK should grow and prosper over the coming decades.[8] It concluded in 2016 with a report which recommended six key projects, which have been integrated into the Plan:MK and are being brought forward by the MK Futures 2050 Programme. These are:

1. making Milton Keynes the hub of the Cambridge–Milton Keynes–Oxford growth corridor

2. enhancing lifelong learning opportunities through the establishment of a new university for Milton Keynes

3. Learning 2050 – providing world-class education

4. smart, shared, sustainable mobility for all

5. Renaissance:CMK, creating an even stronger city centre fit for the 21st century

6. Milton Keynes: the creative and cultured city.

11.5
CENTRE:MK SHOPPING CENTRE, A 650M-LONG STEEL-AND-GLASS STRUCTURE INSPIRED BY MIES VAN DER ROHE. IT WAS DESIGNED BY DEVELOPMENT CORPORATION ARCHITECTS IN 1972–73 UNDER THE DIRECTION OF DEREK WALKER AND IS NOW GRADE II LISTED.

Progress on these projects continues, with a design competition for MK's new university, MK:U, to be located near Central Milton Keynes railway station, launched in 2019.[9] Trials of driverless cars and robotic delivery androids have been taking place in 2018 and a programme of cultural events has been bringing a new offering to the town.

MK's design and architectural heritage has been recognised by the council as an important catalyst for renewal. A recent heritage lottery project led by the council seeks to make it a pilot for future learning and celebration about its new town heritage.

City centre

Central Milton Keynes (CMK) has become an important regional centre and workplace for 30,000 people. It also attracts over 30 million visitors a year, many heading for its covered shopping centre or indoor ski slope. The night-time economy remains limited but has grown markedly over recent years and is likely to develop further. Network Rail recently relocated to CMK, bringing in 3,000 jobs. In 2015 the 'CMK Alliance Plan 2026' – the country's first Business Neighbourhood Plan – received overwhelming support in its referendum. The plan includes a set of policies guiding growth and renewal around the core principles of 'Building on our unique heritage', 'Creating a vibrant regional centre', 'Improving transport and parking' and 'Diversifying the main shopping area'.[10] The Plan claims that it is the quality and extent of the public realm in CMK that asserts its status as a true city centre with great ambitions.[11]

The Centre:MK, CMK's Mies Van de Rohe inspired shopping building (Figure 11.5), was given Grade II listing in 2010.[12] The move was welcomed by many (except its owners), but for many it did not go far enough.[13] Other iconic buildings in MK, such as The Point (see pages 67–8), have not been listed and will soon be lost to redevelopment. A number of recent planning decisions have been made, it is accused by some local residents, in direct conflict with the CMK Alliance

Plan. Meanwhile the extension of permitted development rights is also threatening the loss of some iconic office buildings. The opening of the extended MK Gallery (Figure 11.6) has provided a welcome boost to CMK's cultural offering.

Housing growth and renewal

Milton Keynes has a reputation for innovation in housing, particularly in the promotion of energy conservation. Milton Keynes Development Corporation promoted innovative approaches to the layout of residential development and the design of buildings, including the nation's first energy efficiency standard for buildings – the National Home Energy Rating (NHER), which was used to specify energy efficiency levels in all new housing from 1986 onwards. The individual 'grid squares' (residential areas within the grid road system) vary in design and typology, reflecting the era they were delivered in, by whom and for what purpose (Figure 11.7).[14] They are also, therefore, aging at different rates, with some of the earlier housing, as with other new towns, facing the need for whole estate renewal. MK's first Regeneration Strategy was published in 2009. After establishing Your:MK, a jointly owned partnership with Mears Group plc in 2016, a partnership which has since been broken, Milton Keynes Council is now leading on the regeneration of several of its early housing estates (Figure 11.8). For many people, this is their first experience of regeneration, and the process is raising questions of densification, felt by some to be a direct challenge to the new town vision they bought into. The recognition of MK's important design heritage is also prompting a form of self-regeneration – or gentrification – as there is evidence of a trend for privately owned properties on some of the challenging estates being bought cheaply and restored by design and architecture enthusiasts keen to secure affordable housing in an accessible location.

11.6
THE NEW MK GALLERY, DESIGNED BY 6A ARCHITECTS. IT OPENED TO CRITICAL ACCLAIM IN 2019.

NEW TOWNS: THE RISE, FALL AND REBIRTH

(a)

(b)

(c)

11.7
THE DEVELOPMENT CORPORATION AND THE PRIVATE SECTOR DELIVERED A BROAD RANGE OF HOUSING TYPES IN MK.

HOUSING IN NETHERFIELD (A). NETHERFIELD WAS ONE OF THE EARLIEST RENTAL HOUSING GRID SQUARES IN MILTON KEYNES. IT WAS BUILT BETWEEN 1972 AND 1977, AND ITS 1,043 HOUSES FORM THE LARGEST RENTAL SCHEME IN MK.

A DETACHED HOUSE IN BRADWELL COMMON (B), BUILT IN THE EARLY 1980S BY THE DEVELOPMENT CORPORATION. SOME 31 OF THE HOMES IN BRADWELL COMMON ARE NOW OWNED AND MANAGED BY A HOUSING CO-OPERATIVE, CDS CO-OPERATIVES.

BUNGALOWS IN BEANHILL (C). CONSTRUCTION OF BEANHILL BEGAN IN 1973 DURING A BRICKMAKERS' STRIKE SO HOMES IN PHASE 1 ARE ALL TIMBER-FRAMED BUILDINGS WITH CORRUGATED CLADDING. WITH THE EXCEPT OF TWO STREETS, ALL HOMES IN BEANHILL ARE BUNGALOWS. BEANHILL IS ONE OF THE SEVEN PRIORITY AREAS IN MILTON KEYNES ON WHICH THE COUNCIL'S REGENERATION PROGRAMME WILL BE FOCUSING OVER THE NEXT 15 YEARS.

11 CASE STUDY: MILTON KEYNES, BUCKINGHAMSHIRE

Housing growth is also a key aspect of the new local plan, which includes proposals to deliver land for a minimum of 26,500 new homes within the borough between 2016 and 2031, principally within and adjacent to the city (Figure 11.9). MK also forms a central part of the Oxford–Cambridge Arc, providing an additional layer of impetus for strategic growth.[15]

Green infrastructure and public realm

Milton Keynes' network of parks, green spaces and landscaping is undoubtedly one of its crowning glories, and prior to its wind-up the Development Corporation proposed to the Department of the Environment that a Parks Trust should be created to manage the space 'for use by voluntary groups'. The Parks Trust, formerly known as Milton Keynes Parks Trust, was established to own and manage, in perpetuity, the strategic open space in Milton Keynes. It took a 999-year lease on 4,500 acres of open space and was given an endowment of around £20 million, mainly in the form of commercial property in Milton Keynes, with the rental income providing funding.[16]

Today, the Trust manages over 6,000 acres of parkland in Milton Keynes, which includes more than 200 pieces of public art and provides space for income-generating activities (Figure 11.10) such as the World Picnic. The Milton Keynes Community Foundation was also established in the 1980s, on the initiative of the Milton Keynes Development Corporation's Community Development Team. Pioneering the Community Foundation movement in the UK, it was one of many organisations for which the Development Corporation provided premises (for no or peppercorn rent). The foundation has used property and land endowments from the council, along with commercial and private philanthropic investments, to grow into a profitable enterprise providing a range of support and funding for the voluntary and community sector in Milton Keynes.[17] The Parks Trust model is celebrated as transferable for other places keen to adopt a stewardship model, but is facing its own challenges in the face of developers who favour 'cheaper' options (public parks are passed, without endowment, to the developer's own management company, which can then levy an annual service charge in perpetuity.[18]

11.8
HOMES IN SERPENTINE COURT ON THE LAKES ESTATE ARE TO BE DEMOLISHED AS PART OF A £1-BILLION REGENERATION PROGRAMME.

11.9
NEW HOMES IN ASHLAND, MILTON KEYNES. MILTON KEYNES COUNCIL IS WORKING IN PARTNERSHIP WITH THE PRIVATE SECTOR TO DELIVER NEW HOMES.

11.10
PERFORMERS AT THE MK INTERNATIONAL FESTIVAL. THE FESTIVAL IS ONE OF SEVERAL ARTS EVENTS USING MILTON KEYNES' PARKS AND OPEN SPACES FOR CULTURAL ACTIVITIES.

Movement and transport

Though Milton Keynes' master plan was designed for all modes of transport, the privatisation of bus companies by the Thatcher Government in the 1980s resulted in many residents having to use cars or taxis (or rely on friends and neighbours, or stay at home). The new local plan blames dispersed residential and employment locations for making it difficult to provide a public transport network that links employment areas with residential and other locations – a problem exacerbated by cheap car-parking and multi-destination journeys.[19] It is clear that more can be done to improve the appeal of public transport and make better use of the infamous 'redway' cycle paths by overcoming perceptions of unsafe spaces and ensuring the network remains intact. The council continues to innovate on transport and is focusing on rapid transit as a structuring element, though there is no certainty of the necessary scale of funding. Seeking the status of being a Transport Planning Authority is an obvious next step.[20]

Next steps for Milton Keynes

Milton Keynes' 50th anniversary, and related initiatives such as the 2050 Commission, have provided a positive opportunity for those concerned with the future of MK to reflect on priorities for the next 50 years. From the renewal of its older estates, to the growth of the centre, there is a huge opportunity but also clear and ongoing tension between a desire to develop MK in line with 'traditional' cities, and recognising that MK has a special design ethos and physical framework that is adaptable and a great inheritance for future generations. The council sees these issues, but while wanting to look outwards it can also see the work to be done in completing, or updating, what has already been made, and ultimately 'finishing the job' the corporation started. Key projects – such as MK:U and investment in the cultural offer and celebration of the new town heritage – respect and sustain the original sense of ambition in MK. However, unless lessons learnt on design standards, innovation and stewardship for all new development areas in and around Milton Keynes are applied, the full extent of this opportunity may be missed.

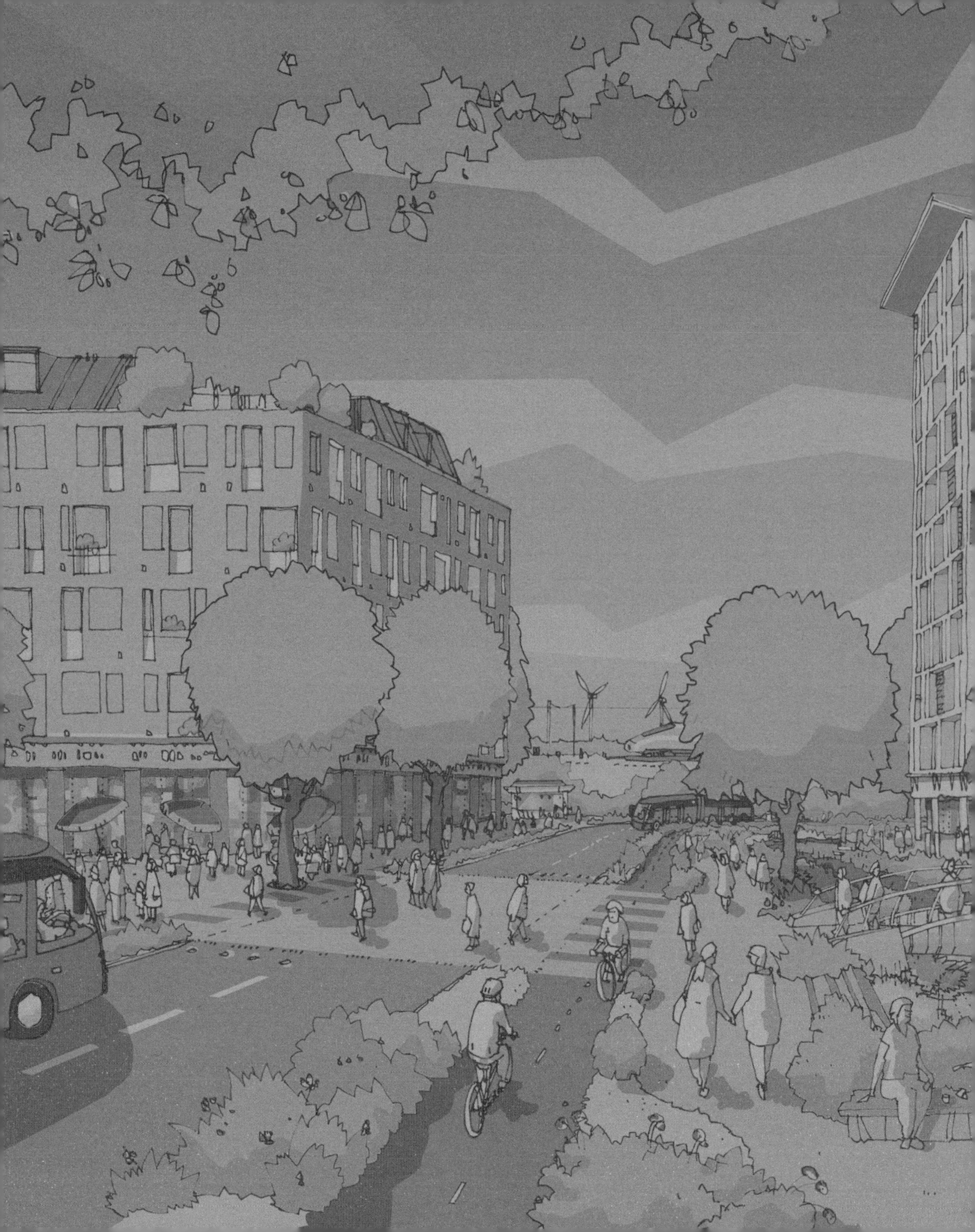

PART III

REBIRTH OF THE NEW TOWNS

12 TOP LESSONS FROM THE NEW TOWNS
13 THE FUTURE OF THE NEW TOWNS IDEAL
14 CONCLUSION

12

TOP LESSONS FROM THE NEW TOWNS

Introduction

This chapter seeks to distil some of the big-picture lessons that flow from the rich story of the British new towns. Given the wealth of experiences from the programme, the choice of these lessons is framed by their relevance to the contemporary debate about creating sustainable communities and the growth and renewal of the new towns themselves.

This book has already demonstrated that there were plenty of mistakes in the delivery of the new towns, just as there are in any complex human endeavour. However, it is equally clear from the evidence set out in Parts 1 and 2 of this book that to regard the New Towns programme as a failed statist experiment, a view held by successive governments, is simply wrong.

In general, policy-makers do not appear to want to confront the scale of the achievement nor the richness and diversity of the approaches and practices which the new towns embodied. While all major public policy areas, such as defence and health, have been subject to the occasional expensive 'failures', we have not concluded that health and defence are choices we can ignore. Neither do we assume that health provision can be delivered solely through local means or solely by the free market. Why, then, do we regard the provision of decent homes, vital to people's health and life chances, as a task firmly in the 'too difficult' box? This question is even more acute given that new towns were, on balance, a remarkable success and continue to provide homes for millions of people. It is also remarkable that in the middle of a long-standing housing crisis we have not, collectively, paid more attention to lessons that the new towns provide for all aspects of making and renewing communities.

This chapter distils the diverse experience of the new towns into six broad lessons, which range from how the location of new towns was agreed to how public consent was, or was not, secured.

NEW TOWNS: THE RISE, FALL AND REBIRTH

12.1
THE COWS, MILTON KEYNES, BY CANADIAN ARTIST LIZ LEYH, 1978. THESE ICONIC SCULPTURES WERE NOT A COMMISSION BY THE DEVELOPMENT CORPORATION BUT A PARTING GIFT FROM THE ARTIST. THEY HAVE BECOME SYNONYMOUS WITH THE IDEA OF NEW TOWNS, AND MORE LOCALLY A TARGET FOR REDECORATION.

Lesson 1: New town design – a concrete cow of despair? The need for innovation not experimentation

It remains difficult to get beyond the public perception of new towns as defined by concrete cows, endless roundabouts and monolithic town centres (Figure 12.1). New towns, it is assumed, are the expression of a Modernist experiment which lacks diversity and humanity. There is no doubt that the New Towns programme was very much of its time and defined by rational and Modernist approaches to design which were playing out in the reconstruction and renewal of many existing cities in the postwar era. Embracing Modernism was both a design and political statement defined by the hope of a new rational and egalitarian society. It was fuelled by the availability of new materials and construction techniques which allowed the delivery of new towns at a price and timescale demanded by Westminster. Some of these iconic Modernist designs have already been swept away in renewal projects, often after long periods of neglect for the reasons discussed later in this chapter. Others are beginning to be recognised for their architectural heritage value. Later master plans also reflected new passions for the private car based on imported assumptions from the US that what was good for the automobile, was good for humanity.

While there are some common design characteristics in the new towns, the approach taken to the design of civic space and housing layout in each place was in fact diverse. Housing types ranged from the traditional semidetached council house to the radical, if short-lived, experiments, such as those designed under the direction of Victor Pasmore in Peterlee (Figure 12.2, and see page 90). In the later stages of the development of 'Mark Three' new towns such

12.2
VICTOR PASMORE'S HOUSING IN PETERLEE, BUILT IN 1960. DESPITE A STUNNING AESTHETIC, THE DESIGN COULD NOT COPE WITH THE CLIMATE OF THE NORTHEAST. THIS PHOTO FROM 2019 SHOWS LATER ADDITIONS OF PITCHED ROOFS AND ATTEMPTS TO 'PRIVATISE' THE OUTSIDE SPACE.

as Milton Keynes, neighbourhood units were being developed by the private sector, resulting in some distinctly mediocre design outcomes. These simply reflected a wider approach to domestic design in the last five decades, which has lacked innovation in construction techniques or commitment to diversity.

The wider design and master-planning of new towns has proved more durable than some of the buildings they contained, not least because of the dubious quality of some postwar building materials. In later examples, initiatives such as Home World and Energy World in Milton Keynes echoed the 'cheap cottage exhibitions' of the garden city movement with their attempts to showcase the latest innovations in domestic architecture. Some of the design approaches applied in the new towns have raised live and contemporary debates on issues such as density, separation of people and traffic, modern heritage and long-term stewardship, issues which also have implications for the renewal of the new towns.

What do these approaches teach us about creating new communities today? Primarily, it is a reminder that the powerful delivery mechanism embodied in the New Towns programme does not imply any fixed approach to design or a single aesthetic. It provides a real opportunity for innovation in design and construction, but it should not be a 'play pen' for the exercise of single design egos experimenting at the expense of people who live there. In the web of ideas that constitute good design, the new town experience appears to reinforce some key principles. Alongside core elements such as a strong vision and designing for climate resilience, these include the need to design with and not for people; the need to reflect local design heritage and local materials; and the need to design places which are adaptable over time. Ironically, many of these ideas were integral to the original garden city design ethos but curiously disregarded in some of the new towns. It is also important to reflect on the design strengths of new towns and particularly the infrastructure-led approach to growth, in stark contrast to most of the homes we build now.

Lesson 2: National government must play a strong role in supporting site identification

Despite a great deal of rhetoric about the housing crisis over the last 10 years and much talk of new cities in the Cambridge–Milton Keynes–Oxford Arc identified in a 2018 report by the National Infrastructure Commission, not one new large-scale settlement has been designated. In this context, the record of the New Towns programme looks extraordinary, with site designation progressing from a recommendation to a confirmed Designation Order in three years, or less.

As we have seen, the need for a state-sponsored new town, together with its location, was typically identified by regional or subregional studies undertaken by various agencies of central and local government. Such studies usually identified the role, purpose and scale of the proposed development. While the process of site identification and designation for the new towns was varied, there are some common and surprising lessons, broadly relating to the role of central and local government in the site-finding process and the role that strategic evidence played in the process.

The first and most important surprise is that the identification of sites for many of the new towns was not a crude top-down imposition but was often led by local authorities. The assumption that the locations for the new towns were determined by central government and imposed on places that didn't want them is simply false. In Milton Keynes and Warrington – two of the fastest-growing towns and cities in the UK – it was county councils who promoted sites for new towns. The same occurred in Wales, though at the invitation of the Welsh Ministry. In Cumbernauld and Craigavon, regional bodies were responsible for identifying needs and locations. While the minister was ultimately the person to designate the new town, the need for a new community had often been established by local authorities or local politicians prior to central government involvement.

The key point is that there was a much more complex and ultimately fruitful dialogue between central and local government than anything we have seen over the last decade. There is no doubt that local authorities would not have embarked on regional studies if central government hadn't made a clear offer to back the process for a designation and hadn't promised the necessary loans and wider investment to the Development Corporations. The role and personality of politicians such as Lewis Silkin (see page 10) and Harold Macmillan (Figure 12.3) were also important,

12.3
STEVENAGE RESIDENTS MEET PRIME MINISTER HAROLD MACMILLAN IN 1959. ALSO PICTURED ARE SIR ROYDON DASH, STEVENAGE DEVELOPMENT CORPORATION CHAIRMAN, AND CONSERVATIVE MP MARTIN MADDEN.

not just in terms of providing the legislative mechanisms for delivery but, in cases such as Warrington or Milton Keynes, in brokering agreements. The minister was able to provide a voice that was independent of local politics and could both inspire action and referee local arguments. Contrary to popular perception, the new towns were not determined by Whitehall but by dialogue between central and local government, backed by both a national and regional evidence base.

While the principle of new towns was established in national policy, it was left to the regional or subregional studies to turn this ambition into a practical reality.

It was through these key studies that the detailed locations were determined as part of the strategic approach that matched housing demand with infrastructure provision, an idea that is both simple and often absent from current debates on housing growth. National government was thinking strategically about the nation as a whole and while this process was far from perfect, the ambition to think about big geographies and the desire for a 'one nation' approach was vital to the success of the new towns. When that ambition was broken in the early 1980s, the subsequent policy vacuum resulted in a piecemeal development, with a consequent and growing public discontent at the lack of affordable and quality homes supported by the right kind of modern infrastructure. The lesson is simply that the government can play a powerful and enabling role in identifying locations, ensuring these locations are linked to wider infrastructure objectives and, as a result, de-risking the development process.

Lesson 3: Modernised Development Corporations are the most effective way to deliver large-scale new communities

Creating a new community is a long-term endeavour that is likely to take at least 50 years to establish. It involves coordinating the creation of housing, public spaces, health facilities, schools, parks, roads and more. A holistic approach is vital to give confidence to investors, local residents, local authorities and all other partners in the enterprise. The New Town Development Corporations proved remarkably successful in providing the necessary conditions to drive delivery. They were the master developers of the town, providing certainty and confidence to the complex web of people and organisation necessary to make the place work.

The success of the corporations was founded on their control of key levers necessary for place-making, a combination of powers that remains a vital precondition for success. In essence, it was the ability to master-plan, design, finance and operate all the functions vital to establishing and sustaining a community which made them so successful.

Importantly, the interlocking nature of the plan-making, development-management and land-ownership powers of Development Corporations made them very effective instruments of delivery. The role of central government was clear, and responsibility for the design, ownership and consent for new development was held by a single public body, ultimately accountable to the minister. This was a total planning approach which represented the first and only time in our postwar history where the ambition of a comprehensive plan was backed by the comprehensive power to deliver it.

Although the corporations were instruments of the government, they were independent and flexible enough to be able to get on with the job. Having the remit to do 'everything necessary' to deliver the town meant that the corporations could, for example, negotiate deals with private investors. But there were also real tensions. The government gave the corporations targets for things such as housing numbers, which even at the time the Development Corporation employees knew were unrealistic. And, as we have seen, the pressure for speed also meant compromising on things like the quality of materials, which led to maintenance problems later.

There were, in some cases, other strained relationships between the Development Corporation and local authorities where the new town was located. One of the primary sources of resentment was that the corporations had the money and powers that local authorities lacked. In many of the new towns, representatives from existing councils were a key part of the board of the

12.4
THE STAFF OF SKELMERSDALE DEVELOPMENT CORPORATION, PHOTOGRAPHED IN THE 1960S.

corporation. In some cases, councillors on the board were perceived to have 'gone native' and to have become closer to the Development Corporation than the council they represented.

The personalities and leadership of the Development Corporations had a profound influence on their effectiveness. The corporations attracted the best young talent in the built environment at the time (Figure 12.4). Young employees were given the means and space to be creative, which led to some fantastic results – but also to some places where the designer has valued aesthetic over the needs of the resident.

This notion of total planning applied by the Development Corporations was, in retrospect, a short-lived experiment and we will never know what might have happened if they had been able to finish the task they were established for. All the New Town Development Corporations (and Commissions) were wound up prematurely between 1982 and 1996 and their assets transferred to existing local authorities or to the Commission for the New Towns; in Scotland, industrial land went to Scottish Enterprise, and in Northern Ireland some assets were transferred to the Ministry of Development.

For the creation of new places today, the stand-out lesson is the way Development Corporations could apply the power of a unified master developer for places on the scale of the original new towns. In practice, this means having dedicated staff and resources to both set a vision and broker the complex relationships necessary to drive delivery. The history of the corporations also illustrates key weaknesses in their long-term commitment to community-led stewardship bodies and their legal vulnerability to being wound up before they had finished the job. A future generation of Development Corporations could have much stronger legal commitments on participation, quality of design, climate resilience and stewardship.

Lesson 4: New towns can pay for themselves

Building new communities requires significant upfront investment in everything from architects to road-building. In recent years these costs have seemed insurmountable, but the long-term creation of new communities can be a highly profitable enterprise. The New Towns programme demonstrates that, far from being a strain on the public purse, investment in new towns can be highly profitable for the government. The dilemma is that this profit relies on strong land value capture tools and cannot be realised without significant upfront investment. The government must stand behind this investment to be the guarantor for growth.

The original new towns were a solid financial success. Assisted by relatively low interest rates, Harlow was able to repay its loans within 15 years and then started to produce a surplus for HM Treasury. It is true that the later 'Mark Three' new towns had to navigate the economic turbulence of the 1970s and 1980s, when interest rates rose dramatically. Above all, it was the forced sale of the Development Corporations' commercial assets (both mature and immature) from 1981 onwards that removed a vital source of income, depriving the towns of the funds for renewal and development.

Any subsequent sales by local authorities of the assets they had received were subject to 'clawback', under which the increase in the value from the sale of any of the liabilities for commercial purposes had to be given back to the Commission for the New Towns or its successors. This limited the ability of the new towns to reinvest in their renewal and upkeep. The total £4.75-billion loan made to the New Town Development Corporations by HM Treasury was repaid in early 1999 (assisted by the sale of sites). It has proved to be one of the most lucrative state investments of modern times. By 2002, land sale receipts had generated around £600 million, of which only £120 million was reinvested in the new towns.[1] Between 2010 and 2014, land sale receipts generated a further £70.3 million for HM Treasury.[2]

Today Homes England (the eventual successor to the Commission for the New Towns) still owns 4,303 hectares of land in the former new towns (see table), though not all of this was former Development Corporation land. The issue of claw-back to HM Treasury of former Development Corporation land remains an important issue for some of the former new town local authorities. The covenants on this land vary from place to place and the requirements are different for every transaction.

HOMES ENGLAND LAND OWNERSHIP IN THE FORMER NEW TOWNS[3]

Note that in addition to land owned by the former Commission for the New Towns (CNT), these figures also include land owned by the former Urban Regeneration Agency and land purchased by Homes England since the CNT ceased to exist.

TOWN	AREA (HA)
Basildon	102.3849
Bracknell	0.2167
Central Lancs	390.1614
Corby	27.2172
Crawley	229.6497
Hatfield	15.8488
Hemel Hempstead	94.4313
Milton Keynes[4]	238.7712
Newton Aycliffe	28.7911
Northampton	529.6844
Peterborough	648.3814
Peterlee	52.166
Redditch	95.5843
Runcorn	95.0443
Skelmersdale	57.6598
Stevenage	64.0976
Telford	901.7945
Warrington	705.0587
Washington	18.0998
Welwyn GC	8.1[5]
Grand total	4303.1431

The heart of this financial success depended on the ability of the early new towns to purchase land at existing-use value. Once this mechanism was broken in 1959 by introducing a compensation regime founded on a distorted view of 'market value', the job of the new towns was made more difficult. There is immense contemporary literature about land value capture and a great deal of complexity about the detail of the issue. However, for the purpose of examining the New Towns programme, the lesson is straightforward. If we want high-quality outcomes in the public interest, we need to decide what is a fair balance between the interests of landowners and the interests of the community.

In the first round of new towns, the government got that balance right by ensuring landowners received payments for the value of their land in its current use. After 1959, we embarked on an era where landowners receive large windfall payments based on increased speculative values for future planning consents which they have not realised and for which they do not have a legal right. These are known as 'hope values' and have to be considered as part of the compensation package when land is compulsory purchased. The increases in land value for which landowners have not contributed are called 'betterment'.[6] The central issue is that these values are created by the actions of public bodies on behalf of the community and deserve, both morally and legally, to be used for community benefit.

Chapter 13 explores how this question is being answered now, but the question of a fair settlement between communities and landowners remains pivotal to all forms of place-making. The New Towns legislation settled the matter in favour of the community, but plainly underestimated the power and sophistication of Britain's land-owning lobby.

What is striking is that even after the return to a 'market' valuation, the later new towns, such as Milton Keynes, which had to consider 'hope value' when purchasing land, were still able to generate profit from the development process.[7]

There are two major caveats to this wider picture of financial success. The first is that just because new towns are new does not mean they can escape the wider national and regional economic forces reshaping our economy. Towns such as Skelmersdale or Peterlee proved vulnerable to the dramatic industrial restructuring of the economy which began in the mid-1970s. The removal of wider measures to rebalance the national economy in the 1980s left a number of new towns in a challenging position, but their fate was often relatively better in terms of accessibility and housing quality than the hundreds of older ex-industrial communities.

The second caveat is more controversial because it relates to a political decision which instructed the winding up of Development Corporations, the early repayment of loans and then the lack of national policy support for the special challenges of renewal that are inevitably associated with the making of new places. This effectively stipped the new towns of assets vital to investing in renewal and removed any possibility of long-term community stewardship funds for community facilities. The opportunity to secure a long-term stewardship model was lost due to political decisions which failed to fully understand or appreciate the benefits of investment in the new towns or the implications of overturning the existing financial model. In the future, the national government needs a genuinely long-term and evidence-based approach and must secure the political consensus to give new communities the continuity they require.

Lesson 5: Stewardship of community assets is vital to a truly sustainable outcome

One of the key lessons of the new towns is that the enormous job of creating them looks easy compared to the job of maintaining and renewing them. This is fundamentally a question of the will and resources to establish a successful stewardship model that can renew and adapt the new town as it matures.

The robbing of new town assets by central government was made easier by the failure of the Development Corporations, with some notable exceptions, to divest their assets to mutual and community organisations during the development process. If greater attention had been paid to that strand of anarchic community self-organisation seen in the original garden cities, the outcomes for the new towns might have been very different. Perhaps the greatest sustained criticism of new towns is their inability to maintain the rich legacy of community assets and parks and gardens to a high standard, which was key to the original design of places like Peterlee. This failure relates to a fundamentally different approach to stewardship from the original garden city ideal and by implication a different view of the citizen as a consumer of services rather than having a stake in controlling them.

New towns have had to deal with a perfect storm of stolen assets, national austerity in local government and simultaneously an aging public realm. Given all of that, they have done surprisingly well but the difference between Letchworth Garden City (Figure 12.5) and Peterlee, for example, reflects the vital importance of and different approach to stewardship of assets.

12.5
HOWARD PARK, LETCHWORTH GARDEN CITY, WHERE THE STEWARDSHIP MODEL ENABLES OVER £4 MILLION A YEAR TO BE REINVESTED IN COMMUNITY ASSETS IN ADDITION TO LOCAL AUTHORITY SERVICES.

Letchworth benefits from having a charitable organisation which uses income from its land and property in the town to provide benefits for residents. This is in addition to the services and facilities provided by the local authority. Letchworth Garden City Heritage Foundation is the successor to the original development company (First Garden City Ltd). The foundation reinvests its income for the long-term benefit of the local people and ensures that key community assets, from the parks to the cinema, are sustained.

When the New Town Development Corporations were building the new towns, they put considerable effort into creating high-quality environments, with generous green space and a wide range of social and cultural facilities that could be enjoyed by residents from the earliest days of moving to the town. They had the resources to pay for everything, from cutting the grass or looking after play areas, to employing artists in residence to add to the cultural vitality of the town. What was not made clear was what was to happen to the Development Corporations, and to the assets they were in charge of, when the new towns reached maturity.

The New Towns Act of 1946 envisaged that the Development Corporations would hand over the assets of mature towns (namely the land, property and financial resources of the Development Corporations) to local authorities.[8] However, this provision was amended by the New Towns Act of 1959, which created the Commission for the New Towns to take over the assets.[9] From this point, the financial benefits of the assets went back to HM Treasury rather than to the places that had generated that value in the first place. When all the Development Corporations were forced to wind up, the remaining assets, after the repayment of the loans, were transferred to the local authority. These 'assets' included, for instance, social housing that quickly became a liability as funding streams to look after it were cut. With the occasional notable exception, the opportunity for a mutualised community stewardship model was broken at precisely the time when the towns began to require renewal.

Today, many of the new towns are in need of restoration and investment. Unlike the Development Corporations, councils do not have the funds to pay the high maintenance costs of huge areas of green space, public art or other public realm that was integral to the new town vision. The lack of a sinking fund during the many years in which the new infrastructure and property needed little maintenance means that today, several decades after they were built, a huge amount of investment is needed, for which there are no special resources. Although the new town assets continued to generate profits for the Commission for the New Towns and its successors, these were used for other projects. The lack of a long-term stewardship strategy for the new towns can be considered one of the major failures of the programme.

There are notable exceptions – in Milton Keynes an endowed Parks Trust and a Community Foundation were among the not-for-profit local institutions set up to receive and maintain in perpetuity some key assets when the Development Corporation was wound up. Today, as a consequence, the Parks Trust is entirely self-financing and maintains over 5,000 acres of parks, meadows, river valleys, woodlands, lakes and the landscaped corridors which run along the main grid roads – about 25% of the new city area.[10]

Lesson 6: People must be empowered to be at the heart of decision-making

A core objective of the garden city movement was to create places where people had a genuine stake in the development process and were able to live happy, healthy and sociable lives. The new towns inherited this ethos, and the creation of 'balanced communities' and opportunities for 'discovering the best ways of living' were core objectives of the Development Corporations.

Despite these good intentions, there were real challenges in public participation, particularly around the designation process. The New Towns Act required that the minister identified and consulted with 'all local authorities affected' but there is little evidence of active consultation with existing residents before designation, beyond an initial public meeting. The public did have the right to comment on the Draft Designation Order through both a public inquiry and the parliamentary process and designation took place in an era of much greater acceptance of the need for decent homes. This is often attributed solely to the wartime experiences of the Blitz and the damage or destruction of hundreds of thousands of homes. But it was due to a wider cultural and political conversation which had begun in the 1930s about the social scandal of poor housing and played out through the mass media of the cinema. This was not solely state-sponsored propaganda but driven by documentaries like *Housing Problems* by John Grierson (1935) and the now long-forgotten but iconic *Land of Promise* directed by Paul Rotha (1946). These arguments were distilled by national figures like J.B. Priestley (Figure 12.6), who made clear the need for a new society at the end of World War II.

The lesson here is that gaining consent for a programme of new towns is not a 'rabbit to be pulled from the hat' by a national politician but is based on a range of complex factors, of which one is the need for national conversation about the need and opportunity for change. As shown in Part 1, the eco-towns programme failed as people had not been properly engaged in the process.

In sharp contrast to many of our debates about housing today, it was also much harder to argue that a new town was simply about profiteering or didn't meet local needs, when a significant proportion of the homes in new towns were for social rent and when supporting infrastructure was so integral to the offer of a new community. That said, the assumption in 1946 was that local authorities asking for a new town's designation spoke for their community and a need for genuine forms of participative democracy was not recognised. Local opposition to some new towns was powerful. Famously, the Minister for Town and Country Planning, Lewis Silkin, had his car tyres let down while he was speaking at a public meeting about the Stevenage new town, and residents also changed the railway sign to read 'Silkingrad'.[12]

The story of post-designation public participation offers a much wider set of lessons for today. Many of the New Town Development Corporations invested in social or community development during construction, including employing officers to welcome new residents, publishing newsletters, organising community events or establishing neighbourhood councils. This was designed to address what had come to be known as the 'new town blues' – a consequence of moving to a new community, usually away from existing social networks and activities. Many development corporations funded community meeting places and accelerated the establishment of networking institutions such as mother-and-toddler groups, Scout and Guide troops, allotment societies, local history associations and music, dance and singing groups.

12.6
J.B. PRIESTLEY, PLAYWRIGHT AGITATOR FOR BETTER LIVING CONDITIONS.

Later new towns also put specific efforts into considering the views of residents. As part of the process of developing the master plan for Milton Keynes, a survey was undertaken of residents living in the villages within the potential designated area. Annual surveys of the views of new residents were also conducted by the Development Corporation. This included views on everything from the design of homes to whether 'housewives' felt they had enough employment opportunities.

The emphasis that the Development Corporations put on community development is one of the key positive legacies in the new towns and may have contributed to the strong sense of civic pride in many new town residents today. This pride comes as a surprise to many outsiders but it has to be balanced by the stigma attached to some of the less successful new towns. Several, such as Craigavon, face significant challenges of overcoming the stigma associated with their 'new town' title. In some cases, these views are based on real problems but in others negative media preconceptions are not consistent with the sense of civic pride felt by many new town residents.

New towns themselves have fallen in and out of love with their pioneering heritage. Now the concept has returned to political favour, many new towns are once again proud of their heritage. Many Development Corporation employees have always called their new towns 'new cities'. Milton Keynes is one of the fastest-growing cities in the UK but it does not officially have 'city status', something it is acutely aware of.

The civic identity of the new towns has not always been helped by their fragmented governance. In some cases, such as Stevenage, the areas of the town are controlled by a single local authority. In other cases, the new town is part of a wider district with no single local authority control. In other cases, the assets and land ownership are fragmented between differing private and public institutions. In Peterlee, land is owned by the county and town councils, as well as Natural England, while the town centre is in private ownership. This fragmentation and complexity is profoundly unhelpful in creating a clear line of sight for democratic and practical renewal.

Conclusion

So, where does the new town learning leave us? With three dominant and uncomfortable questions:

1. If the new towns were so successful in meeting housing needs, why can't we apply our learning to the creation of a new generation of places?

2. Why don't we apply the lessons of what made the creation of new towns so successful to their renewal and regeneration?

3. If we truly want to create quality, inclusive and affordable places (Figure 12.7), why don't we apply the lesson of the new towns' development model, which created a fair financial balance between the needs of the community and the needs of landowners and developers?

Chapter 13 attempts to answer these questions in the context of Britain's contemporary political realities.

12.7
A 'MARCH FOR HOMES' PROTEST HELD IN LONDON IN 2015. THE SHORTAGE OF DECENT HOMES IS A CRISIS THAT WON'T GO AWAY.

13

THE FUTURE OF THE NEW TOWNS IDEAL

Introduction

During the last decade there has been a tendency, particularly in England, to prioritise the number of housing units built rather than their quality, affordability or sustainable location (Figure 13.1). Getting planning 'out of the way' still hasn't produced the number of homes we need but has ensured many of them lack the breadth of social infrastructure that was seen as essential for the new towns. None of the great prizes that result from high-quality design, including the opportunity to transform people's health and wellbeing, have been secured. This resulted from a profound and longer-term failure by the government to learn the importance of the whole complex narrative of place-making, from strategic coordination to the provision of art and culture and, perhaps above all, the vital role of the public sector as an enabler and de-risker in the development process. It is interesting to reflect that in a decade dominated by chronic housing shortage and with rhetoric about a million new homes between Oxford and Cambridge, we have designated not one new community on the scale of any of the new towns. In the 10 years after 1946, we had designated and started to build 14 new towns in a much more challenging context for investment, materials and labour supply. So far, the plans for the Cambridge–Milton Keynes–Oxford Arc (Figure 13.2) have ignored almost all the key lessons of the New Towns programme.

This chapter examines our current policy responses to the existing new towns and to the delivery of new places. For both challenges it seeks to explore current government policy before setting out how we might address some of the issues explored in previous chapters. If there is a single common theme in these suggestions, it is that the government needs to play a much more effective role in enabling and supporting growth. To do this, the government must create the strategic policy coordination and investment offer to encourage local action. It must also talk to people, beginning the process of national conversation about our homes and communities.

NEW TOWNS: THE RISE, FALL AND REBIRTH

13.1
A MODERN 'BRICK BOX', IN THE MIDLANDS. THE STANDARD OF MANY MODERN HOUSING DEVELOPMENTS IS UNACCEPTABLE.

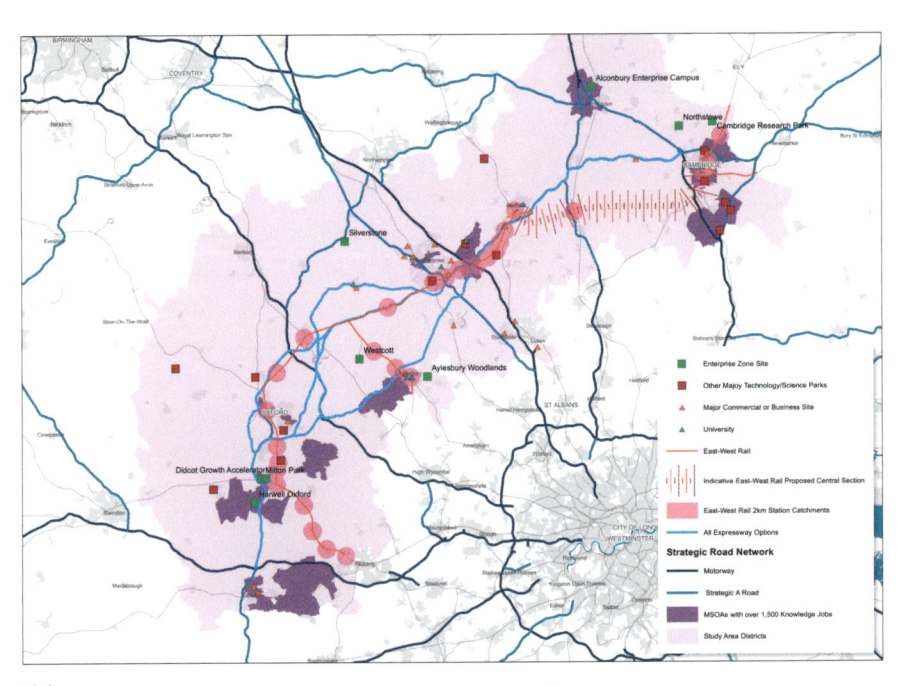

13.2
MAP OF THE PROPOSED CAMBRIDGE–MILTON KEYNES–OXFORD ARC, 2019.

The fate of our existing new towns

Today the new towns exhibit a range of successes and failures – including, as they do, both the fastest-growing and most successful yet also some of the most deprived communities in the UK. While their economic context is diverse, we have seen that they share common challenges and opportunities and have embedded in their DNA a distinct heritage which flows from how and when they were built.

While responsibilities for planning and regeneration are devolved in the UK, it is curious that no nation or region has developed a package of policy to address the specific needs of new towns. In England there isn't even a ministerial post with responsibility for new towns. Neither is there any wider cultural recognition of the programme. While events and institutions of the same era – such as the 1951 Festival of Britain, the NHS or national parks – are rightly seen as core to our national identity, new towns have been forgotten.

Of course, the new towns themselves have been celebrating various anniversaries, but it's surprising that there is no national association of new towns and therefore no network to advocate their needs to the government. Efforts to restore such a network form a positive step but new towns have been disavowed by successive governments, despite their record for dealing with growth and their ability to survive the confiscation of their assets.

Only in the last two years has there been the beginning of a shift in attitudes, with the establishment of an All-Party Parliamentary Group (APPG) on New Towns which has begun to attract national political attention (Figure 13.3).

In July 2018 the All-Party Parliamentary Group on New Towns, which was set up to celebrate the contribution made by the UK's new towns and to highlight the challenges they face, launched a new manifesto with three key asks:

1. New towns should be included in a Ministry of Housing, Communities and Local Government (MHCLG) Minister's list of key responsibilities, to help unlock their potential and give new towns the national attention and focus they need and deserve.

2. The government should publish a new towns prospectus setting out how they can support existing new towns to regenerate and grow through providing tailored government support to local areas with ambitious and innovative proposals. This would include capacity funding.

3. The government should review the tools and powers local authorities need to transform the town centres of new towns in order to unlock their potential for growth and renewal, including the regeneration of shopping areas.

Government recognition of the unique challenges of the new towns, particularly around their town centres and the need to replace infrastructure and the public realm, which is all aging at the same rate, would be a major step forward. Above all, giving back the remaining new town assets owned by Homes England to create stewardship funds could have a transformational impact on renewal, as well as being some form of reparation for the way the new towns have been dealt with by central government. Some 4,303 hectares of land in the new towns is still owned by Homes England (see page 150).[1] But the spirit of innovation in the new towns offers other opportunities.

Faced with the systemic renewal problems of some of our new towns, what would happen if we re-designated Development Corporations to drive change? How could these corporations be more sensitive to community needs and be genuinely participative? How could we learn from the American model of community development corporations which operate at a street and neighbourhood level? How might this experience help us deal with the apparently intractable problems of many ex-industrial towns? Addressing fragmented governance and complex land ownership are core renewal problems which need strong public intervention to transform.

It is significant that most of what we know about town centre renewal is defined by the re-creation of civic space through art, culture and leisure, in order to make it less dependent on retailing. To do this comprehensively requires either a private owner with strong social responsibility or, more likely, a strong public-sector body with a clear vision for creative place-making. The pioneers of growth are now the pioneers of renewal and should be recognised as such. This, of course, would require a seismic change to our wider political culture to see public bodies as master developers working in a strong democratic context.

Some of the new towns have begun the process of regaining control of civic space after the failed experiment of privatisation. Milton Keynes Futures 2050 Commission explored options for the city's future and has set ambitious objectives to embrace growth and change.[2] Milton Keynes Council purchased its former new town assets back from the government and is exploring how best to make that work. But renewal in such a young place comes with its own specific challenges, including how to accommodate economic renewal while honouring the very DNA that makes Milton Keynes so special.

13.3
THE MANIFESTO LAUNCH OF THE ALL-PARTY PARLIAMENTARY GROUP ON NEW TOWNS, IN 2018. FROM LEFT: LUCY ALLAN MP (CHAIR OF THE APPG), RT HON SAJID JAVID MP (THEN SECRETARY OF STATE FOR HOUSING, COMMUNITIES AND LOCAL GOVERNMENT) AND KATE HENDERSON (THEN CHIEF EXECUTIVE OF THE TOWN AND COUNTRY PLANNING ASSOCIATION).

13.4
THE NATIONAL INFRASTRUCTURE COMMISSION'S PARTNERING FOR PROSPERITY REPORT. THE NIC HAS SET OUT A STRATEGIC CASE FOR THE CAMBRIDGE–MILTON KEYNES–OXFORD ARC.

Whole estate renewal is also a major challenge for the new towns. Should these neighbourhoods be densified? How does that affect the vision of place that people wanted to be part of? What is the best way to accommodate this feeling? These questions are perhaps even harder to address, as for many residents this is the first time they have experienced regeneration of any sort. Like Harlow, Milton Keynes has recognised the importance of its built heritage to the community's sense of identity. The council has a range of initiatives, such as a project exploring new town heritage, a process which has led many to conclude that the city centre's infrastructure is perhaps its most important asset. Discussions are under way about an Infrastructure Trust to protect and manage these assets in a similar way to Milton Keynes' parks.

Specific interventions, such as the repurposing of some green space in new town estates – for food growing or energy or biodiversity – could maximise the multiple benefits of this important new town asset. And it is clear that drawing on the current interest in postwar architecture and public art, using new town heritage as a catalyst for renewal, provides a specific and exciting opportunity.

It takes time to unpick the mythology that surrounds the new towns and so it is perhaps unsurprising that in a time of wider political crisis national government has, so far, chosen not to engage with the places that house 2.8 million of our citizens. In fact, there is growing interest in the existing new towns at the highest level of government, even if that interest is still informed with outdated views of the New Towns programme. Speaking in 2018, the then Secretary of State for Housing, the Rt Hon Sajid Javid MP, stated:

There's little doubt that there are valuable lessons to be learned from new towns ... Many ... are home to successful companies, offer affordable homes and job opportunities that attract inward commuters. But the downsides of the rapid development and, in particular, centralised planning, that underpinned new towns are all too evident. Dated, often identikit housing, infrastructure and town centres that, too often, look like everywhere and nowhere. That doesn't just make these towns the butt of lazy jokes ... but makes it harder for them to be seen as truly aspirational and attract the investment they need to grow and thrive. Like you, I want this to change. And I can see that many new towns are stepping up to the challenge.[3]

The Secretary of State's views summarise the current national political approach to new towns. Recognised for their economic contribution, they are, in the same breath, dammed for being the product of 'centralised' planning. This is a prime example of our continued and collective failure to let go of the myths of the new towns and to understand them with the objectivity they deserve. Of all the places in the Cambridge–Milton Keynes–Oxford Arc, it is significant that it is a new town that has the highest productivity. Powerful public-sector-led planning works.

The prospects for a 21st-century New Towns programme?

There is an intimate connection between the complex fate of our existing new towns and the wider political enthusiasm to back a new generation of communities. The myths this book has tried to address are powerful and politicians might be forgiven for not wanting to be associated with what some regard as a damaged 'brand'. The relationship between central and local government is also strained, particularly in England, so that the kinds of fruitful relationships that resulted in the designation of Milton Keynes are hard to achieve. Local government in general and new towns in particular are cautious about the stop-start nature of central government's policy initiatives. The lesson of abandonment of the new towns casts a shadow on those in local government trying find the courage and consent to bring forward new communities. Central government can be equally frustrated at what it sees as the slow pace of action by local government on housing delivery. Above all, there is an absence of the most important commodity in making long-term change happen: trust.

Current government policy

As we saw in Chapter 3, the main focus of the debate about large-scale new settlements in the UK is focused on the high-demand areas of the Southeast of England. Here, recent government policy can most charitably be described as complex and conflicted. The shorthand version is that there is a major gap between the rhetoric of ministers on the potential of new places and the detailed measures necessary to deliver on that ambition.

Among the various recent policy strands to promote growth there are four dominate themes:

- an emphasis on the Southeast rather than on one nation
- an emphasis on localism
- an emphasis on private-sector delivery
- an emphasis on deregulation.

A one-nation growth strategy?

The period after 2010 was defined first by the abandonment of any urban policy or national development strategy and then by a slow return to focused support on enabling growth in high-demand areas of the Southeast. There was and remains no serious attempt to deal with systemic regional inequalities. The single biggest idea was that of devolution, with a series of complex city deals offered to combined authorities and city mayors. It is now for these bodies to reinvent regional plans and strategies in a multitude of ad hoc approaches. Central government, despite the importance of the industrial strategy or the need for strategic response to climate change, is not developing a national development plan. Those initiatives that have been introduced, such as the Northern Powerhouse or Midlands Engine, are an accretion of measures and investments each with a very different character. The one strategic idea in which government is most interested is the Cambridge–Milton Keynes–Oxford Arc (Figure 13.4), where a million additional new homes are to be planned.[4] Homes England, the Infrastructure Planning Authority, the National Infrastructure Commission, various government departments and agencies such as Network Rail and Highways England, and a private rail investment company, plus 34 local councils and multiple private-sector planning consultancies have all come together to deliver this growth. But by ignoring the lessons of the new towns, the government has made three potentially key mistakes:

- It has not set the plan for the Arc in any wider regional and national policy context.
- It has not made any plans as yet for use of Development Corporations to manage growth points as part of a portfolio of options to manage growth.
- It has not built any public consent for plans, which are largely being developed out of public view.

One might add that the ambition for action on climate change, affordability or technological change is sadly absent from documents that are in the public domain. It may be that the Arc proves successful in the long term. However, when measured against the foundational work for the new town designations, the Cambridge–Milton Keynes–Oxford Arc feels half baked.

Localism

The government has committed to continuing its support for the locally led 'garden communities' and further funding support was announced in the first half of 2019, although the process of identifying successful places remains piecemeal.[5] Critically, there has appeared to be a lack of a clear plan by the government to indicate the best areas of search for these places, nor an adequate package of investment or policy to build confidence for locally led places to come forward.

With the exception of places like Ebbsfleet (Figure 13.5), which is being delivered by an Urban Development Corporation, the majority of large-scale developments currently in planning are being delivered by the private sector, with the involvement, encouragement and sometimes limited participation of the local authority. There are important exceptions to this, such as the sites at Bicester and Northstowe, where the local authority is taking a more significant lead. It is also true that Homes England is playing an increasingly active role in supporting growth. But there are still currently a very limited number of proposals for large-scale development of more than 10,000 housing units in the planning process, and none on the scale of an original new town.[6]

13 THE FUTURE OF THE NEW TOWNS IDEAL

13.5
AN ARTIST'S IMPRESSION OF PROPOSALS FOR EBBSFLEET. THE EXPANDED COMMUNITY IS BEING DELIVERED BY AN URBAN DEVELOPMENT CORPORATION.

The dominant role of the private sector

Despite government dependence on the volume housebuilders, the lack of larger-scale projects suggests that the private sector is unable to assemble, promote and deliver schemes for more than 5,000–8,000 homes. Relying on the private sector alone has also been vulnerable to the stop-go of national economic cycles. It now seems clear that if a new settlement on the scale of a new town is going to be built, the government will have to underwrite the main risk: private capital from institutional investors will then follow.

Deregulation

The final major policy strand from the government is focused on deregulation. The dismantling of the planning system was laid out in detail in the Raynsford Review in 2018.[7] The summary of this analysis was a system in England which was complex, ineffective, underfunded and focused on the numbers and not the quality of new homes. The expansion of permitted development rights was the most striking example of deregulation and has led to the creation of very large numbers of substandard housing units, which the Raynsford Review concluded would be the 'slums of the future'. It is true that this headlong drive to get planning 'out of the way' has now run its course. In its place we can see the slow re-invention of ad hoc strategic planning and a growing concern at the outcome of poor housing. While none of this activity reflects the systematic approach of the New Towns programme, it does, perhaps, illustrate the beginning of greater openness to the lessons of successful strategic growth.

Where next for new towns?

Any government that is serious about dealing with the housing crisis in a period of economic and environmental challenge should have new towns in its armoury of solutions. It is not hard to learn the lessons of the original programme and to improve all aspects of the process and outcome of building new places. Imagine how extraordinary a new community might be if that learning were fused with the advances we have made in technology.

As the years of inaction have passed and the housing crisis has intensified, it is now clearer than ever that the nation needs a modernised New Towns programme in which central and local government work together to deliver communities using the Development Corporation approach.

The future of new towns in the UK depends on our capacity to answer two questions. What measures do we need to take to learn the lessons of the existing programme? Is there a compelling political case for a new programme?

In learning the lessons, national governments should look to address four immediate challenges:

1. committing to a national policy context for designating locations, setting ambitious standards and defining a package of financial support
2. making the New Towns Act fit for purpose
3. securing the skills and capacity to deliver
4. delivering the right financial model.

13 THE FUTURE OF THE NEW TOWNS IDEAL

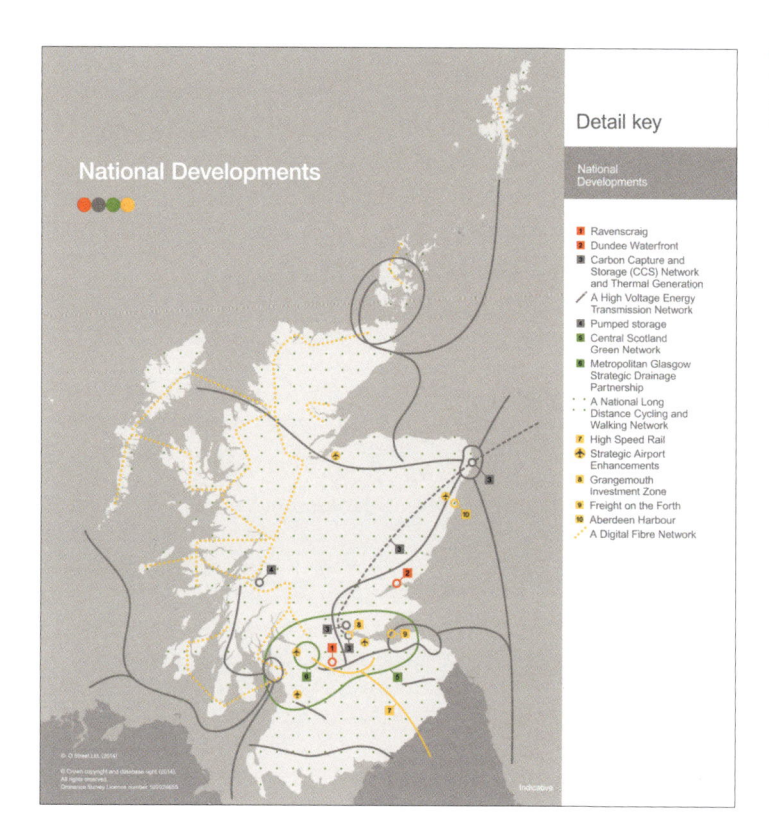

13.6
THE SCOTLAND SPATIAL PLAN (2014) OFFERS A STRATEGIC VISION FOR THE NATION.

1 National policy

Unlike Scotland (Figure 13.6), Wales and Northern Ireland, England does not have any systematic national or regional strategic planning. The Raynsford Review was just one of a growing chorus of voices advocating why such a plan could make our lives better by helping to support more balanced national development in the context of the future pressures facing the nation. Such a plan would set the broad context for growth areas in England and create the foundation for areas of search for new communities. It would rule out areas where costs, environmental limits or other vulnerability make development unwise and identify the magic moments where planned infrastructure, housing needs and land availability come together. It should be the role of the government to select areas of search for new communities and provide the confidence to subregional and local plans to define the precise location.

A national plan would also need to be accompanied by a national policy framework which set out the support national government would offer for local action, including how government departments would be forced to work together to join up investment decisions and deal with the blockages so often created by failure to align infrastructure investment. Finally, national government would need to set out the kinds of ambitious quality standards based on the Garden City Principles, which would include enhanced national design standards and compliance with ambitious targets for zero-carbon and climate-resilient places.

2 Reforming the New Towns Act

We have already made clear that a locally led new towns approach which shifts the burden of the delivery solely to local authorities is unlikely to be used extensively. Instead, the best approach is to update the legislation that successfully built 32 new places. There are a number of key changes that should be made, including:

- updating the designation process to ensure that it is based on robust strategic evidence and powerful and participative community rights
- new duties on Development Corporations to ensure the critical issues such as equality and climate change (Figure 13.7) are front and centre of the corporations' outcomes
- a new and much more robust approach to stewardship so the assets created through the development process are mutualised for the benefit of the community over the long term.

So, what would a 21st-century New Town Development Corporation look like?

The result of these changes would be a dynamic body capable of the long-term and complex job of creating new places by:

- being committed to the long-term project of building a new community (50+ years)
- being legally bound to deliver all the high standards framed by the Garden City Principles at the outset and with the financial and governance arrangements to do so in perpetuity
- establishing a master plan with a strong vision and structure but which provides the flexibility for the place to evolve over time
- having the power to do everything necessary to deliver the town, including planning and compulsory purchase powers, and social and economic development
- enabling existing authorities to feel actively engaged in the development of the town
- allowing for real public participation throughout the development process
- being focused on creating the stewardship bodies with communities to hold and protect the assets for the benefit of the community.

3 Skills and capacity

The public service contains some brilliant and committed people but it has lost an immense amount of expertise and capacity as a result of austerity. For example, basic expertise on the compulsory purchase of land is now a rare asset in many local authorities. Rebuilding this capacity is a critical problem for an ambitious programme of new communities and requires new partnerships with private-sector consultancies. The hugely successful model of Public Practice has sought to address these capacity challenges and there are opportunities to explore how this could be expanded with specific support for those planning at scale {endnote: Public Practice is a not-for-profit social enterprise with a mission to improve the quality and equality of everyday places by building the public sector's capacity for proactive planning. Find our more at: http://www.publicpractice.org.uk/]

In fact, we are short on skills of all kinds, from community development to engineering, from artists to strategic planning, and solving this problem in the long term requires a new approach to how we educate the people who will design and build new communities. One positive

13 THE FUTURE OF THE NEW TOWNS IDEAL

13.7
FREIBURG, A CITY WHERE ALL THE ELEMENTS OF COMPREHENSIVE PLANNING
HAVE DELIVERED ONE OF EUROPE'S MOST SUSTAINABLE COMMUNITIES.

opportunity is that this demand for skills and talent to work on real change could attract the enthusiasm of a new generation of creative thinkers and doers, recapturing the excitement of the original Development Corporations.

4 Who's going to pay?

Access to land in the right location and at the right price is the foundation of successful new places. Both local authorities and Development Corporations have the power to use compulsory purchase to assemble the land needed for a new community. The issue of how much it is reasonable to pay for land is much more complex. The issue is vital because the capture of the uplift in land values which the granting of planning permission and development creates is crucial to fund debt repayment and long-term reinvestment in a new community. Changes are needed now to create a fairer balance between landowners and the community. Some positive steps have been taken in relation to viability testing in the planning system and there is now greater acceptance that strong requirements in planning policy will result in more realistic expectations of returns from landowners. But there remain key barriers that need to be dealt with, including dealing with 'hope value' through changes to the compensation code.

HM Treasury investment in new communities

The financial history of the new towns shows that they can pay for themselves over time but they need upfront investment and the government will have to play a role in supporting new places. HM Treasury could make available long-term, low-interest loans to new Development Corporations, with more flexibility for borrowing from different sources than was the case in the new towns. Even without providing loans, the government could guarantee (explicitly or implicitly) long-term 'patient' private-sector investment. This would not only assist with upfront finance but would help to 'de-risk' the process and encourage private-sector investment.

Private-sector-led finance

The private sector could have an important role to play in financing new communities, and initiatives such as the Wolfson Economics Prize prompted thinking on whether new garden cities could in fact be entirely funded by the private sector.[8] The need for upfront investment in infrastructure and the need for investors to be patient in terms of expectation of a return on their investment appears to suit the business model of pension funds. Some of these (such as Legal & General) have already expressed interest.[9] Private-sector investment could play an important role in a new programme of new towns but it is unlikely to be realised without the ability of a New Town Development Corporation to de-risk a scheme by creating real confidence that it will be delivered. The private sector alone cannot provide the heavy lifting to deliver but it can be part of a fruitful relationship in shaping a new community in terms of patient investment and as a key partner in delivery of homes and infrastructure and ultimately the employment of a new community.

Making it happen and politics of new towns

Building a new generation of new towns would provide an opportunity to offer people a better way of living, but while we have all the technical and financial solutions we need to create genuinely sustainable living, we don't have public consent for such a programme. Unlike the 1940s, there is no civil society debate about our collective future, and while there is growing public awareness on issues such as climate change, there remains a lack of detailed dialogue on how our homes, streets and communities might change to respond to the forces that are reshaping our society. New towns have always been places where we try to work these problems out, providing much-needed learning for existing communities. If there is to be any future for new towns, public understanding will have to change in two key ways:

- Change is possible. We don't have to put up with the unsustainable and damaging lifestyles we lead now. A better condition of life is attainable and we have the practical mechanisms for delivering it.

- Change is necessary. We can't go on with our current chaotic and low-quality delivery model if we are to be ready for climate challenges and for the technological changes that will reshape the nature of work and redefine many human relationships.

It is significant that at the time of writing the wind is blowing in the new towns' direction, partly because it seems to be the only way to get the housing delivery the nation so desperately needs. The politics of housing, like public attitudes to climate change, will finally shift only when a critical mass of people see the opportunity of a new, more sustainable, more equitable and more rewarding way of living.

14
CONCLUSION

The story of the British new towns shows what our society can achieve when confronted with existential challenges of renewal and reconstruction. It illustrates how the complexity of making places that have to reflect all aspects of the human condition is a monumental task requiring sensitivity, ambition and patience. It is hard to get all of this right all of the time, but the new towns battled to create balanced communities offering economic, recreational and cultural opportunities for all of their citizens.

We hope this book has gone some way to disrupt the wider mythology of the new towns. We wanted to get behind the conferences of concrete cows to reveal a landscape populated with remarkable success as well as some real setbacks. Above all, we wanted to challenge four commonly held assumptions about the New Towns programme which have proved to be completely wrong:

1. **New Towns were not centrally imposed.** They resulted in most cases from the aspiration of local government to solve particular growth and renewal needs in the context of a powerful package of central government support.

2. **The New Towns programme was not a financial disaster.** In fact, it proved to be self-financing and the assets still yield incomes to the government. This is despite the fire sale of assets forced by the derailing of the programme in 1980.

3. **The New Towns programme is not 'finished'.** New Towns should not be regarded as a historical curiosity. They are living and breathing places with major challenges around renewal. They are also places of growth opportunity, both in meeting the ambitions of their original population targets and because, in some cases, there remains a strong spirit of ambition for the future development of the town.

4. **New towns were not just about growth in the Southeast of England.** The relevance of the New Towns programme is not simply about dealing with overspill from London in an overheated Southeast. New towns had a number of reasons to be, including industrial modernisation and social renewal. Even in this context, their objectives were complex and, in the case of Central Lancashire, had an ambition to knit together the fragmented pattern of a swathe of ex-industrial communities whose economic future was uncertain. New Town Development Corporations are still a more effective route for regeneration than their diluted cousin the Urban Development Corporation.

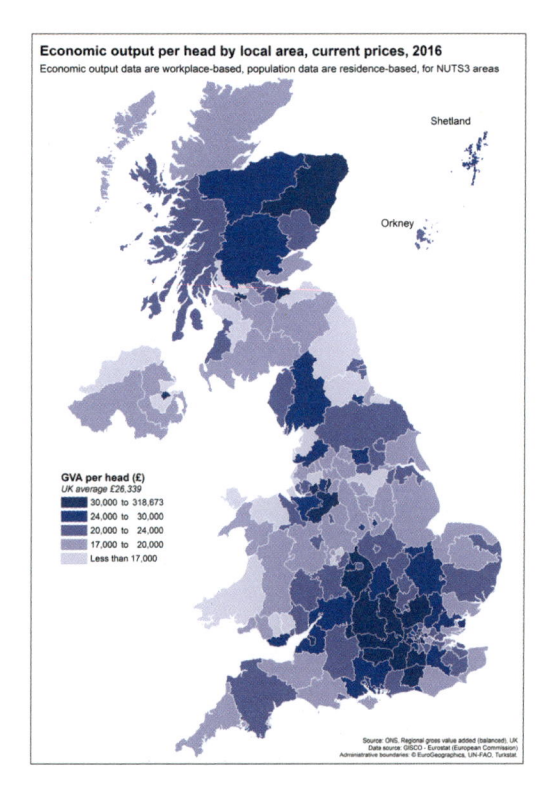

14.1
A MAP SHOWING ECONOMIC OUTPUT PER HEAD, BY LOCAL AREA (2016). SHOWING A STARK PICTURE OF ENGLAND'S REGIONAL INEQUALITIES.

The success and failures of individual new towns are, of course, as much to do with their regional, economic and social circumstances in a nation which is defined by stark regional inequalities (Figure 14.1). New towns cannot escape this economic geography of neglect despite their new town heritage. However, their specific circumstances of delivery, across these different socio-economic contexts, allows conclusions to be made about the impact of their approach to delivery, and therefore how to learn the lessons of the past and to help their renewal in the future.

As we have seen, new towns have common challenges around their town centres, (mis)management of their public realm, aging infrastructure and fragmented land ownership resulting from the dispersal of assets when their Development Corporations were wound up. Meanwhile the 'Right to Buy' has had a significant impact on places which have a high proportion of social housing, making estate renewal beyond the public realm a huge challenge in all the new towns. Despite these challenges and lack of any interest in the existing new towns on the part of central government, they remain places with remarkably strong identity and loyalty from residents. Many continue to economically outperform their regional neighbours and their design legacy gives them the opportunity to adapt to changing needs for healthy environments and technological innovation.

Off the fence?

Although the new town ideal is gaining support, there is little sign that the main Westminster parties have addressed the question of how to deliver high-quality and comprehensively planned new communities, which can take more than 50 years to deliver and transcend electoral cycles. This is, of course, because it involves addressing the difficult and politically sensitive issues of consent, land value (and compensation) and ensuring high standards of development within environmental limits.

Instead of taking responsibility for the long-term progress and organisation of new towns, the approach, particularly in England, has been defined by confused objectives, fragmented governance and a stark gap between the rhetoric of growth and a systematic approach to delivery. The lessons of the new towns have been largely forgotten and there is a risk that the wider programme will soon be regarded as a historical curiosity. Does that matter? Yes, it does. The changing dynamics of demography, the need to reorganise our population in relation to climate change and sea-level rise, the multiple and deep-seated needs for renewal in ex-industrial Britain require a comprehensive planning approach.

For all these practical reasons, we will see a new kind of New Towns programme for growth and renewal inside the next decade. We hope it will set behind us the chaos that pervades our current approach to organising England. The removal of strategic planning after 2010 and longer-term refusal to consider the new towns as a way of transforming delivery has exacerbated the housing crisis. We have experimented with a short-term and deregulated approach to housing growth and in terms of numbers, quality and affordability it has failed. If we want practical solutions in which public and private resources are harnessed effectively together, we need to revisit the new town model. Derwenthorpe, near York, is one example that shows that some councils and private-sector delivery partners are working hard to try to build well-designed and inclusive places despite confused policy.

But there is one final moral reason for taking the new towns' legacy out of its box and putting it to work in the 21st century. Shouldn't our ambition be to build places that offer the very highest standards of design to support people's wellbeing and life chances? Shouldn't we be seeking to offer this to everyone in socially mixed communities? There is evidence for the dramatic impact that the design of places has on the health and wellbeing of residents. Further, reports such as the Raynsford Review (see page 164) show that our current speculative housing delivery model frequently produces soulless, bolt-on housing estates of brick boxes with no walkable access to social facilities and a chaotic process of planning for schools and health care. All of this leaves many existing and new residents frustrated and car dependent.

There is a real urgency to find new solutions to building the communities we need. It is not only the scandal of homelessness. It is also the inhumane standards of the 'homes' we are creating. In the summer of 2019, the Planning Inspectorate approved the conversion of a commercial building in Watford into residential units.[1] Some of these units had a total living area of only 16sq m and had no windows. It is a shocking illustration of how we seem to have lost our moral compass when it comes people, homes and communities. While not all these deregulated conversions are as bad as this example, we have allowed more than 100,000 housing units to be created since deregulation began in 2013. Three 'Mark One' new towns would have delivered the same amount of homes and would have created an immeasurably better quality of life for future generations.

14.2
AN EXTINCTION REBELLION PROTEST IN LONDON 2019. A DEMAND FOR A NEW WAY OF LIVING?

In 1946, under much harsher economic conditions, we could have chosen slums instead of new towns but we didn't. We risked a great deal to try to build the best for ordinary people. But despite all the learning that the creation of 32 new towns should have given us, we have chosen now, in England, to build what Nick Raynsford has described as 'a new generation of slums.'[2] The fact that we failed to build on the success of the new towns' legacy is one of the UK's great missed opportunities and one with real consequences for those most in housing need. Failing to value our existing new towns is also a lost opportunity. Their story is not 'finished' and in many cases they offer the potential for growth, innovation and renewal which could be at the cutting edge of, for example, how we reinvent civic space or transform how we produce local food.

The growing interest in new towns fulfils a collective responsibility to explore how the programme worked and the lessons it provides, as well as to support the real and diverse needs of the communities as they exist now. This is part of a long-term reconnection with the new towns' legacy which is both challenging and ultimately hopeful. Above all, new towns should be celebrated as one of the great national achievements of the UK.

There are so many 'What ifs?' that surround the New Towns programme, not least, what would have happened if we had continued the programme on a modest scale? One final question is what would have happened if the new towns had stuck more closely with the Garden City Principles? There may have been good reasons to play down the transformative ideals of Ebenezer Howard in a bid to normalise the idea of new towns in the 1930s. But while some were ashamed of the 'sandal-wearing vegetarians' in Letchworth, it turns out that future cities will be filled with just these kinds of people searching for better, more sociable and sustainable lives in era that will have to be defined by new ways of living within our very limited natural resources (Figure 14.2).

NOTES AND REFERENCES

INTRODUCTION

1. K. Henderson, K. Lock and H. Ellis, *The Art of Building a Garden City: Designing New Communities for the 21st Century*, RIBA Publishing, 2017.

CHAPTER 1

1. House of Commons Debates, 1946, vol. 422, col. 1091.

2. P. Hall and C. Ward, *Sociable Cities: The 21st-Century Reinvention of the Garden City*, 2nd Edition, Routledge, 2014, p. 2.

3. K. Henderson, K. Lock and H. Ellis, *The Art of Building a Garden City: Designing New Communities for the 21st Century*, RIBA Publishing, 2019.

4. P. Ackroyd, *The Life of Thomas More*, Vintage, London, 1998.

5. Formal definition adopted by the Garden Cities and Town Planning Association in 1919, and quoted by C.B. Purdom in C.B Purdom, W.R. Lethaby, G.L. Pepler, T.G. Chambers, R. Unwin and R.L. Reiss, *Town Theory and Practice*, Benn Brothers, 1921.

6. E. Howard, *To-morrow: A Peaceful Path to Real Reform*, Swann Sonnenschein & Co. Ltd., 1898.

7. G. Orwell, *The Road to Wigan Pier*, Victor Gollancz, 1937.

8. R. Unwin, *Nothing Gained by Overcrowding!*, P.S. King & Son, 1912.

9. F.J. Osborn, *New Towns after the War*, 2nd Edition, J.M. Dent & Sons Ltd., 1942, http://cashewnut.me.uk/WGCbooks/web-WGC-books-1942-1.php (accessed 30 April 2019).

10. Hall and Ward, *Sociable Cities*, p. 37.

11. Ibid, p. 39.

12. Ibid, p. 35.

13. C.B. Purdom, *The Building of Satellite Towns*, J.M. Dent & Sons, 1925.

14. *Report of the Royal Commission on the Distribution of the Industrial Population*, Barlow Report, Cmd 6378, HMSO, January 1940.

15. J.H. Forshaw and P. Abercrombie, *County of London Plan 1943*, Macmillan, 1943.

16. Once land has been given planning permission, its value increases, usually considerably (this increase in value is called 'betterment'). For instance, a hectare of agricultural land costing a few thousand pounds could subsequently be worth several million pounds if planning permission for development upon it were granted.

17. Town and Country Planning Association (TCPA), *New Towns and Garden Cities – Lessons for Tomorrow. Stage 2 Report: Lessons for Delivering a New Generation of Garden Cities*, TCPA, 2015, p. 56, https://www.tcpa.org.uk/research-gcnt (accessed 18 September 2019).

18. Myers v Milton Keynes Development Corporation, 1974, 2 All ER 1096. A legal ruling which meant that when land was valued for purchase by Milton Keynes Development Corporation, they could disregard the new town scheme, but had to account for other potential uses that might be permitted on the site. From this point on, valuation became even more complicated – and opportunities for land value capture decreased – as account had to be made for other potential uses.

19. Memorandum NT33, submitted by the Department for Transport, Local Government and the Regions to the House of Commons Transport, Local Government and the Regions Committee, within New Towns: Follow-Up, HC 889, Ninth Report of Session 2007–08, House of Commons Communities and Local Government Committee, TSO, 2008, http://www.publications.parliament.uk/pa/cm200102/cmselect/cmtlgr/603/603m38.htm (accessed 20 August 2019).

20. Figure provided by the Homes and Communities Agency, July 2015. Includes all land in the new towns, and not just land formerly in the ownership of the Commission for the New Towns.

21. D. Lyddon, New Towns in Scotland, undated paper, collected in the New Towns Record, a CD-ROM of information about new towns authorised and edited by Idox Information Services – see https://theknowledgeexchangeblog.com/2014/02/25/a-unique-insight-into-uk-new-towns (accessed 1 October 2019). See also 'Pathfinder pack on Scottish New Towns', Resources for Learning in Scotland, http://rls.org.uk/database/record.php?usi=000-000-001-504-L (accessed 2 October 2019).

22. Lewis Silkin MP, New Towns Bill debate, House of Commons Debates, 1946, vol. 422, col. 1090.

23. A. Alexander, *Britain's New Towns: Garden Cities to Sustainable Communities*, Routledge, 2009, p. 74.

24. A. Ravetz, *Council Housing and Culture: The History of a Social Experiment*, Routledge, 2001, p. 103.

25. David Lock Associates, *Forward into the Past: Garden Cities*, 2014, p. 22.

26. See Alexander, *Britain's New Towns*, for a more detailed analysis of the design characteristics and influences of the garden cities and new towns.

27. For more information see http://www.discovermiltonkeynes.co.uk/uploads/1/0/3/9/10393340/10h.pdf (accessed 18 September 2019).

28. Statistics from Census data cited within the New Towns Record. The 2011 Census records Basildon as having a population of 110,762, in 45,558 households, and Peterlee a population of 26,633, in 11,462 households – see Town and Country Planning Association (TCPA), *New Towns and Garden Cities – Lessons for Tomorrow. Stage 1 Report: An Introduction to the UK's New Towns and Garden Cities*, Appendix: The New Towns: Five-Minute Fact Sheets, TCPA, 2014, https://www.tcpa.org.uk/research-gcnt (accessed 18 September 2019).

CHAPTER 2

1. M. Strong, An Overview of New Towns in Northern Ireland, 1995, written for the New Towns Record, a CD-ROM of information about new towns authorised and edited by Idox Information Services – see https://theknowledgeexchangeblog.com/2014/02/25/a-unique-insight-into-uk-new-towns (accessed 1 October 2019).

2. Nathaniel Lichfield & Partners, *Start to Finish: How Quickly do Large-Scale Housing Sites Deliver?*, 2016, https://lichfields.uk/media/1728/start-to-finish.pdf, p. 3 (accessed 20 April 2019).

3. A. Alexander, *Britain's New Towns: Garden Cities to Sustainable Communities*, Routledge, 2009, p. 95.

4. Figures from the New Towns Record. Note that a summary table of delivery is currently being compiled.

5. Nathaniel Lichfield & Partners, *Start to Finish*, p. 3.

6. M. Clapson, 'Suburban paradox? Planners' intentions and residents' preferences in two new towns of the 1960s: Reston, Virginia, and Milton Keynes, England', *Planning Perspectives*, vol. 17, no. 2, 2002, pp. 145–62.

7. J. MacGuire, 'The elderly in a new town. A case study of Telford', *Housing Review*, vol. 26, no. 6, 1977, pp. 132–36.

8. Department for Communities and Local Government, *Transferable Lessons from the New Towns*, 2006, p. 41.

9   For example, see http://www.talkingnewtowns.org.uk and http://www.livingarchive.org.uk (both accessed 30 April 2019).

10 F. Schaffer, *The New Town Story*, Paladin, 1972, p. 123.

11 Alexander, *Britain's New Towns*, p. 137.

12 M. Aldridge, *The British New Towns: A Programme without a Policy*, Routledge and Kegan Paul, 1979, p. 85.

13 New Towns Act 1959, para. 2.

14 Quoted in *The Journal of the Town and Country Planning Association*, January 1967, and cited in Alexander, *Britain's New Towns*, p. 139.

15 Aldridge, *The British New Towns*, p. 90.

16 Alexander, *Britain's New Towns*, p. 140.

17 https://protect-eu.mimecast.com/s/QoqHCDkOnuZ2PPiWf4I_" https://api.parliament.uk/historic-hansard/commons/1980/mar/26/stevenage-development-authority-bill-by (accessed 20 September 2019).

18 Nene Park, *History and Heritage in Nene Park*, 2013, https://www.nenepark.org.uk/storage/History_and_Heritage_in_Nene_Park.pdf (accessed 30 April 2019).

19 Ibid.

20 Further information is available from The Parks Trust website, https://www.theparktrust.com/ (accessed 20 September 2019).

21 Further information is available from the Milton Keynes Community Foundation website, https://www.mkcommunityfoundation.co.uk/ (accessed 20 September 2019).

22 Memorandum by North Lanarkshire Council (NT 44) submitted to the Select Committee on Transport, Local Government and the Regions Inquiry on New Towns, The New Towns: Their Problems and Future, HC 603-I, Nineteenth Report of Session 2001–02, House of Commons Transport, Local Government and the Regions Committee, TSO, July 2002, Appendices to the Minutes of Evidence, https://publications.parliament.uk/pa/cm/cmtlgr.htm (accessed 1 October 2019).

23 Alexander, *Britain's New Towns*, p. 141.

CHAPTER 3

1   Town and Country Planning Association (TCPA), *New Towns and Garden Cities – Lessons for Tomorrow. Stage 1 Report: An Introduction to the UK's New Towns and Garden Cities*, TCPA, 2014, p. 20, https://www.tcpa.org.uk/research-gcnt (accessed 18 September 2019).

2   Office of the Deputy Prime Minister, *Sustainable Communities: Building for the Future*, 2003, https://webarchive.nationalarchives.gov.uk/20120919140956/http://www.communities.gov.uk/documents/communities/pdf/146289.pdf (accessed 25 April 2019).

3   Henry Cleary, who had responsibility for housing growth programmes at the Department for Communities and Local Government 2001–11, provides a useful overview of the lessons from the Growth Areas and Growth Points programmes in H. Cleary, 'Large-scale housing growth: Learning lessons from the last 15 years', *Town and Country Planning*, May 2015, pp. 222–26.

4   Economist Kate Barker authored two reviews for the government, the Barker Review of Housing Supply published its final report on 17 March 2004, presenting recommendations to the UK government for securing future housing needs. In December 2005, Barker was asked to conduct an independent Review of Land-Use Planning, and she reported on 5 December 2006.

5   H. Cleary, 'Garden Cities: What can we learn from eco-towns and growth points?', *Planning*, 10 February 2014.

6   Department for Communities and Local Government (DCLG), *Homes for the Future: More Affordable, More Sustainable*, 2007, http://webarchive.nationalarchives.gov.uk/20120919132719/www.communities.gov.uk/documents/housing/pdf/439986.pdf (accessed 25 April 2019).

7   Communities and Local Government, Planning Policy Statement, 'Eco-towns: A supplement to Planning Policy Statement 1', 2009.

8   For a transcription of the process see Communities and Local Government, 'Written Statements: Friday 24 January 2014', *Written Ministerial Statements*, 2014, http://www.publications.parliament.uk/pa/cm201301/cmhansrd/cm140124/wmstext/140124m0001.htm (accessed 25 April 2019).

9   Department for Communities and Local Government (DCLG), *Locally-led Garden Cities: Prospectus*, 2014, https://www.gov.uk/government/publications/locally-led-garden-cities-prospectus (accessed 25 April 2019).

10 Ibid.

11 Ibid, p. 1.

12 HM Treasury, *Budget 2016*, 2016, https://assets.publishing.service.gov.uk/government/uploads/system/uploads/attachment_data/file/508193/HMT_Budget_2016_Web_Accessible.pdf (accessed 25 April 2019).

13 Department for Communities and Local Government (DCLG), *Locally-led Garden Villages, Towns and Cities*, 2016, https://www.gov.uk/government/publications/locally-led-garden-villages-towns-and-cities (accessed 25 April 2019).

14 Ministry of Housing, Communities and Local Government (MHCLG), 'The New Towns Act 1981 (Local Authority Oversight) Regulations 2018', *UK Government*, 2018, http://www.legislation.gov.uk/ukdsi/2018/9780111169995/contents (accessed 25 April 2019).

15 Ibid.

CHAPTER 4

1   Town and Country Planning Association (TCPA), *New Towns and Garden Cities: Lessons for Tomorrow. Stage 2 Report: Lessons for Delivering a New Generation of Garden Cities*, TCPA, 2015, p. 2, https://www.tcpa.org.uk/Handlers/Download.ashx?IDMF=62a09e12-6a24-4de3-973f-f4062e561e0a (accessed 10 May 2019).

2   HM Government, Government's Response to the Transport, Local Government and the Regions Committee Report: The New Towns: Their Problems and Future, 2002, https://publications.parliament.uk/pa/cm200102/cmselect/cmtlgr/newtowns.pdf (accessed 24 September 2019). House of Commons Communities and Local Government Committee, New Towns: Follow-Up, 2008, (accessed 24 September 2019).

3   Town and Country Planning Association (TCPA), *TCPA New Towns Network*, TCPA, 2019, https://www.tcpa.org.uk/tcpa-new-towns-network (accessed 10 May 2019).

4   The TCPA's research explores what experience of delivering new communities from across the UK and beyond can teach us about delivering new garden cities today, see https://www.tcpa.org.uk/research-gcnt (accessed 5 October 2019).

5   Town and Country Planning Association (TCPA), *New Towns and Garden Cities – Lessons for Tomorrow. Stage 1 Report: An Introduction to the UK's New Towns and Garden Cities*, Appendix: The New Towns: Five-Minute Fact Sheets, TCPA, 2014, https://www.tcpa.org.uk/Handlers/Download.ashx?IDMF=19cba732-e704-4b33-9c3c-43edbcbeca03 (accessed 10 May 2019).

6   Town and Country Planning Association (TCPA), *New Towns and Garden Cities – Lessons for Tomorrow. Stage 1 Report: An Introduction to the UK's New Towns and Garden Cities*, TCPA, 2014, p. 25, https://www.tcpa.org.uk/lessons-for-tomorrow-stage-1-report (accessed 10 May 2019).

7   Ibid.

8   Ibid.

9   Ibid.

10 TCPA, *New Towns and Garden Cities – Lessons for Tomorrow. Stage 1 Report*, Appendix: The New Towns: Five-Minute Fact Sheets.

11 Housing, Communities and Local Government Committee, *High Streets and Town Centres in 2030*, House of Commons, 13 February 2019, https://publications.parliament.uk/pa/cm201719/cmselect/cmcomloc/1010/1010.pdf (accessed 10 May 2019).

12 https://www.hatfield2030.co.uk (accessed 5 October 2019).

13 https://www.gov.uk/government/news/homes-england-funds-first-homes-through-local-authority-accelerated-construction-programme (accessed 5 October 2019).

REFERENCES

14 J. Averill, 'Neighbourhood plan is "weakened" by intu Milton Keynes scheme say critics', *MK Citizen*, 29 July 2017, https://www.miltonkeynes.co.uk/news/neighbourhood-plan-is-weakened-by-intu-milton-keynes-scheme-say-critics-1-8078608 (accessed 10 May 2019).

15 The Town and Country Planning Association (TCPA), 'Stevenage – A journey to utopia', *The Journal of the Town and Country Planning Association*, December 2018, vol. 87, no. 12, p. 492.

16 Allies and Morrison Urban Practitioners, *Harlow Town Centre – Area Action Plan: Issues and Options Report*, June 2018, p. 130, http://www.harlow.gov.uk/sites/harlow-cms/files/files/documents/files/HTCAAP%20Issues%20and%20Options%20Report.pdf (accessed 10 May 2019).

17 T. Wall, 'Milton Keynes: UK capital of "right-to-buy-to-let"', *The Guardian*, 20 January 2018, https://www.theguardian.com/money/2018/jan/20/milton-keynes-uk-capital-of-right-to-buy-to-let (accessed 10 May 2019).

18 C. Reid, 'Build it and they will come? Why Britain's 1960s cycling revolution flopped', *The Guardian*, 19 September 2017, https://www.theguardian.com/cities/2017/sep/19/britains-1960s-cycling-revolution-flopped-stevenage (accessed 10 May 2019).

19 'Schools have fun up-cycling Stevenage's dark underpasses', *The Comet*, 15 October 2016, https://www.thecomet.net/news/schools-have-fun-up-cycling-stevenage-s-dark-underpasses-1-4736569 (accessed 10 May 2019).

20 TCPA, *New Towns and Garden Cities – Lessons for Tomorrow. Stage 1 Report*, p. 25.

21 D. Lock, 'Fleecehold – creeping forward on stewardship', *The Journal of the Town and Country Planning Association*, February 2019, vol. 88, no. 2.

22 Skemster, 'Skelmersdale: A New Town', 20 November 2015, http://picturenewtown.org (accessed 10 May 2019).

23 http://capturingcraigavon.com/about (accessed 24 September 2019).

24 Somerset House, *Out there: Our post-war public art*, Somerset House Trust, 2018, https://www.somersethouse.org.uk/whats-on/out-there (accessed 10 May 2019).

25 As part of Stage 1 of the research project *New Towns and Garden Cities – Lessons for Tomorrow*, the TCPA conducted surveys with the heads of planning in the local authorities where the new towns were located to gather their views on the legacy.

26 Debate with Lee Shostak, David Lock and John Walker at TCPA Conference on 'A New Future for New Towns', London, March 2019.

27 The MK Futures 2050 Commission was set up in September 2015 as a way of thinking about the future of Milton Keynes, helping to create a long-term vision for the way MK should grow and prosper over the coming decades, see https://www.mkfutures2050.com (accessed 5 October 2019).

CHAPTER 5

1 'Figure for the tightly defined Harlow District area' in Town and Country Planning Association (TCPA), *New Towns and Garden Cities – Lessons for Tomorrow. Stage 1 Report: An Introduction to the UK's New Towns and Garden Cities*, Appendix: The New Towns: Five-Minute Fact Sheets, TCPA, 2014, https://www.tcpa.org.uk/research-gcnt (accessed 18 September 2019).

2 Harlow Local Development Plan Pre-Submission Version – May 2018, available at https://www.harlow.gov.uk/local-development-plan-examination-submission-documents (accessed 27 February 2019).

3 F. Gibberd, B.H. Harvey, L. White et al, *Harlow: The Story of a New Town*, Publications for Companies, 1980, p. 10.

4 Allies and Morrison Urban Practitioners, *Harlow Town Centre Area Action Plan: Issues and Options Report*, final consultation, June 2018, p. 8, https://www.harlow.gov.uk/aap (accessed 27 February 2019).

5 Other examples of high-rise in Harlow can be found at: https://municipaldreams.tumblr.com/post/146934255434/high-rise-in-harlow-new-town-for-more-on-the-new (accessed 7 October 2019).

6 Department of Planning Oxford Brookes University for Department for Communities and Local Government: London (July 2006) Transferable Lessons from the new Towns, page 38. https://www.westminster.ac.uk/sites/default/public-files/general-documents/Transferable-Lessons-from-the-New-Towns.pdf

7 Harlow Local Development Plan Pre-Submission Version – May 2018.

8 Allies and Morrison Urban Practitioners, *Harlow Town Centre Area Action Plan: Issues and Options Report*.

9 'Guidance – PHE Harlow', updated 10 January 2018, available at https://www.gov.uk/government/publications/phe-harlow-science-hub-proposals/phe-harlow-science-hub-proposals (accessed 24 September 2019).

10 https://www.harlow.gov.uk/housing-investment-programme (accessed 7 October 2019).

11 Harlow Council, sculpture collection, (accessed 27 February 2019).

12 Sir Frederick Gibberd's description of Harlow, 1950, quoted in Harlow Local Development Plan: Pre-Submission Publication, May 2018, p. 2, https://moderngov.harlow.gov.uk/documents/s12412/Appendix%20A%20-%20Local%20Development%20Plan.pdf (accessed 7 October 2019).

CHAPTER 6

1 Totals for the following wards: Peterlee East, Peterlee West, Horden, Wingate, Shotton.

2 County Durham Plan available at https://www.durham.gov.uk/cdp (accessed 24 September 2019).

3 C.W. Clarke, *Farewell Squalor: A Design for a New Town and Proposals for the Re-Development of the Easington Rural District*, 1946.

4 G. Philipson, *Aycliffe and Peterlee: New Towns 1946–1988*, Publications for Companies, 1988, http://balticplus.uk/aycliffe-and-peterlee-new-towns-1946-1988-c18252 (accessed 7 October 2019).

5 Ibid, p. 101.

6 Ibid, p. 117.

7 Ibid, p. 119.

8 http://www.apollopavilion.info/history/apollo-pavilion/restoration (accessed 24 September 2019).

9 https://www.castledeneshoppingcentre.co.uk/news/protect-peterlee-town-centre-save-our-stores (accessed 24 September 2019).

10 2011 Census totals for Peterlee East ward, Peterlee West ward, Horden ward, Wingate ward, Shotton ward.

11 G. Banks, 'Drug use in Peterlee woods prompts police and council crackdown', *The Northern Echo*, 9 February 2018, (accessed 24 September 2019).

12 The programme of current and past projects can be viewed at: https://www.eastdurhamtrust.org.uk/projects.html (accessed 24 September 2019).

CHAPTER 7

1 Office for National Statistics, *Table KS101EW: Usual resident population*, 2011 Census, 2011, data retrieved from https://www.nomisweb.co.uk/census/2011/ks101ew (accessed 10 May 2019). (The total population figure for Cwmbran comprising the following wards: Upper Cwmbran, Pontnewydd, Croesyceiliog North, Croesyceiliog South, Fairwater, St Dials, Llanyrafon North, Llanyrafon South, Llantarnam, Greenmeadow, Coed Eva, Two Locks.)

2 Torfaen County Borough Council, *Local Development Plan (to 2021) Written Statement*, 2013, https://www.torfaen.gov.uk/en/Related-Documents/Forward-Planning/Adopted-Torfaen-LDP-Writen-Statement.pdf (accessed 10 May 2019).

3 Torfaen County Borough Council, *Replacement Torfaen Local Development Plan*, 2019, https://www.torfaen.gov.uk/en/PlanningAndDevelopment/Planningpolicy/Local-Development-Plan-Review/Replacement-Torfaen-Local-Development-Plan.aspx (accessed 10 May 2019).

4   F.J. Osborn and A. Whittick, *The New Towns: The Answer to Megalopolis*, Leonard Hill, 1969, p. 345.

5   Ibid, p. 346.

6   T. Alwyn Lloyd and H. Jackson, for the Minister of Town and Country Planning, *South Wales Outline Plan for the South Wales and Monmouthshire Development Area (excluding the Borough of Pembroke)*, HMSO, 1949 (commissioned in 1946 by the Ministry of Town and Country Planning).

7   Draft Cwmbran New Town (Designation) Order, 1949, Explanatory Memorandum, HLG 91/577 14605, New Towns Act, 1946. In the New Towns Record, a CD-ROM of information about new towns authorised and edited by Idox Information Services – *see* https://theknowledgeexchangeblog.com/2014/02/25/a-unique-insight-into-uk-new-towns (accessed 1 October 2019).

8   Cwmbran New Town Designation Order – Brief for Opening Statement by Minister's Representatives, Draft Cwmbran New Town (Designation) Order, 1949, Explanatory Memorandum, HLG 91/577 14605, New Towns Act, 1946. In the New Towns Record.

9   RTPI, *History of Planning in Wales*, 2014, p. 8, http://www.rtpi.org.uk/media/1238497/wales_centenary_history_project.pdf (accessed 7 October 2019).

10 Osborn and Whittick, *The New Towns: The Answer to Megalopolis*, p. 348.

11 P. Riden, *Rebuilding a Valley: A History of Cwmbran Development Corporation*, Cwmbran Development Corporation, 1988, p. 135.

12 Ibid, p. 131.

13 Ibid, p. 131.

14 Osborn and Whittick, *The New Towns: The Answer to Megalopolis*, p. 349.

15 Ibid.

16 https://www.southwalesargus.co.uk/news/16156200.cwmbran-centres-monmouth-square-set-for-revamp-to-change-weary-and-dated-appearance and http://vitalize.org.uk/exclusive-check-out-these-redevelopment-plans-for-cwmbran (both accessed 24 September 2019).

17 Torfaen County Borough Council, *Cwmbran Regeneration*, 2019, https://www.torfaen.gov.uk/en/PlanningAndDevelopment/Regeneration/Cwmbran-Regeneration/Cwmbran-Regeneration.aspx (accessed 10 May 2019).

18 The Town and Country Planning Association (TCPA), 'Cwmbran – The valley new town at 70', *The Journal of the Town and Country Planning Association*, December 2018, vol. 87, no. 12, p. 498.

CHAPTER 8

1   Town and Country Planning Association (TCPA), *New Towns and Garden Cities – Lessons for Tomorrow. Stage 1 Report:* Appendix: The New Towns: Five-Minute Fact Sheets, TCPA, 2014, p. 18, https://www.tcpa.org.uk/Handlers/Download.ashx?IDMF=19cba732-e704-4b33-9c3c-43edbcbeca03 (accessed 10 May 2019).

2   Glasgow and the Clyde Valley Strategic Development Planning Authority, *Welcome to Clydeplan*, 2019, https://www.clydeplan-sdpa.gov.uk (accessed 10 May 2019).

3   D. Lyddon, 'Cumbernauld: Underlying principles of housing', 1994, updated with assistance from North Lanarkshire Council, 1997. In the New Towns Record, a CD-ROM of information about new towns authorised and edited by Idox Information Services – *see* https://theknowledgeexchangeblog.com/2014/02/25/a-unique-insight-into-uk-new-towns (accessed 1 October 2019).

4   D. Lyddon, 'Cumbernauld town overview', 1994, updated with assistance from North Lanarkshire Council, 1997. In the New Towns Record.

5   Ibid.

6   J.R. Gold, 'The making of a megastructure: Architectural modernism, town planning and Cumbernauld's central area, 1955–75', *Planning Perspectives*, 21, pp. 109–31, 2006, https://www.academia.edu/2184522/The_making_of_a_megastructure_architectural_modernism_town_planning_and_Cumbernauld_s_central_area_1955-75 (accessed 7 October 2019).

7   Ibid.

8   D. Cowling, *An Essay for Today: Scottish New Towns 1947–1997*, Rutland Press, 1997, p. 53.

9   Ibid.

10 Ibid, p. 54.

11 Ibid, p. 55.

12 Ibid.

13 Ibid.

14 New Towns Record, Cumbernauld Master Plan 1962, Prologue, Summary.

15 New Towns Record, Cumbernauld Master Plan 1962, p. 17. Form of Town.

16 D. Cowling, *An Essay for Today*, p. 56.

17 A. Alexander, *Britain's New Towns: Garden Cities to Sustainable Communities*, Routledge, p. 113.

18 C. Buchanan, *Traffic in Towns*, Ministry of Transport, Penguin Books, 1964.

19 J.R. Gold, 'The making of a megastructure'.

20 BBC, 'Cumbernauld voted best town after double "plook" shame', *BBC*, 25 May 2012, https://www.bbc.co.uk/news/uk-scotland-glasgow-west-18200899 (accessed 10 May 2019).

21 As noted at the Town and Country Planning Association (TCPA) Roundtable on Lessons from Cumbernauld New Town, held in Cumbernauld on 10 July 2015.

22 Memorandum by North Lanarkshire Council (NT 44) submitted to the Select Committee on Transport, Local Government and the Regions Inquiry on New Towns, The New Towns: Their Problems and Future, HC 603-I, Nineteenth Report of Session 2001–02, House of Commons Transport, Local Government and the Regions Committee, TSO, July 2002, Appendices to the Minutes of Evidence, https://publications.parliament.uk/pa/cm/cmtlgr.htm (accessed 1 October 2019).

23 http://news.bbc.co.uk/1/hi/scotland/4519084.stm (accessed 26 September 2019).

24 North Lanarkshire Council, *Cumbernauld Town Centre Action Plan Framework*, 9 December 2015, https://www.northlanarkshire.gov.uk/CHttpHandler.ashx?id=18391&p=0 (accessed 10 May 2019).

25 ENGIE, *Cumbernauld poised for £11.7m investment*, 2019, https://www.engie.co.uk/about-engie/news/cumbernauld-poised-for-11-7m-investment (accessed 10 May 2019).

26 Further details are available from the Cumbernauld Living Landscape webpages, at http://cumbernauldlivinglandscape.org.uk (accessed 26 September 2019).

CHAPTER 9

1   Totals for the following wards: Ashurst, Birch Green, Tanhouse, Moorside, Digmoor, Skelmersdale South, Skelmersdale North, Up Holland.

2   West Lancashire Borough Council, *Spatial Evidence Papers: Skelmersdale*, 2011, https://www.westlancs.gov.uk/media/94839/LDF_SP_Skelmersdale.pdf (accessed 27 February 2019).

3   F. Osborn and A. Whittick, *New Towns: Their Origins, Achievements and Progress*, 3rd edition, Leonard Hill, 1977, p. 294.

4   Ibid, p. 296.

5   Ibid.

6   C. Dunn, '*Is Skelmersdale one of the most overlooked towns in the North West*', Liverpool Echo, 31 December 2017, (accessed 27 February 2019).

7   https://wellnorthenterprises.co.uk/stories/creating-a-bright-future-together (accessed 7 October 2019).

8   Well Skelmersdale, '*Welcome to the official Well Skelmersdale blog*', 2019, (accessed 27 February 2019).

9   Rosie Cooper MP, in A. Brown, 'Skelmersdale "failed by a lack of foresight" says town's MP, *Southport Visiter*, 21 July 2017, (accessed 27 February 2019). See also https://hansard.

parliament.uk/Commons/2017-07-12/debates/17071239000001/NewTowns (accessed 26 September 2019).

10   West Lancashire Borough Council, *The Local Plan 2012–2027: Chapter 2 – Spatial Portrait.*

11   Supporting evidence from West Lancashire Local Plan Review: Preferred Options Evidence Base.

12   Rosie Cooper MP, in Brown, 'Skelmersdale "failed by a lack of foresight" says town's MP'. *See also* https://hansard.parliament.uk/Commons/2017-07-12/debates/17071239000001/NewTowns (accessed 26 September 2019).

13   West Lancashire Borough Council, *The Local Plan 2012–2027: Chapter 2 – Spatial Portrait*, p. 11.

14   West Lancashire Borough Council, *West Lancashire Local Plan Review: Preferred Options*, 2018, pp. 39–42, (accessed 27 February 2019).

15   West Lancashire Borough Council, *The Local Plan 2012–2027: Chapter 2 – Spatial Portrait*, p .7.

16   The Tawd Valley Park Project, https://www.westlancs.gov.uk/leisure-recreation/parks-and-countryside/parks-and-countryside-sites/tawd-valley-park-skelmersdale/tawd-valley-park-project.aspx (accessed 26 September 2019).

17   https://www.lancashire.gov.uk/media/313320/DRAFT-West-Lancashire-Masterplan-FINAL.pdf (accessed 26 September 2019).

18   Notes from conversation with local community representatives from West Lancashire Council for Voluntary Services.

CHAPTER 10

1   *The Planning Service*, Craigavon Area Plan (CAP) 2010, 2004, https://www.planningni.gov.uk/index/policy/development_plans/devplans_az/craigavon2010-adopted-plan.pdf (accessed 10 May 2019).

2   Armagh City, Banbridge and Craigavon Borough Council, *Preferred Options Paper (POP)*, 2018, https://www.armaghbanbridgecraigavon.gov.uk/resident/local-development-plan-residents/#1522162519976-f43e6047-05a2 (accessed 10 May 2019).

3   Town and Country Planning Association (TCPA), *New Towns and Garden Cities – Lessons for Tomorrow. Stage 1 Report: An Introduction to the UK's New Towns and Garden Cities*, TCPA, 2014, p. 9, https://www.tcpa.org.uk/lessons-for-tomorrow-stage-1-report (accessed 10 May 2019).

4   House of Commons debate, 17 April 1978, Hansard, vol. 948, para. 216, http://hansard.millbanksystems.com/commons/1978/apr/17/craigavon#S5CV0948P0_19780417_HOC_390 (accessed 10 May 2019).

5   M. Strong, 'An overview of New Towns in Northern Ireland', 1995. In the New Towns Record, a CD-ROM of information about new towns authorised and edited by Idox Information Services – see https://theknowledgeexchangeblog.com/2014/02/25/a-unique-insight-into-uk-new-towns (accessed 1 October 2019).

6   House of Commons debate, 17 April 1978, Hansard, vol. 948, para. 217, http://hansard.millbanksystems.com/commons/1978/apr/17/craigavon#S5CV0948P0_19780417_HOC_390 (accessed 10 May 2019).

7   New Towns Record, Craigavon Master Plan 1967, The Concept of the City, The Rural City.

8   Ibid.

9   New Towns Record, Craigavon Master Plan 1967, The Concept of the City, 2. Accessibility.

10   New Towns Record, Craigavon Master Plan 1967, The Concept of the City, The Rural City.

11   Craigavon (and separately Lurgan) were identified as two of the most desirable postcodes in the UK in March 2015: 'Royal Mail said the study, conducted by the Centre for Economic and Business Research, looked at green spaces, affordable housing and commuting times' – see http://www.bbc.co.uk/news/uk-32016713 (accessed 10 May 2019).

12   Paul Hogarth Company, with Gareth Hoskins Architects, *Living Places: An Urban Stewardship and Design Guide for Northern Ireland*, CUi & WYG, for Department of the Environment Northern Ireland, 2014, http://www.planningni.gov.uk/index/policy/supplementary_guidance/guides/livingplaces_-_web.pdf (accessed 10 May 2019).

13   *Capturing Craigavon*, 2019, http://capturingcraigavon.com (accessed 10 May 2019).

14   Tribal, *Central Craigavon Masterplan Report*, January 2010, p. 10, https://www.communities-ni.gov.uk/sites/default/files/publications/dsd/rdo-craigavon-masterplan.PDF (accessed 10 May 2019).

CHAPTER 11

1   Totals for the following 'urban' wards: Bletchley and Fenny Stratford, Bradwell, Campbell Park, Denbigh, Eaton Manor, Emerson Valley, Furzton, Linford North, Linford South, Loughton Park, Middleton, Stantonbury, Stony Stratford, Walton Park, Whaddon, Wolverton, Woughton.

2   Milton Keynes Council, *Plan:MK Examination*, 2019, https://www.milton-keynes.gov.uk/planning-and-building/planning-policy/plan-mk-examination (accessed 10 May 2019). https://www.milton-keynes.gov.uk/planning-and-building/plan-mk (accessed 9 October 2019).

3   For example, Milton Keynes was home to the world's first solar house in 1972, and to the first UK door-to-door recycling scheme, from 1989.

4   T. Bendixson and J. Platt, *Milton Keynes: Image and Reality*, Granta, 1992, pp. 265–66.

5   L. Shostak and D. Crewe, '*Here comes Maggie!*', Essay for Milton Keynes Development Corporation. Cited in Bendixson and Platt, *Milton Keynes: Image and Reality*, p. 109.

6   Milton Keynes Council, *Plan:MK Sustainability Appraisal Scoping Report*, 2014, p. 13, https://www.milton-keynes.gov.uk/planning-and-building/planning-policy/evidence-base-documents (accessed 9 October 2019).

7   Milton Keynes Development Partnership LLP (MKDP) was established by Milton Keynes Council to hold undeveloped land that was formerly owned by MK Development Corporation. It promotes that land for development, along with other land owned by MK Council with commercial value: https://protect-eu.mimecast.com/s/HjQECNkrAupKkAi48eT3" https://www.mkdp.org.uk/about-us/

8   Milton Keynes Council, '*About the Commission*', Milton Keynes Futures 2050, 2019, https://www.mkfutures2050.com/about (accessed 10 May 2019).

9   https://www.cranfield.ac.uk/about/mku (accessed 9 October 2019).

10   CMK Town Council, *The CMK Business Neighbourhood Plan*, 2014, http://cmktowncouncil.gov.uk/referendum-on-cmk-business-neighbourhood-plan/#toggle-id-1 (accessed 10 May 2019).

11   https://www.milton-keynes.gov.uk/planning-and-building/planning-policy/cmk-alliance-business-neighbourhood-plan (accessed 7 October 2019).

12   Historic England, '*Shopping Building*', 2019, https://historicengland.org.uk/listing/the-list/list-entry/1393882 (accessed 10 May 2019).

13   M. Kennedy, 'Milton Keynes shopping centre becomes Grade II listed', *The Guardian*, 16 July 2010, https://www.theguardian.com/artanddesign/2010/jul/16/milton-keynes-shopping-centre-grade-listed (accessed 10 May 2019).

14   Document MK/HOU/007 at: https://www.milton-keynes.gov.uk/planning-and-building/planning-policy/plan-mk-evidence-base (accessed 7 October 2019).

15   National Infrastructure Commission (NIC), *Partnering for Prosperity: A New Deal for the Cambridge–Milton Keynes–Oxford Arc*, 17 November 2017, https://www.nic.org.uk/publications/partnering-prosperity-new-deal-cambridge-milton-keynes-oxford-arc (accessed 10 May 2019).

16. Further information is available from the Parks Trust website, https://www.theparkstrust.com/our-work (accessed 7 October 2019).

17. Further information is available from the Milton Keynes Community Foundation website, (accessed 10 May 2019).

18. D. Lock, 'Fleecehold – Creeping forward on stewardship', *The Journal of the Town and Country Planning Association*, February 2019, vol. 88, no. 2, p. 48.

19. Milton Keynes Council, Plan:MK, adopted March 2019, section 8.17, p. 126, https://www.milton-keynes.gov.uk/planning-and-building/planning-policy/dpd-s-and-spds-spgs (accessed 7 October 2019).

20. Milton Keynes Council, for the National Infrastructure Commission, 'Strategy for First Last Mile Travel', 17 November 2017, https://www.nic.org.uk/publications/milton-keynes-first-last-mile-strategy-report (accessed 9 October 2019).

CHAPTER 12

1. Submitted by the Department for Transport, Local Government and the Regions to the House of Commons Transport, Local Government and the Regions Committee, within New Towns: Follow-Up, HC 889, Ninth Report of Session 2007–08, House of Commons Communities and Local Government Committee, TSO, 2008, http://www.publications.parliament.uk/pa/cm200102/cmselect/cmtlgr/603/603m38.htm (accessed 26 February 2019).

2. Figure from Homes and Communities Agency, July 2015. Includes all land in the new towns, not just former Commission for the New Towns land.

3. Figures provided to the Town and Country Planning Association by the Homes and Communities Agency (predecessor to Homes England), 2015.

4. When Milton Keynes Council bought land in the city from the Homes and Communities Agency (and subsequently the MK Development Partnership) some areas were already 'commercially advanced' and so not made available for the council to purchase.

5. Figure for town centre only; figure from Homes and Communities Agency Herts & Bucks Team, August 2015.

6. Betterment is an increase in land value created not by the actions of the landowner but by the actions of a public authority in granting consent for new development and/or providing new infrastructure.

7. 'Hope value' is value over and above any value created by any existing planning permission: it is the value that may be created by the hope of future development. The Myers case (Myers v Milton Keynes Development Corporation, 1974, 2 All ER 1096) over compulsory purchase in Milton Keynes illustrates the complexity.

8. Town and Country Planning Association (TCPA), *New Towns and Garden Cities – Lessons for Tomorrow. Stage 1 Report: An Introduction to the UK's New Towns and Garden Cities*, TCPA, 2014, p. 19,(accessed 16 February 2019).

9. R. Thomas, *The Economics of the New Towns Programme*, 1996, accessed from the New Towns Record, a CD-ROM of information about new towns authorised and edited by Idox Information Services – see https://theknowledgeexchangeblog.com/2014/02/25/a-unique-insight-into-uk-new-towns (accessed 1 October 2019).

10. For more on the MK Parks Trust see TCPA Stewardship Guide, https://www.tcpa.org.uk/built-today-treasured-tomorrow2014 (accessed 4 October 2019) and https://www.theparkstrust.com/our-work/about-us/the-parks-trust-model (accessed 1 May 2019).

11. Town and Country Planning Association (TCPA), *New Towns and Garden Cities – Lessons for Tomorrow. Stage 1 Report: An Introduction to the UK's New Towns and Garden Cities*. Appendix: The New Towns: Five-Minute Fact Sheets, TCPA, 2014, p. 4, https://www.tcpa.org.uk/Handlers/Download.ashx?IDMF=19cba732-e704-4b33-9c3c-43edbcbeca03 (accessed: 26 February 2019).

CHAPTER 13

1. Figure provided by the Homes and Communities Agency, July 2015. Includes all land in the new towns, and not just land formerly in the ownership of the Commission for the New Towns. In Town and Country Planning Association (TCPA), *New Towns and Garden Cities – Lessons for Tomorrow. Stage 2 Report: Lessons for Delivering a New Generation of Garden Cities*, TCPA, 2015, p. 20, https://www.tcpa.org.uk/Handlers/Download.ashx?IDMF=62a09e12-6a24-4de3-973f-f4062e561e0a (accessed 27 September 2019).

2. Milton Keynes Council, 'Home: Milton Keynes Futures 2050', 2019, http://www.mkfutures2050.com, (accessed 25 April 2019).

3. Ministry of Housing, Communities and Local Government (MHCLG) and Rt Hon Sajid Javid MP, 'New Towns: launch of the All-Party Parliamentary Group', *UK Government*, 2018, https://www.gov.uk/government/speeches/new-towns-launch-of-the-all-party-parliamentary-group (accessed 25 April 2019).

4. HM Treasury, '*Helping the Cambridge, Milton Keynes and Oxford corridor reach its potential*', 2017, https://assets.publishing.service.gov.uk/government/uploads/system/uploads/attachment_data/file/661401/Helping_the_Cambridge_Milton_Keynes_Oxford_corridor_reach_its_potential_digicomms.pdf (accessed 7 May 2019).

5. Ministry of Housing, Communities and Local Government (MHCLG) and Kit Malthouse MP, '£3.75 million to fund 5 new garden towns across the country', 25 March 2019, https://www.gov.uk/government/news/37-million-to-fund-5-new-garden-towns-across-the-country (accessed 26 April 2019).

6. 'Special Report: The 100 Biggest Planning Permissions', *Planning Resource*, 23 May 2014, http://offlinehbpl.hbpl.co.uk/NewsAttachments/RLP/Housingtables2.pdf (accessed 7 May 2019).

7. Town and Country Planning Association (TCPA), *Planning 2020 – Final Report of the Raynsford Review of Planning in England*, 2018, https://www.tcpa.org.uk/Handlers/Download.ashx?IDMF=30864427-d8dc-4b0b-88ed-c6e0f08c0edd (accessed 7 May 2019).

8. Policy Exchange, 'Wolfson Economics Prize 2014', 2014, https://policyexchange.org.uk/wolfson-economics-prize-2014 (accessed 25 April 2019).

9. P. Inman, 'Legal & General wants to create five new towns in UK in next 10 years', *The Guardian*, 19 January 2014, http://www.theguardian.com/business/2014/jan/19/legal-and-general-build-new-towns (accessed 25 April 2019).

CHAPTER 14

1. https://www.watfordobserver.co.uk/news/17776352.tiny-flats-no-windows-get-green-light-watford-appeal (accessed 27 September 2019).

2. Town and Country Planning Association (TCPA), *Planning 2020 – Final Report of the Raynsford Review of Planning in England*, 2018, https://www.tcpa.org.uk/Handlers/Download.ashx?IDMF=30864427-d8dc-4b0b-88ed-c6e0f08c0edd (accessed 7 May 2019).

INDEX

Abercrombie, Patrick 9, 15, 17, 22, 28, 104
accessibility 71–72
Addison Act (1919) 8
Alconbury Weald 48
All-Party Parliamentary Group (APPG) on New Towns 61, 158–159, *160*
Antrim 28, 62
Apollo Pavilion, Peterlee 91, *91, 94*
Arts and Crafts movement 6, 16
asset transfer and disposal 35–37, 38–44, *39,* 64, 70, 152–153
Aycliffe 27

Ballymena 28, 62
Barker, Kate 49
Barlow Commission 9, 33
Basildon *21,* 25, *60,* 63, *67,* 68, 70, 76, *77*
betterment 6, 11, 12, 151
Bicester 162
Blair, Tony 48–51
Bracknell 63
build quality 69–71
built heritage *see* design and built heritage

Cambourne 48
Cambridge–Milton Keynes–Oxford Arc 133, 137, *146,* 157, *158,* 160, 162
Cameron, David 52
cars 18, 22, 64, 72
Castle Dene Park, Peterlee 94, *94*
Central Lancashire 28
Churchill, Winston 35
Clarke, C.W. 88
Clyde Valley Regional Plan (1946) 15, 22, 28, 104
Commission for the New Towns (CNT) 35, 36–37, *36,* 41, 44, 77
community development 26, *26,* 31, *31, 32,* 154
community stewardship bodies 6, 34, 35, 73, 152–153, *152*
construction speed 29
Copcutt, Geoffrey 107–108, *108*
Corby 27, 62
Cowling, David 105
Craigavon 28, 62, 72, 121–128, *123, 146,* 155
 employment and industry 63, 124
 green infrastructure and public realm 128, *128*
 heritage assets 75, 126, *126*
 housing 127–128, *127, 128*
 master plan 123–125, *124, 125*
 town centre 126–127, *127*
Crawley *26,* 36, 63
Crossman, Richard 130
cultural regeneration 67
Cumbernauld 27, 28, 62, *73,* 103–112, *105, 146*
 community development 108–109
 governance and stewardship 112
 green infrastructure and public realm 111–112
 housing 20, *106,* 111, *111, 112*
 master plan *105,* 106–109
 town centre 69, 107–108, *107, 108, 109, 110*
Cwmbran 27, 64, 95–102, *97*
 employment and industry 33, 48

governance and stewardship 101–102
 green infrastructure and public realm 100–101, *101*
 heritage assets 100, *100*
 housing 70, 99, 101, *102*
 master plan 97–99, *98*
 town centre 100, *100*

delivery of new towns 27–33, *28*
deprivation statistics 62
deregulation 52, 70, 164
 permitted development rights 52, 68, 70, *71,* 86, *86,* 135, 164
Derry–Londonderry 28–29, 62, 63
design and built heritage 66, 69, 74–75
 Craigavon 75, 126, *126*
 Cwmbran 100, *100*
 Harlow 66, *67,* 69, 81, 85
 Milton Keynes 69, 134, 135
 Peterlee 91, *91,* 94, *94*
design of new towns 16–26
Designation Orders 12, 29, 154
designation process 29, 154, 166
Development Corporations 11, 12–13, 147–149, 153
 asset transfer and disposal 35–37, 38–44, *39,* 70, 152–153
 autonomy and life span of 33, 34–35
 community development 26, 31, *31, 32,* 154
 financing 14–15
 future of 166, 168
 'locally led' 54–55
 public engagement 32, 155
 in Scotland 41
 social housing 25, 30–31, 41
 winding up of 19, 38–44, *39*
Dudley Report (1944) 17

East Kilbride 27, 28, 62
Ebbsfleet 53, 162, *163*
eco-towns programme 49, 50, *50,* 51
employment and industry 4, 9, 13, 20, 25, 33, 48, 62–63, 76–77
 Craigavon 63, 124
 Cwmbran 33, 48
 Harlow 77, 82, 83
 Milton Keynes 48, 63, *78*
 Peterlee 48, 63, 92, 93
 Skelmersdale 33, 48, 115, *116*

financing
 garden cities 6, 34
 new towns 14–15, 37, 149–151, 167–168
future growth 75–76
future of new towns 157–168

garden cities 4–7, *5,* 8, *9,* 16, 34
 financial and governance model 6, 34, 152–153
 green belt 22
 Letchworth 5, *6, 7,* 28, 34, 152–153
 locally-led garden communities 52–54, *53, 54,* 162
 Welwyn Garden City 8, *28*
Garden Cities Association 5, 7, 9
Gibberd, Frederick 80, 86
Glasgow Eastern Area Renewal (GEAR) 37
Glenrothes 27, 28, 62, 63
Greater London Plan (1944) 9, *9,* 17, 22, 28
green belt 9, 12, 22
green infrastructure and public realm 19, 22,

23, 39–41, 73
 Craigavon 128, *128*
 Cumbernauld 111–112
 Cwmbran 100–101, *101*
 Harlow *23,* 80–81
 Milton Keynes 40–41, *40,* 73, *74,* 137, *138*
 Peterlee 73, 93, *94*
 Skelmersdale *115,* 118
Grenfell-Baines, George 89
Grierson, John 154
Growth Areas programme 48, 49, *49*
Growth Points programme 49, *49*

Harlow 79–86, 149
 community development *32*
 employment and industry 77, 82, 83
 future growth 76, 82–83, 84, 85
 green infrastructure and public realm *23,* 80–81
 heritage assets 66, *67,* 69, 81, 85
 housing 20, *30,* 68, 69, *82,* 83–85, *85*
 master plan 80–81, *81*
 movement and transport *20,* 72
 permitted development rights 68, *71,* 86, *86*
 sculpture 74, *75, 76,* 81, *82,* 85, *86*
 town centre *20,* 83, *84*
Hatfield 36, 63, 65
Hemel Hempstead 36, 63, 66, *67,* 76, 77
heritage assets *see* design and built heritage
Homes England *42–43,* 44, 65, 150, 159, 162
housing
 build quality 69–71
 Craigavon 127–128, *127, 128*
 Cumbernauld 20, *106,* 111, *111, 112*
 Cwmbran 70, 99, 101, *102*
 estate renewal 68–71
 Harlow 20, *30,* 68, 69, *82,* 83–85, *85*
 low-density 20
 Milton Keynes 31, 69, *69,* 70, *70,* 71, *71,* 135–137, *136*
 Peterlee 25, 69, 93, *145*
 Skelmersdale 118, *120*
 social 25, 30–31, *30,* 41, 44, 62, 170
 statistics 62
 tenure mix 30–31
Housing Market Renewal Initiative 48
Howard, Ebenezer 4–7, 8, 21, 22, 34, *34*

industry *see* employment and industry
infrastructure *see* green infrastructure and public realm; movement and transport
inner-city regeneration 37, 48
innovation and experimentation 6, 22, *23,* 24–25, 144–146
interest rates 15, 37
Irvine 28, 62, 63

Javid, Sajid 160–161, *160*
Jellicoe, Sir Geoffrey 66, *67*

land ownership 64–65, 150
Le Corbusier *16,* 107
Letchworth Garden City 5, *6, 7,* 28, 34, 152–153
Livingston 28, 62
localism 52–55, 162
locally-led garden communities 52–54, *53, 54,* 162
Location of Industry Act (1946) 33

179

Longstanton-Oakington 48
low-density living 20
Lubetkin, Berthold 88, 89, *89*, 90

Macfarlane, Peter 97
Macmillan, Harold 35, *36*, 146
master plans 18–19, *19*
    Craigavon 123–125, *124*, *125*
    Cumbernauld *105*, 106–109
    Cwmbran 97–99, *98*
    Harlow 80–81, *81*
    Milton Keynes 32, 130–132, *131*
    Peterlee 88, 89, *89*
    Skelmersdale 114–115, *115*
Matthew, Robert 15
Matthew Report (1963) 28, 122
Milton Keynes *24–25*, 28, *29*, *31*, *37*, *39*, *60*, 64, 129–139, 146, 151, 155
    Business Neighbourhood Plan 65
    city centre 65, *131*, 134–135, *134*
    Community Foundation 41, 137, 153
    cultural facilities 67, *68*, 135, *135*
    delivery 132–133, *132*
    employment and industry 48, 63, *78*
    future growth 76, 133, 137
    green infrastructure and public realm 40–41, *40*, 73, *74*, 137, *138*
    heritage assets 69, 134, 135
    housing 31, 69, *69*, 70, *70*, 71, *71*, 135–137, *136*
    master plan 32, 130–132, *131*
    movement and transport 71, 72, 138
    Parks Trust 40–41, *40*, 73, *74*, 137, 153
Milton Keynes Futures 2050 Commission 133–134, 159
Minoprio, Anthony 97
Modernism 16–17, *16*, *17*, 144
More, Thomas 4
movement and transport 64, 71–72
    accessibility 71–72
    cars 18, 22, 64, 72
    ease of movement 22, *22*, 71–72
    pedestrianised town centres 21, *21*, 64
    underpasses 22, 64, 72, *73*
    walkable neighbourhoods 17, *17*, 19, 20, *20*

national urban policy 45–55
    Blair administration 48–51
    existing new towns 47–48, 158–161
    future of new towns 157–168
    post-2010 locally led approach 52–55, 162
neighbourhood units 17, *17*, 19, *20*
Nene Park Trust, Peterborough 39
'new town blues' 31
New Town Commissions, Northern Ireland 13, 16
New Town Development Corporations *see* Development Corporations
New Towns Act (1946) 3, 10, 11–12, 35, 153, 154
New Towns Act (1959) 35, *36*, 153
New Towns Act (1981) 54–55
New Towns Act (Northern Ireland) (1965) 16, 122
New Towns (Amendment) Act (1968) 29
New Townsmen 8
Newton Aycliffe 64, *65*
Newtown 28
Northampton 28, 37
Northern Ireland 13, 15–16, 28–29, *28*, 47

asset transfer 41
deprivation 62
employment 63
Troubles 37, 124, 125
see also Craigavon
Northstowe *42–43*, 48, 162

Osborn, Frederic James 7, *7*, 8

Parker, Barry 7, 16, 17
Parker Morris design standards 69, 89
Pasmore, Victor 22, 69, 90–91, *90*, *91*, 145
pedestrianised town centres 21, *21*, 64
permitted development rights 52, 68, 70, 71, 86, *86*, 135, 164
Perry, Clarence 17
Peterborough 28, 37, 39, 73
Peterlee 13, 27, 29, 71, 87–94, 154
    Apollo Pavilion 91, *91*, *94*
    employment and industry 48, 63, 92, 93
    governance and stewardship 94, *94*
    green infrastructure and public realm 73, *93*, *94*
    heritage assets 91, *91*, *94*
    housing 25, 69, 93, *145*
    master plan 88, 89, *89*
    town centre 92–93, *92*
    Victor Pasmore and 22, 69, 90–91, *90*, *91*, 145
Pickles, Eric 52
The Point, Milton Keynes 67, *68*, 134
policy *see* national urban policy
Pooley, Fred 130
population 61
Priestley, J.B. 154, *155*
private sector 10, 162, 164, 168
    sale of assets to 38, 41, 64
public art 22, *24–25*, 31, *74*
    sculpture in Harlow 74, *75*, *76*, *81*, *82*, *85*, *86*
public engagement and participation 32, 154–156
public realm *see* community development; green infrastructure and public realm; town centres
Purdom, C.B. 8, *9*

Radburn, New Jersey 17, *17*
Raynsford Review (2018) 164, *165*, 171
Redditch 28
Regional Spatial Strategies 48, 49, 51
Reith, Lord 10, 34
Reith Committee 10, 22, 33, 34–35
'Right to Buy' scheme 62, 70, *71*, 170
Runcorn *23*, 28, 62, 63, 76

Scotland 15, 27, 28, *28*
    asset transfer 41
    deprivation 62
    devolution 47–48
    employment 63
    urban regeneration 37
    see also Cumbernauld
Scottish Wildlife Trust 112
self-containment 25, 33
shared-ownership tenure 31
Shore, Peter 37
Silkin, Lewis 3, 10, *10*, 16, 35, 80, 88, 146, 154
site identification 27–29, 146–147
Skelmersdale 28, 75, 113–120
    employment and industry 33, 48, 115, *116*
    future growth 76, 118
    governance and stewardship 119
    green infrastructure and public realm *115*, 118
    housing 118, *120*
    master plan 114–115, *115*
    movement and transport 71, 118–119
    town centre 117, *117*, *119*
social and community development 26, *26*, 31, *31*, *32*, 154
social balance 13
'Social City' concept 5, *5*
social housing 25, 30–31, *30*, 41, 44, 62, 170
Spencley, Hugh G.C. 97
Stein, Clarence 17
Stevenage *22*, 32, 38, 48, 63, 64, 66, *66*, 68, 72, 77, *77*, 154, 155
Stonehouse 28, 37
Sustainable Communities Plan 48, 49, *49*
sustainable design 22

Taylor, W.G. 8
Telford 28
tenure mix 30–31
Thatcher, Margaret 31, 37, 38, 132, 138
Town and Country Planning Act (1947) 11
Town and Country Planning Association 7, 35, 38, 54, 61
town centres
    Craigavon 126–127, *127*
    Cumbernauld 69, 107–108, *107*, *108*, 109, *110*
    Cwmbran *100*, 100
    Harlow *20*, 83, *84*
    Milton Keynes 65, *131*, 134–135, *134*
    pedestrianised 21, *21*, 64
    Peterlee 92–93, *92*
    renewal of 64–68, *65*, *66*, *67*, *68*
    Skelmersdale 117, *117*, *119*
Town Development Act (1952) 27
transport *see* movement and transport
Tudor Walters Committee 8

underpasses 22, 64, 72, *73*
Unwin, Raymond 7, 8, 16, 17
Urban Development Corporations 36, 37, 51, 53, 162, *163*
urban regeneration 37, 48

walking
    ease of movement 22, *22*, 64
    pedestrianised town centres 21, *21*, 64
    underpasses 22, 64, 72, *73*
    walkable neighbourhoods 17, *17*, 19, 20, *20*
Warrington 12, 28, 48, 63, 71, 76, 77, 146
Washington 28, 62
Waterbeach 48
Welwyn Garden City 8, *28*
Wilson, Harold 37
Wilson, Sir Hugh 114
Wilson Report (1965) 28

zoning 20